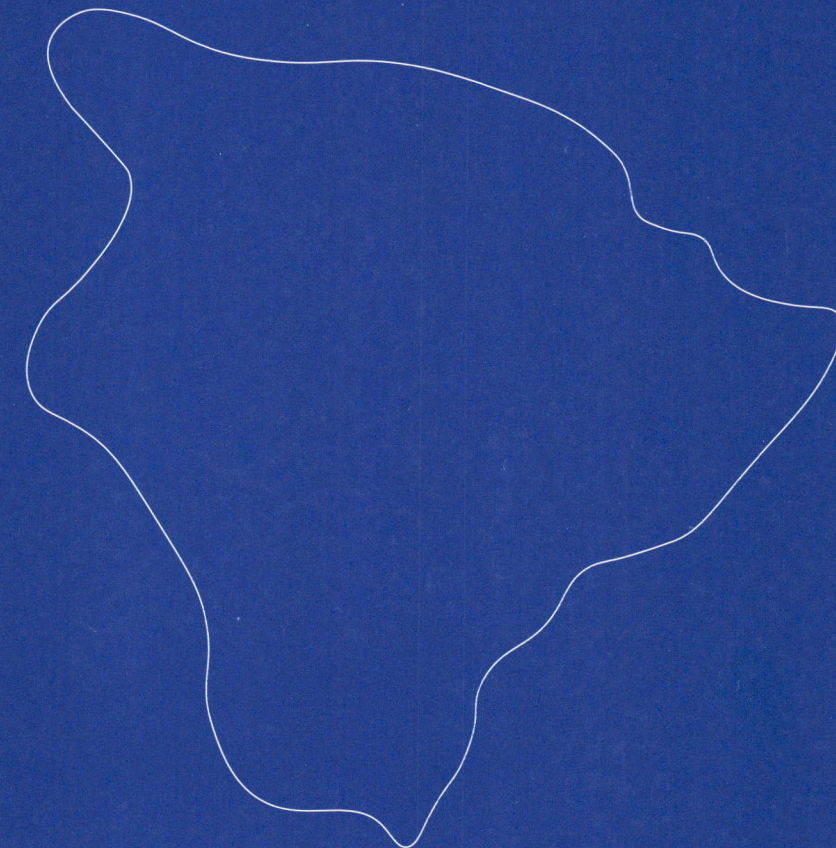

This book is dedicated to the most amazing freediver to be, my beautiful daughter, Rosa. Amore mio.

THE BLUE ON FIRE

HAWAI'I

Ni'ihau

Kaua'i

O'ahu

Moloka'i

Lanai

Maui

Island of Hawai'i

THE BLUE ON FIRE
HAWAI'I

Enzo Barracco

Foreword by Lorenzo Bertelli

CONTENTS

FOREWORD 08

INTRODUCTION 09

NOT JUST A SPORT 10
THE LAST TOUCH OF ENERGY

LASTING IMPACT 11

"DON'T MESS WITH MY WORLD" 12
CLIMBING THE OCEAN

PORTAL TO ANOTHER REALM 13
NOT JUST A RAW MATERIAL

IT'S NO JOKE 14
GREEN FIREWORKS

LOOK HARD 15

COMING TOGETHER FOR HAWAI'I 18

BLUE VOICES 24

THE BLUE ON FIRE: HAWAI'I 166

ACKNOWLEDGMENTS 167

FOREWORD

The sea has always been a strong passion of mine. Like so many Italians, this began as a child, but as an adult I still feel that same enduring connection to the ocean. I've been fortunate enough to embrace this in my professional career, extending the legacy of my father, whose own passion for the sea led him to establish the Luna Rossa Prada Pirelli sailing team.

In 2019, the Prada Group decided to launch a collection made of regenerated nylon from recycled post-consumer plastics, (including fishing nets abandoned on the seabed). I quickly realized that the project could not be limited merely to product innovation. It presented an opportunity to create culture, to educate people on the health of our sea, its importance, and our collective responsibility to preserve it. Thus, we developed SEA BEYOND: the program which, since 2019, in partnership with UNESCO's Intergovernmental Oceanographic Commission (IOC), has been supporting the promotion of ocean literacy among the younger generation, confident in the belief that the best way to communicate with adults is to talk to children. In November 2023, I was appointed by UNESCO as "Patron of the Ocean Decade Alliance" and in this role I feel the responsibility of making a positive contribution to society as a whole. Thus, our Group continues to be committed to this partnership to amplify the messages of ocean education.

SEA BEYOND now works with more than 35,000 young people worldwide. Through the program we are able to educate them on how the ocean is changing under the influence of climate change, about the urgent need to act so we can protect that which constitutes 71% of our planet, and of the danger of this beauty disappearing. Knowledge gives us the extraordinary power to intervene, to inspire and enact change and to correct our behavior. Education spreads through different forms – I'm proud that SEA BEYOND is one of them. So too is the photography of Enzo Barracco, whose pictures capture the beauty and contrasts of nature, as well as the impact of climate change. With the disruptive power of the images you will find in this book, his art is capable of conveying the fragility of the Hawaiian Islands, an outpost of biodiversity at risk.

For me, Enzo's work is an example of how a photographer's talent, combined with passion for the environment, can help to develop knowledge and awareness, working in the interest of humanity and our future on this planet.

Lorenzo Bertelli, PRADA Group Head of Corporate Social Responsibility

INTRODUCTION

As someone deeply committed to addressing climate change, I've come to realize that storytelling is one of our most powerful tools in inspiring action. Facts and data are essential, but they often fail to resonate on a personal level. It's the stories we tell—about the places we cherish and the people who are impacted—that truly inspire action. Through storytelling, we can transform the abstract challenges of climate change into something that touches our hearts and compels us to act, transforming abstract concepts into tangible, relatable experiences. The natural world is a source of awe and wonder, and by sharing its stories, we foster a deep emotional connection that drives us to preserve it.

Enzo Barracco's work is a testament to the power of storytelling through the lens of photography—and it serves as a powerful reminder of what we are working so hard to preserve. His photographs capture the profound beauty that exists in every corner of our world. They remind us that every image tells a story, and every story has the power to inspire action.

Hawai'i's breathtaking landscapes and vibrant ecosystems are more than just beautiful—they are vital to the health of our planet. The ancient rainforests, coral reefs, and volcanic mountains of Hawai'i are not just natural wonders; they are living stories of resilience and harmony. The people of Hawai'i, with their deep connection to the land and sea, exemplify a way of life that respects and honors nature. Their culture, rooted in a profound understanding of the environment, reminds us of the wisdom in living sustainably.

By sharing Hawai'i's stories—its beauty, its people, its challenges—we can inspire others to see the value in protecting our planet and remind the world of what is at stake. As we share the stories of places like Hawai'i, we also highlight the interconnectedness of all life on Earth. The protection of our natural world is not just an environmental issue; it is a human one. Through storytelling—and through the powerful imagery of artists like Enzo Barracco—we can inspire a movement that values and preserves the beauty of our planet for generations to come.

Shyla Raghav, Chief Climate Officer, TIME

NOT JUST A SPORT

How many secrets can a wave keep?

I think everyone is born an artist and explorer. I see this every day with my beautiful daughter but after I spent a day with Laird Hamilton in Hawai'i, I think everyone is born a surfer … it is interesting to see how a sport can shape and become an integral part of a place's culture. But Hawai'i is not only surf and surf is not just a sport.

The positive contribution that Hawaiians make to the preservation of nature is incredible. Do you think you love the ocean? If you do, go to Hawai'i and think again. The Hawaiians are an example to us all of what our relationship with the ocean should be. For them, the ocean is a member of the family. They have the ocean in their veins. This is how the ocean should be for all of us.

Just less than a month after I went to Hawai'i to start my project about the islands and the vital importance of the ocean, a devastating wildfire hit the island of Maui. This dramatic event changed the direction of my project profoundly. This land which is surrounded by an intense blue has a very close relationship with fire, but this fire was different. This fire was a desperate call to remember that when we change the dynamic of the natural world and destroy its balance, it will inevitably have a catastrophic impact on people's lives. Our day-to-day actions can significantly affect and impact it's people and its place, even a place so beautiful, wild, and remote as Hawai'i.

THE LAST TOUCH OF ENERGY

This land was made by fire, a fire surrounded by blue and amazing, majestic waves. I have been in the middle of the ocean many times, but I have never had an experience like this. On a morning with very bright light which was reflected on the surface of the sea I arrived at a beach to take some photos and immediately realized that I was in a special place.

The waves constantly and desperately tried to touch the coast, apparently without leaving any sign of their presence. They seemed to say, "I'm on the move for you", but in some cases the faint roar of the waves was a scream.

The waves were so high that they seemed to merge with the clouds. I saw mountains of water full of energy emerging from the surface of the ocean. The waves hit the coast with what appeared to be extreme violence, everything seemed to boil, but in reality, it was a loving embrace. As they crashed on the shore, they created a work of art like Jackson Pollock's paintings. They mixed roughly with the sand but at the same time their touch was tender. A touch that they yearned for from far away. After their very long journey they greeted the coast in a passionate embrace, as if to say, "Please remember me". The frenzied impact lasted for a few seconds and then the waves said a delicate goodbye. And, as if they wanted to put on one last show, they shouted out distantly before retreating into the vastness of the ocean, seemingly losing their majestic power and energy - the last touch of energy.

After spending half an hour observing and studying waves that looked like towering marble sculptures, I decided to dive into them to try to take some photos. As soon as I immersed myself within them, I realized that it was not just their appearance that resembled marble, but also that their strong and hard impact reminded me of the very essence of the marble.

A force that gives you no respite
A force that takes your breath away
A merciless force that does not grant you grace
Violent, strong, without compromise

If you are in the wrong place and time in the middle of a wave, you have to get out on your own. No one can help you. The incredible force is greater than you can control.

Wrong timing, wrong place is definitely what happened to me. I decided to take a photograph in the middle of the wave. Being a free diver, I thought I knew a little about ocean wave dynamics but actually, I had barely scratched the surface of this world. I could not imagine the violent force that is unleashed inside the apparently delicate blue waves here in Hawai'i. It was a terrifying, electrifying experience, I very nearly broke myself in two. In the middle of the wave, I lost control of my position and was spinning in all directions. I thought let's hope the impact isn't too violent. I couldn't see at all, and I didn't know where I was going. Everything happened fast and everything was very confusing, both astonishing and dangerous. I was engulfed in the blue in an extremely dangerous place in the middle of a very bold, unforgiving chain reaction. I hoped that everything would end soon and tried to prepare myself for a brutal impact. In the middle of the wave, I was rotating in all directions. With my head down it felt like I was under a train. The violent blows continued until the wave crashed savagely onto the shore. I felt excited and alive, but it was a very intense race.

Ironically, I don't know why, I returned to the ocean but immediately afterward a gigantic wave which looked like a wall caught me and then I understood that there was nothing I could do apart from take as much air as possible not knowing how long I would be underwater. I knew more or less what to expect.

I began to be hit very hard everywhere, and if I say everywhere, I mean it. I took hits to my body in places that I did not know existed. The wave threw me onto the bank, and I tried to protect the camera with one hand and my head with the other. In practice, if a wave catches you, it will flip you over, swamp you and make you spin until you make yourself crash to the bottom of the ocean which gradually becomes shallower until you slam into the beach. I almost saw sparks and the air was forced out of me by the violent impact.

After that gigantic wave we all stayed out of the ocean on shore waiting for the moment when we could return because the conditions were very difficult. A week before a surfer had a dangerous accident and broke his helmet. He was saved by a miracle. It goes without saying that I didn't even have a helmet. I felt a strong sensation of fear but at the same time the waves attracted me like a magnetic force. Now I understand why during the winter all the greatest surfers gather in Hawai'i to ride these colossal waves. Surfers have always had my respect for their athletic gesture and the relationship that they have with the ocean but now that I understand a little of what happens down there, they have my deepest respect.

Brave people do beautiful things
As my beautiful daughter Rosa says

Immediately after I had finished taking the photos, the surfers told me that this place is one of the most dangerous beaches in the world where many people do not return to the shore. I have no difficulty understanding why they say this. Next winter I will try again but maybe with a helmet. As Robert Capa said, "If your pictures aren't good enough, you're not close enough". I am not sure if the photo of the wave is good but for sure I was very, very close to it, so very close.

Now every wave I see I know what happens. After the wave messes you up and flips you in all directions it crashes you onto the shore, and when you have checked that everything is pretty much ok, you look at the ocean and it steals a smile from you in a mix of emotions. And the waves still keep their secrets inside. Waves are a world unto themselves with their own rules. They touch the coast everyday a thousand and a thousand times, but a wave is never the same as the previous one. It is a world where gigantic forces operate. When you are exposed to this immense energy you realize the true scale of the ocean's power. The waves are like an endless sculpture between the sky and the sea. Now I understand why for surfers the search for waves lasts a lifetime.

LASTING IMPACT

On a rainy, cloudy morning I set sail in a dinghy with my team in search of whales. They did not keep us waiting. I immediately began to see several specimens of this wonderful animal on the surface but nothing of their majestic tails. After a long wait one whale finally revealed its tail. Then, as if to greet me and give me a precious gift the enormous creature raised its magnificent tail as disappeared into the abyss, sliding into the depths of the ocean with formidable delicacy and agility. Whales do not always do this, but when it happens, it is as if they are saying, "arrivederci". In the background the mountain ranges of the coast imitate the crests of the whales' spines as they bend to dive. They displace a huge amount of water without making a splash with the agility of a free diver. Or rather, we free divers try to imitate this creature when we dive.

After spending some time deep in the ocean, the whale came to the surface once again. The sound of its first breath after the long dive was full of energy and life and echoed round the bay. Not happy with this already grandiose spectacle, whales sometimes jump almost completely out of the sea when they reach the surface, as if to say we are here … and I must say when they do this, they do create some modest splashes … Diving again, the whale showed the end of its tail, becoming a bull for a moment before slowly disappearing into the abyss.

I realize now why anyone who meets a whale has their life changed forever. The experience will remain with them for life, and it belongs to us more than we think. I would like to say the same thing for a whale when it encounters man. But in certain cases when they cross paths with us, our activities in the ocean have consequences that are often the opposite of positive, as they did for an unfortunate whale that I saw during the expedition when I was taking photographs.

I caught a glimpse of the magnificent creature holding a bizarre orange yellow object in its mouth. I could not make out what it was. It was far away; everything was happening quickly. I changed the camera lens to zoom in on the whale and saw something I wished never to see. I don't have the words to express how abnormal and disturbing it was. The whale had a fishing net caught in its mouth. My team immediately called the coast guard in the hope that they would arrive soon to free it. I saw the massive effort the whale had to make to drag the buoys which prevented it from diving properly, exhausting it, while hoping that meeting us and our civilization would not negatively affect its destiny and have a lasting impact.

"DON'T MESS WITH MY WORLD"

After spending a wonderful day with the whales but unfortunately also with the unpleasant incident, we headed to another island in the Hawaiian archipelago and another unique spot, the North Shore, which is a mecca for surfers and a hot spot for sharks. Particularly the beautiful Galápagos shark that I was lucky to see in the Galápagos Islands for my previous project, The Skin of Rock: Galápagos. Unlike the dark water and strong currents of the Galápagos, in Hawai'i I had a chance to see the sharks immersed in a particular shade of deep blue.

After navigating for several miles, we found ourselves in a spot where we could dive. I started to prepare all the equipment and to watch out for a fin on the surface, while feeling a special sense of excitement. As I always do when I dive with sharks, I prepared myself to jump into a very different world with very sophisticated animals. Once in the water I was surrounded by an intense deep blue, another dimension of blue with incredible visibility. I saw the sun disappear in the dark blue below me and after a few minutes, out of blue in front of me, I saw a very familiar shape that slowly became bigger and bigger … a Galápagos shark. Finally, I can see them, unlike in the Galápagos Islands. Now, immersed in this intense blue, it is a unique spectacle.

Very curiously but always with a certain distrust the shark began to circle me. Starting a dance, it took turns checking out what I was. It is always electrifying to be in the water with this extraordinary creature. Soon after another one arrived from my right and another below me. The next thing I knew I was surrounded by them. Practically a living fossil and a great master of adaptability, the shark is an animal to take inspiration from and protect at all costs. In this electric dance they seemed to slowly twirl and cross paths like super jets traversing the sky. Then, emerging from the blue frenzy the least shy aimed at me with extraordinary agility and precise and accurate movements until it almost touched me but at the last moment, it shaved past me with incredible control, turning and missing me with its tail by a few centimeters. Its sharp severe gaze penetrated me, creating a hint of healthy fear, a fundamental buzz of adrenaline as if it were saying, "Don't mess with my world". There is a real sense of ancient mystery behind sharks' eyes. To understand sharks, you need to become one.

When they turned and had their backs to me the tension eased a little but soon after another shark tried again. They are so genuinely curious, they cannot resist. I love them. It is wonderful to see these animals lording it over their territory in a distant world. Stories of stories that belong to us that are part of our memories and our future.

Between the circling sharks and the deep blue, a gap opened, and a trumpetfish appeared. I could not believe my eyes, a little fish among so many sharks. It ventured from the depths of the ocean to the surface, and I could not help but root for the brave little fish. Even though I love sharks, I really admire courage in animals and people.

I moved among the sharks until I reached the surface where blending into the waves, I approached and saw this very fine, thin fish with eyes larger than its body. Despite its courage, I sensed a little terror in its eyes, but it swam on without stopping. To finally be on the surface among the giants was a surreal moment, and a moment of real life. After a few minutes all the sharks disappeared into the deep water again. All I had left was to watch them swim away with respect and admiration. There is something pure and mysterious about this extraordinary animal. What remained was only the blue, a decidedly intense blue, but after this experience I found another dimension of blue.

CLIMBING THE OCEAN

After resting on the coast for a few hours we left early for another island. Direction Kaua'i to explore the majestic and unique Nāpali coast. After a short car journey, we arrived at a little port where my team and I boarded a small boat. Immediately after leaving the port, I realized "we need a big boat". We found ourselves in the middle of a storm, with the wind against us and the impetuous sea tossing the boat up and down. We had to cross this stretch of water as quickly as possible and take shelter under the coast where it acted as a natural barrier for us. But with a strong wind against us and the storm in front of us, it felt like climbing the ocean.

As soon as you approach this incredibly beautiful prehistoric coastline, it seems too perfect, too beautiful to be true. The forests are very green and the rocks an acid red. The mysterious caves and waterfalls surrounding us confirm that we are in one of the rainiest areas of the world. Its beauty is shocking, everything is in its place in perfect harmony. I felt like I was in front of a huge painting by Caspar David Friedrich. Meanwhile we almost forgot about the storm, everyone except my friend Claudio and his stomach… he gave a lot, almost everything, as we crossed the turbulent water. Even though we were slightly protected by the coast the ocean was still very raw. In the general chaos with the storm still raging, I was trying to take photos by moving rapidly from one side of the boat to another. Getting the perfect angle for the photos required a team effort between me, the ocean and the captain who flawlessly followed my directions, skillfully placing the boat at the perfect angle and velocity for me to shoot. As I tried to describe what I was experiencing, my photographic needs sometimes led us to take small risks. Sailing dangerously close to the coast we entered a cave while albatrosses flew above us mastering the wind, as only they can do.

The storm was getting stronger and stronger, and we had a window of less than two hours. Then we had to leave immediately before conditions became prohibitive. We returned to port riding the waves in a race against time. The images I had taken were imprinted in my mind and I hoped that the photos were also imprinted on my memory card. Amidst the chaos and excitement, it was hard to tell if everything was working perfectly. But if you are reading this book, it means that, most likely, all had gone well.

PORTAL TO ANOTHER REALM

As soon as we reached the port, I felt that I needed to see the coast again. Luckily, I was already planning to explore it by helicopter so that I could see this astonishing place from another perspective. We took a car to the waiting helicopter, and I quickly checked the equipment. The salt water which was still on the lenses reminded me of the climbing ocean. I cleaned them very quickly; I think too quickly. The wind was still strong, and I wondered for a few seconds whether we could travel by helicopter in these conditions. The weather was just at the limit for flying. To avoid the reflection of the windows of the helicopter that can compromise the quality of the photos, I decided to remove the helicopter's doors. I thought that salt on the lenses was enough. So, ready, off we went without the doors … to the happiness of my team. We approached the Nāpali coast from the east flying for 20 minutes over the very thick, green forest and waterfalls of the truly grand Waimea Canyon. We were flying at around 1,000 meters with a few gusts of wind that made the helicopter a bit shaky. But even though we were high above sea level the forests and rocks gave us a sense of security. When we finally got to the coast, we were still at 1,000 meters but with the endless ocean below and a stormy blue, strangely, fear slowly began to build creating a feeling of precariousness. Yet until a few minutes before we had been above forests and mountains as sharp as blades – not exactly an ideal place to land a helicopter.

It was a reminder that the ocean imposes fear and respect not only when you dive into it or when you find yourself on its surface but also when you are far away at more than 1,000 meters above it. Passing the coastline seemed like crossing the border of another world, just as diving through the surface of the ocean feels like entering the gate to a new world. It is the portal to another realm, and you can feel this when you are close to it or more than 1,000 meters above it.

At that height the storm had almost disappeared apart from a few gusts of wind which reminded us of it. The thing that we noticed were the white fins of the whales which appear blue when they are seen under the surface of the ocean.

NOT JUST A RAW MATERIAL

The ocean is so astonishingly beautiful I hope it will not give up in the face of our daily attacks. It is fundamental to our existence; we cannot afford to lose it and yet we belittle the unconditional love that it offers us. We need to feel the ocean even if we do not see it. Let's try to imagine it through the eyes of sharks, whales and octopuses and maybe we can understand what they are feeling. Let's hope the ocean does not surrender and goes on masking our impact until we change our attitude. Otherwise, the ocean will return to the wild but without us.

The ocean has been part of our planet for billions of years, and it will find a way to outlive our stupid and obtuse behavior. However, I don't know if we can adapt to the drastic changes that the ocean will experience. We need to change if we don't want to die. We need to change if we want to keep the world in balance. We need to make sacrifices and refuse to have everything right away. We must return to respecting the timing of the oceans, grow sustainably and work with nature not against it.

We don't realize that used wisely nature is the best product, the best advanced technology that we have, and the only technology that will enable us to bring our planet back into balance. Nature is not just raw materials that we can use. The natural world is the best start up that we have had the opportunity to meet. Even if it's only been around for billions of years of evolution, let's start investing in it, let's invest in our future.

IT'S NO JOKE

It was time to return. On our way back as we left the coast behind and started to approach the forest and mountains once again, in the distance we saw an extinct volcanic crater. We decided to investigate it a little more closely and we literally entered it. I could not believe that we were doing this with the helicopter blades almost touching the wet, rocky walls. As soon as we entered the crater we were surrounded by thick fog and none of us could see anything at all. Apparently, the pilot could. The fog disappeared but then we were surrounded by sprays of water coming from every direction. After making a rotation the pilot exited the crater with great skill. It was an unreal experience; it was like a video game. Even though I have never played a video game, you will know what I mean. The ocean inspires fear and respect, but I have to say that a volcano, even if it is not active, is no joke.

GREEN FIREWORKS

After so many days of strong wind, a faint breeze was enough to make the palms dance creating delicate green fireworks, perpetuating a dance between the wind and the palm trees that has taken place for millennia.

One day by a fjord among the forest trees I saw a leaning palm tree on the shore. It touched the surface of the water as if to caress the blue, as if it wanted to connect the two worlds. Leaving the fjord, I headed into the vastness of a lava field. It was a sea of lava that stretched out of sight but in the distance, on the horizon, in contrast with the sharp, hot lava scorching in the beating sun I glimpsed palm trees shimmering in the heat released by it.

After a few hours in the car crossing this endless lava bed, the landscape changed and in total contrast an area of beautiful expansive plains began, made more beautiful by the gold light of the sun that was almost ready to set. But before it went down, it wanted to paint those fantastic hills once more. Totally in contrast with the landscape I found myself in a few hours before, slowly, we approached the night.

But before night fell, an incredible sunset with a very intense gold light invaded the ocean and for a split second it sparkled all over with gold and once again the surface of the ocean became something else before everything disappeared in the dark. It disappeared from our eyes, but under the surface another world was slowly waking up to create an astonishing show of life.

LOOK HARD

Many battles are fought, many struggles endured, to leave the place where you were born and get as far away as possible. But then there comes a moment in life when you struggle equally relentlessly to return to the land of your birth. I hope it's not too late to realize that we have only one place that we can return to, just one place. The ocean is our home, and it is worth fighting for, and protecting. We can try to live 1,000 lives without the ocean, but the truth is we only have one life and that depends on the unconditional love that the ocean gives us, which we scorn.

The ocean provides this incredible stability. We need to change our system which does not work. We take from the ocean but do not give anything back. We need a radical transformation: we need to value living trees and living fish. It is bizarre how we place more value on a felled tree and a dead fish than on living creatures. We all need to make the ocean part of our culture. If the Hawaiians lose the ocean, they will lose their culture. We need to feel the ocean even when we cannot see it.

We listen when there is an image and when we start to look, it is difficult to stop. We do not understand how much power a story and an image have. A story and a photo can change us. Photography has the capacity to communicate a very complex story. Its stillness and silence move us and create a very strong connection between the image and the viewer. It can change our perceptions. This reminds me of what the world saw in 1968 for the first time: a photo of our planet from space, from the Moon, 1.3 light seconds away from the Earth. It was December 24, 1968, when the Apollo 8 crew immortalized "Earthrise", the historic image of our planet taken by the Australian Bill Anders which portrays the spectacular sunrise of Earth seen from the Moon. It has become an iconic image of the 20th century. That photograph immediately changed our understanding, our perspective, as we became aware of its significance: that our home, our planet with its power, fragility and strange delicacy is a limited and confined world. Now, this makes me think, "Houston, we have a problem".

As a photographer I am a co-author with the audience in order to create a different point of view. The audience completes my work.

Photography doesn't need translation

I hope my work accelerates the momentum to take collective action for our natural world and our ocean, and that it stimulates surprise and curiosity, which is one of the driving forces of humanity. Let us use our creativity to make everyone value the ocean.

If you see, you connect
If you see, you care
If you see, you think differently

If we had to pay the natural world to do the job of sequestering carbon it would cost trillions. Instead, it does it for free. What we must do is leave our natural world alone and use our wisdom to inspire new possibilities.

The climate crisis is not a crisis of knowledge, it is a crisis of sensibility and soul. We know what we risk. We need to change the way we experience the natural world; we need social change. I truly believe the young generations will create this social change. It is already happening now because they are very, very angry about the oceans they have inherited. It's as simple as that.

I am happy and honored to be part of this conversation and to contribute what I can to bring about the social change that we need. We are all marine animals … we just forgot.

COMING TOGETHER FOR HAWAI'I

We are proud to support the work of Enzo, an artist who cares as much about the planet and its people as we do. His photography captures the heart of humanity and the grand expanse of nature, blended together to tell an incredibly important story.

At Lavazza, we strongly believe that the art of coffee cannot exist without protecting coffee-growing communities and their farms. That's why sustainability is at the forefront of all we do. Since 2004, the Lavazza Foundation has led 30 social, environmental, and economic projects in over 20 countries worldwide, impacting over 100,000 people. As we continue to grow globally, we endeavor to provide the care and support needed for our coffee farmers to grow with us.

It is an honor to join Enzo Barracco in celebrating the beauty and splendor of our planet.

Daniele Foti, VP of Marketing, Lavazza North America

Oceans and Hawai`i

Many people have said "water is life" but when you hear someone from Hawai`i or a Pacific nation say this, know that they are expressing a practical, existential reality.

As the planet warms and the oceans rise, many Pacific nations and the state of Hawaii face transformational changes to their way of life. Some people will become climate refugees, others will have to move their homes and villages to survive. Economies will be forced to evolve to address the imminent change as the ocean weighs ever heavier on their way of life.

Still, the ocean has shaped the magnificent cultures of all these sacred places for thousands of years, so this change will need to be embraced in a way that empowers people who live near the sea and draw their sustenance from it.

Climate pressures will shape political discourse in the region in the coming decades and wise nations and states will integrate these forces into their policy decisions to help their people survive.

Often an overlooked part of the world, the Pacific region will likely have an outsized impact on geopolitical futures for the world. How the Pacific nations and Hawai`i fortify themselves against sea level rise and climate change will play a major role in how history takes shape.

Food security derived from the ocean, housing that is sustainable near the sea and the ability to pivot an economy despite sea level rise, will determine survival for many.

Josh Green M.D., Governor of Hawai`i (Ke Kia`aina o Hawai`i)

Since the invention of photography, intrepid camera operators have shown us the world. The desire to create a record of our planet is inextricably linked to an awareness that the world is constantly changing, owing to forces of climate, modernization, migration, and so on. Going beyond awareness to advocacy, Enzo Barracco's photographic projects are aligned with global environmental preservation efforts. Whether seen in books, exhibitions or online, Barracco's photographs circulate widely and spark action. As he puts it, "photography doesn't need translation".

Barracco has earned his recognition as one of the world's leading climate artists, undertaking physically demanding expeditions to the Antarctic, the Galápagos Islands and now the islands of Hawai'i. Connecting these bodies of work is Barracco's view of the world's oceans as embodiments of energy, which he has felt metaphorically and viscerally. Just as significantly, contemplating the oceans has given him a deep sense of environmental interconnectedness. An event or action in one location has an impact many miles away, just as past histories continue to resonate in present time.

As a Pacific-facing museum, LACMA's commitment to the artistic culture of Hawai'i is reflected in our collections and exhibitions. International contemporary artist Enzo Barracco shows us the islands as he encountered them, inviting us to focus on their beauty, power and vulnerability at this moment. Infused with passion and executed with technical finesse, each photograph is an immersive world in itself, while the entire series is a sweeping survey. These photographs of Hawai'i speak urgently to the present and profoundly to the future.

Britt Salvesen, Curator and Department Head, Wallis Annenberg Photography Department and Prints and Drawings Department, LACMA Museum, Los Angeles

We're standing at a precipice. There are two possible scenarios: we go over the edge by continuing to burn fossil fuel, waste resources, overdevelop, and keep destroying nature at an ever faster speed, causing increasingly irregular weather patterns and pollution that make large areas of this Earth uninhabitable and generate millions more climate refugees.

The other option is to build a bridge to the other side into the future. This requires the recognition that if we continue business as usual, we, too, will disappear as a species. But what will make us stop in our track, change, and invest in alternatives?

Almost two decades ago, shortly after Al Gore's An Inconvenient Truth came out in 2006, I felt compelled to make people see and feel what they were about to lose. The best way to achieve this, I thought, was through art. I co-founded ARTPORT_making waves, an organization on art and climate change, at a time when it wasn't a hot topic in the art world. In 2009, we were invited to curate an exhibition on gender and climate change at the United Nations Climate Conference in Copenhagen. A delegate, after seeing (Re-) Cycles of Paradise, said: "Now I understand what's at stake. Seeing your art exhibition, I can feel it in my gut—all our hundreds of pages of reports weren't able to achieve this."

When we captivate people's imagination and stir their emotions, they will become passionate about a cause. Whether capturing the majestic icebergs of Antarctica, the sublime island creatures of Galápagos, or the powerful ocean waves in Hawai'i, Enzo Barracco's photographs pull us into the magic of nature and closer to our own humanity. And that's when we begin to realize what it means to lose all of that.

As the Chief Curator of the Parrish Art Museum, I am surrounded by architecture and landscape that respect and reflect the singular natural beauty of Long Island's East End. From where I work inside the galleries I can see 14 acres of native grasses and wildflowers framed by various hues of blue sky and ocean. Here I am reminded daily of how art can be a part of the solution. In 2026, we will present a comprehensive exhibition with artists imagining a sustainable future through earth art, installation, performance, and interactive community projects. Art can be the inspiration to build the bridge that gets us to the other side.

Corinne Erni, The Lewis B. and Dorothy Cullman Chief Curator of Art and Education, Deputy Director of Curatorial Affairs, Parrish Art Museum, Water Mill, NY

Enzo Barracco's commitment to the environment and climate permeate his artworks, but the Hawai'i project presents his entire vision for the future of our planet. Enzo's work offers the possibility of an environmentally friendly progress of humankind, with this astonishing, unique series of images.

Hawai'i is about the overwhelming beauty of nature and its complicated relationship with humans, but it also seems to tell us that the better we understand our position within the natural environment, the more able we will be to do our best to preserve the Earth's treasures.

The Hawai'i project comes at a time when everyone should contribute to the fight against climate change, even artists. Through his majestic images of the ocean and the flora and fauna of the remote Hawaiian Islands, Enzo is significantly raising global awareness on this crucial topic.

Sergio Strozzi, Consul General of Italy in San Francisco

Hawaiʻi is a special place, with a diverse community, diverse environment, and rich culture and history that together amaze and inspire all who grace her shores.

At the University of Hawaiʻi at Mānoa, we take pride in our role, described in our Mission as "… UH Mānoa is a globally recognized center of learning and research with a kuleana (responsibility and privilege) to serve the people and places of Hawaiʻi, and our neighbors in the Pacific and Asia." This commitment is evident in all that we do, whether it is our work in supporting the health and wellbeing of the communities we serve, or our work in understanding and protecting the environments that host these communities.

The indigenous people of this place, now called Native Hawaiians, understood the intrinsic connection between people and the land. This has remained a core value that informs the community's (and university's) efforts towards preserving Hawaiʻi's precious land. This land is the most ecologically diverse on earth, with habitats that include rain forest and tundra, and physiographic regions ranging from vibrant deep coral reefs to mountains exceeding 4,000 meters (13,000 feet) in elevation. Numerous plants and animals found here are endemic to Hawaiʻi, with some species that are unique to individual islands. As we work together to preserve these treasures and this place for future generations, it is vital that we acknowledge that generations of Indigenous Hawaiians and their knowledge systems shaped Hawaiʻi in sustainable ways that allow us to enjoy her gifts today, and learn from
their ways of knowing.

The world is at a crossroads, a place in time where we must choose to preserve the only planet we have. This is nowhere more evident than in the Pacific Islands, where land that is considered sacred to its people, and ocean waters that have sustained these people for millennia, are now threatened by the impacts of climate change. Enzo's remarkable artistic project is a stunning presentation of the natural beauty of Hawaiʻi, and a reminder of the places that are most at risk.

The work of Enzo is at once stunningly beautiful and bittersweet, as his images remind us of the precious places in the Pacific that are most at risk of the impacts of climate change.

**Michael Bruno, Provost and Professor of Ocean Engineering,
University of Hawaiʻi at Mānoa**

BLUE VOICES

When I traveled to Hawai'i, I met Native Hawaiians and others who call the islands home. Laird Hamilton, the internationally renowned big wave surfer, is among those who have settled in Hawai'i. He feels like an islander but is always conscious that he is a guest, when he is in the Ocean surfing.

Terry Chung, Henk Rogers, Kevin Aoki, and Jon Bryan all have different stories but they are united by their respect and love for the ocean, and their deep understanding of how indebted we are to it.

In Conversation: Enzo Barracco with Laird Hamilton

Enzo Barracco: If I say ocean, you say?
Laird Hamilton: I might say … God.

EB: What is your first memory of the ocean?
LH: Movement. Water hitting me, then seaweed. A wave grabbing and taking me. The Hawaiian beaches where I learned to swim were dangerous. I was young and needed to be rescued a lot, but the love I experienced being rescued was the start of my fascination with the ocean.

EB: What does the ocean mean to you now, and to your community?
LH: The ocean is the source of life. It supplies us with our physical and emotional needs. It produces oxygen, regulates the climate and affects the weather. It also stores information about the history of our planet, past and present. I call it nature's 'cloud'.

EB: When you leave Hawai`i, what is the first thing you do when you return?
LH: Just breathe the air in. Take a big breath.

EB: Your first memories of the ocean are interesting. Do you ever fear for your life when you are in the ocean now?
LH: Too many times to count. You would be stupid not to be fearful for your life within such power.

EB: Which ocean creature do you respect the most?
LH: The orca, the 'killer whale'. People don't realize they are not whales but the largest dolphins. It is the most intelligent predator, the apex predator. It hunts and eats the liver of great white sharks.

EB: Are you ever afraid of sharks?
LH: Of course. They are everywhere, but what you do is more important than how you feel, and admitting you are scared is a sign of courage.

EB: I agree. Are there lessons that we can learn from the ocean?
LH: It is the place where you can learn the most important skills and behaviors, about respect, responsibility, courage and endurance. We need to learn about the ocean environment and the information it holds and be less abusive toward it before it is too late. We've only explored five percent. We know more about Mars than we do about the ocean.

EB: My favorite things to photograph are waves and one of the most joyous moments in my life was surfing in Italy, even though we don't have big waves like Hawai`i.
LH: The whole objective of surfing is to be in the moment when you can only think about the present. It's like Formula 1 or being in a fighter jet when you are in flow state but in the ocean on a wave, it's so simple, so pure. You are riding the energy that is traveling through the water. There are very few things that bring you quite into that state and the waves are free.

EB: Let me ask you another question. You have experienced the ocean, and you know the benefits. What can we say to people in New York? In London?
LH: There's a beautiful book called Blue Mind* that talks about how good it is for us to look out at the horizon of the ocean and to feel what it does to our brains and bodies. We are all connected to the ocean. It is important for everybody to have a relationship with it in some way no matter where they are. We need to take greater care of it because it is as vital to our lives as the organs in our body.

EB: When did you realize the connection with Hawai`i?
LH: It started from so young. My mother brought me to Hawai`i when I was a baby so my relationship started before a time that I can remember. I was always in Hawai`i.

EB: Do you feel this place is your place?
LH: I wouldn't say my place because I'm not Hawaiian. I am an outsider, but I think that made me more observant, more interested and more aware of the culture and environment.

EB: You don't take it for granted.
LH: No, I am a guest and as a guest I conduct myself in a certain way. That's how I conduct myself in the ocean. I'm from the land. When I'm in the ocean, I'm a guest of the ocean. But since I was a young child whenever I was traveling, I would say that I was from Hawai`i not America. Hawai`i is completely different culturally. The people who grew up on the islands have an islander's mentality. It's a different approach.

EB: How can we inspire love for the ocean in others?
LH: I think by encouraging participation. The more people swim, kayak, wind surf in the ocean, kite surf, sail, go to the beach, whatever it is, the more they will start to care about the beauty of the beach and water and keep them clean. Fishermen are concerned about the fish disappearing. Maybe we can catch less, only catch what we need. The more we integrate the more concerned we are.

EB: We have touched on the joy and fear that you feel in the ocean, what other emotions does it inspire in you?
LH: The first thing that comes to me is – I don't even know the word for the emotion. It's like a draw, a lure, a beautiful woman, like a trap …

EB: How do you see the future of the ocean and the future of Hawai`i?
LH: Hawai`i is special. It can be a sanctuary in the middle of chaos because of its location and natural resources but it must be protected. It needs people that are there for the right reasons. The ocean is going to be under attack more than ever before because of its resources. Our biggest concern is that the world is going to start mining the seabed and unleashing who knows what kind of environmental disasters. It's going to be like opening Pandora's box. You don't know what is going to come out of it.

EB: Do you see any hope? Is there something positive or do you think it will be devastation?
LH: I think there is a great awakening happening right now. Our technology is allowing us to learn so much so quickly and that makes me optimistic but there's so much more we don't know and don't understand. And there's some things about humans … you know we have a war between good and evil.

EB: The last question I want to ask you is specifically about your work, what is a good day as a surfer, and what is a bad day?
LH: I think you should cherish the good days and not always be looking for the next and the next. There's no end to that. Today's the day and you get what you get. It is a formula for life.

EB: I like that. You need to make a good day every day. It's on you to try do that. Thank you, Laird, for your time, support and inspiration.

Laird Hamilton, American big-wave surfer

*Wallace J. Nichols, with a foreword by Céline Cousteau,
Blue Mind: How Water Makes You Happier, More
Connected and Better at What You Do, Boston: Little, Brown
& Company, 2014.

In Conversation: Enzo Barracco with Terry Chung

Enzo Barracco: If I say ocean, you say?
Terry Chung: Horizon.

EB: What is your first memory of the ocean?
TC: North Shore huge surf.

EB: What does the ocean mean to you, and to your community?
TC: Resources for food.

EB: When you leave Hawai`i, what are the first things you do when you return to Hawai`i?
TC: Relax and be grateful for where we live.

EB: Do you ever fear for your life in the ocean, and if yes, when?
TC: Actually, yes. Whenever I enter the ocean, I am careful. The ocean has no mercy.

EB: Which animal in the ocean do you respect the most, and why?
TC: That would be the porpoise. It is an intelligent mammal living off the ocean.

EB: What lesson can we learn from the ocean?
TC: Respect the ocean and all that comes from it.

EB: Why should people care about the ocean?
TC: The reason we humans should care for the ocean is because it is a lifeline to living on the Earth in every way.

EB: When did you realize the connection with Hawai`i?
TC: Here in Hawai`i we are surrounded by the Pacific Ocean. In my case I have access to it. We make it a big part of our life, fishing for food resources, surfing for pleasure and fun, swimming in it for relaxation and saltwater therapy.

EB: How can we inspire love for the ocean in others?
TC: The way to inspire love for the ocean is the way we use it for our enjoyment and the way we depend on it to fulfill our lifestyle. Like I said, we are surrounded by it. Do not avoid it, love everything about it.

EB: What emotions does the ocean provoke in you?
TC: The dependability of being able to enter the water and have undeniable access to it, and to look out to the horizon, the almighty of the sea and earth.

EB: How do you see the future of the oceans and Hawai`i?
TC: I see the future of the world's oceans as worse than in the past. They have been drained of the fish stocks that were so massively plentiful, and the pollution caused by mankind is still on the rise. As for Hawai`i, the ocean surrounding it where we live

Terry Chung, Kaua`i Waterman

will probably remain the same as it has always been, but the fish that used to be so abundant will continue to be depleted in a declining trend towards the future.

In Conversation: Enzo Barracco with **Henk Rogers**

Enzo Barracco: If I say ocean, you say?
Henk Rogers: Blue.

EB: What is your first memory of the ocean?
HR: I remember going to the beach in Scheveningen, the Netherlands, and playing in the waves.

EB: What does the ocean mean to you, and to your community?
HR: The ocean means life. The ocean is the source of all life on Earth. The ocean produces most of the oxygen we terrestrial beings depend on.

EB: When you leave Hawai`i, what are the first things you do when you return to Hawai`i?
HR: I look to see my children and my grandchildren. I appreciate the paradise, the rocks, the plants, the animals and the people of Hawai`i.

EB: Do you ever fear for your life in the ocean, and if yes, when?
HR: I feared for my life in the ocean several times. I almost drowned while surfing on the North Shore of O`ahu. I was almost sucked into a hole in the reef on Swain's Island while sailing with Hōkūle`a, the Polynesian Voyaging Society canoe.

EB: Which animal in the ocean do you respect most, and why?
HR: Of all animals in the ocean, I respect the octopus the most. They are a species that has evolved intelligence separately from vertebrates. They learn and do many interesting clever things. I have great respect for them. They are like aliens.

EB: What lesson can we learn from the ocean?
HR: We can learn that, like Mother Nature, the ocean can be gentle and sweet, but also merciless and terrifying. We should treat it with love and respect.

EB: Why should people care about the ocean?
HR: The ocean is the source of our wellbeing. If the ocean changes, weather and climate will change. If weather and climate change, the places that provide for us will no longer do so. So, if we want to continue living on this planet in the way we have been, we should be very careful in dealing with the ocean.

EB: When did you realize the connection with Hawai`i?
HR: When I was 18, I moved from New York City to Hawai`i. I lived on the beach for a year. During that year I was in the ocean every day. I was either surfing or skin diving. I learned to love and respect the ocean. Hawai`i is in the middle of the biggest ocean in the world. We can feel the rhythm, the breathing of the ocean in Hawai`i as if she is alive more than anywhere else in the world.

Henk Rogers, Founder Blue Planet Companies

EB: How can we inspire love for the ocean in others?
HR: We can inspire love for the ocean by showing them the beauty of the ocean. They should swim around the coral reef and experience the wonderful biodiversity, the amazing colors, the coral, the fish, the invertebrates, the life.

EB: What emotions does the ocean provoke in you?
HR: The ocean provokes oneness with Mother Nature in me.

EB: How do you see the future of the oceans and Hawai`i?
HR: I see lots of damage in the near term and lots of regeneration in the long term for both Hawai`i and the oceans.

In Conversation: Enzo Barracco with **Kevin Aoki**

Enzo Barracco: If I say ocean, you say?
Kevin Aoki: Togetherness, Unity, Community.

EB: What is your first memory of the ocean?
KA: Some of my most fond, and earliest memories of the ocean date back to the late '70s at the Grand Prix in Pleasant, New Jersey. I remember being with my father and siblings and going to watch the races that Benihana would sponsor every year.

EB: What does the ocean mean to you, and to your community?
KA: The ocean is a source of vitality for the community on the island. Everything is surrounded by the ocean, and it is our duty as locals to preserve it. Being a restaurateur, Hawai`i is a prime marketplace for sourcing seafood. Being transparent with food, and supporting locals is a core value of ours. At Aoki Group, we pride ourselves on fresh, premium cuts that we acquire from our home.

EB: When you leave Hawai`i, what are the first things you do when you return to Hawai`i?
KA: One of the first things I like to do upon arriving home is allowing myself to reset by taking a stroll around Ala Moana Beach Park. The ocean and nature are so enchanting; looking at all the nature and the vast ocean provides me with a moment of stillness amongst the everyday chaos that comes with being a business owner.

EB: Do you ever fear for your life in the ocean, and if yes, when?
KA: The ocean is paradoxical. It is simultaneously so boundless and terrifying, yet beautiful and exciting. The juxtaposition between such contrasting attributes is what makes the ocean a special place. Synonymous with life, and yin and yang—the bad would not exist if it were not for the good, and vice versa.

EB: Which animal in the ocean do you respect most, and why?
KA: I had the opportunity to swim with tiger sharks and it was an incredible, eye-opening experience. It made

Kevin Aoki, Owner Aoki Group

me realize our misconstrued perception of sharks. It is sad to see such an integral part of the ocean ecosystem in declinine, but with enough awareness we can change the misconception of sharks and save them. In honor of the great respect I have for these creatures, I will be using sharks as a label on my whisky bottles set to launch soon.

EB: What lesson can we learn from the ocean?
KA: Life is precious and delicate. We are given this great resource, and we have to respect it before it is too late.

EB: Why should people care about the ocean?
KA: We are surrounded by the ocean. It is the biggest resource that we have. A resource that if we lost would change Hawai`i drastically. We as locals need to do our part in respecting our home and saving our oceans.

EB: When did you realize the connection with Hawai`i?
KA: The main thing that drew me to Hawai`i was my first born Noa. While taking trips here, the island gradually became my home. I saw great potential for a Japanese American fusion restaurant due to the island's unique position between Asia and North America. Now, after 20 years, we have over eight different concepts, and 12 restaurants in Hawai`i, Las Vegas and Florida.

EB: How can we inspire love for the ocean in others?
KA: Cultivate love, remind people it is our duty to care for and respect our home.

EB: What emotions does the ocean provoke in you?
KA: The ocean is immeasurable, inspiring us to look beyond what is in front of us. It motivates me to break away from monotony and come up with greater and grander ideas.

EB: How do you see the future of the oceans and Hawai`i?
KA: There is enough understanding of how important the ocean is to local communities. People will continue to respect the ocean and even educate and advocate for future generations. The sentiment will stay the same, and locals will play a big influence on how much we can preserve and protect our oceans.

In Conversation: Enzo Barracco with Jon Bryan

Enzo Barracco: If I say ocean, you say?
Jon Bryan: My church … my happy place … where I feel free and with nature.

EB: What is your first memory of the ocean?
JB: Growing up at Outrigger Canoe Club and my family visits to Tahiti.

EB: What does the ocean mean to you, and to your community?
JB: A lifeline of food and resources … a passageway to another place … a place that brings happiness and fun. A place to train, paddle, surf and rejuvenate.

EB: When you leave Hawai`i, what are the first things you do when you return to Hawai`i?
JB: Jump in the ocean … eat local food.

EB: Do you ever fear for your life in the ocean, and if yes, when?
JB: Yes, of course. With fear comes respect. The ocean is powerful and much greater than I. This fear has occurred during canoe surfing big surf or during a Moloka'i Hoe channel crossing on a 6-person outrigger canoe.

EB: Which animal in the ocean do you respect most, and why?
JB: I respect all animals in the ocean. It is their ocean not mine. I love and respect whales, dolphins and sharks. They all can be 'aumākua (ancestor gods).

EB: What lesson can we learn from the ocean?
JB: Always be respectful. Observe the ocean before you enter. Be aware of the tides, currents, wave size and direction, and wind.

EB: Why should people care about the ocean?
JB: The ocean is our source for food. We have more oceans on this planet than we have land. It is imperative that we protect this valuable resource and not destroy it with pollution and global warming.

EB: When did you realize the connection with Hawai`i?
JB: Living in Hawai`i requires you to respect and honor the ocean. It is our lifeline and connects us to the rest of the world. It provides food and nourishment, and it provides enjoyment and peace. The Hawaiian people have historically respected the ocean because of all it provides.

EB: How can we inspire love for the ocean in others?
JB: We need to expose them to the ocean and share all that it gives back to us. The ocean cleanses your body and soul and can be so tranquil and yet so powerful.

Jon Bryan, Outrigger Canoe Surfer

EB: What emotions does the ocean provoke in you?
JB: Happiness, tranquility, calmness, joy and love.

EB: How do you see the future of the oceans and Hawai`i?
JB: The future of our oceans is in danger. We need to do more with the creation of laws that protect the ocean and its resources. As Hawai`i is in the most remote place on earth, the ocean means everything to our existence and survival. We need to protect, honor and cherish the ocean so future generations can benefit from it as well.

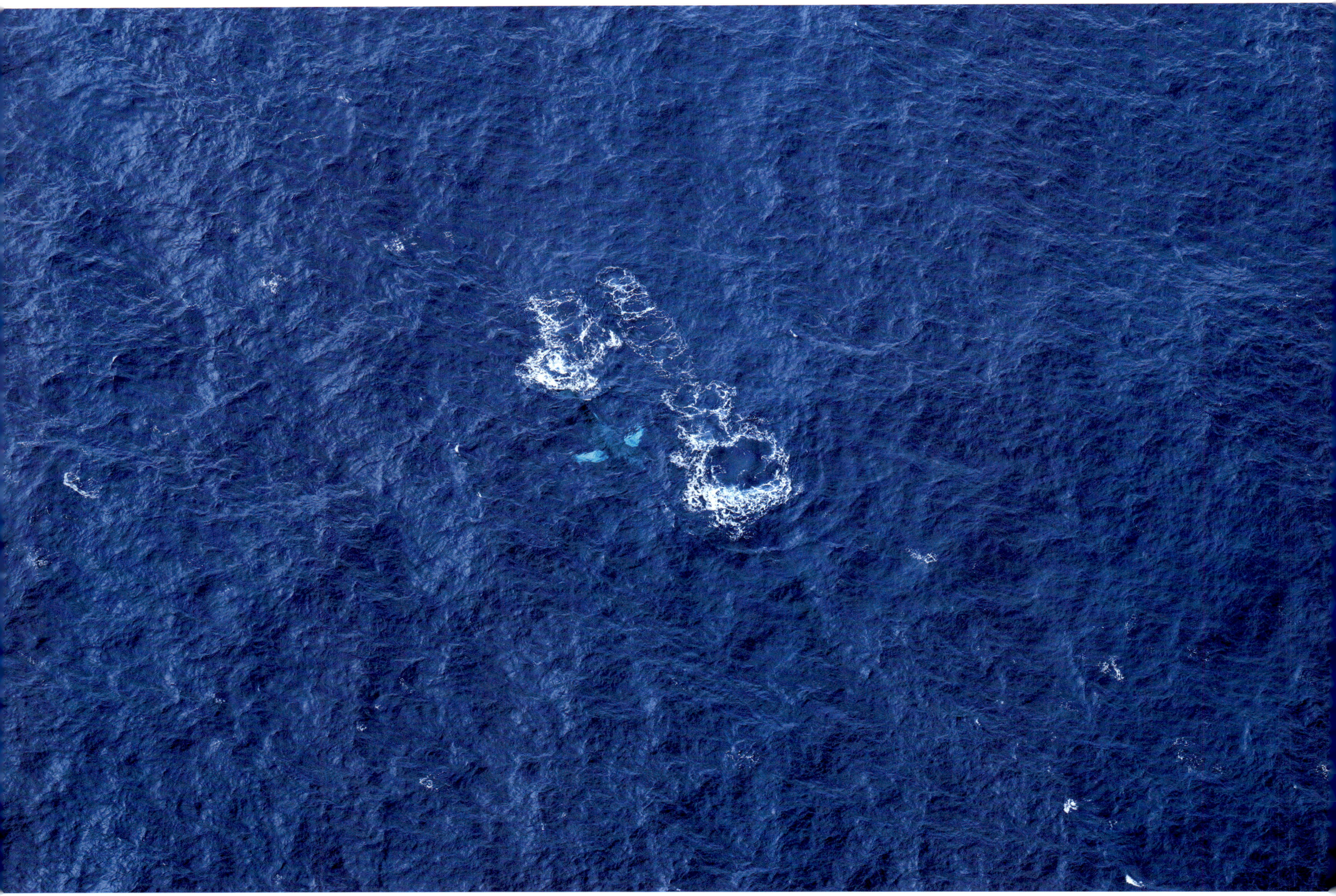

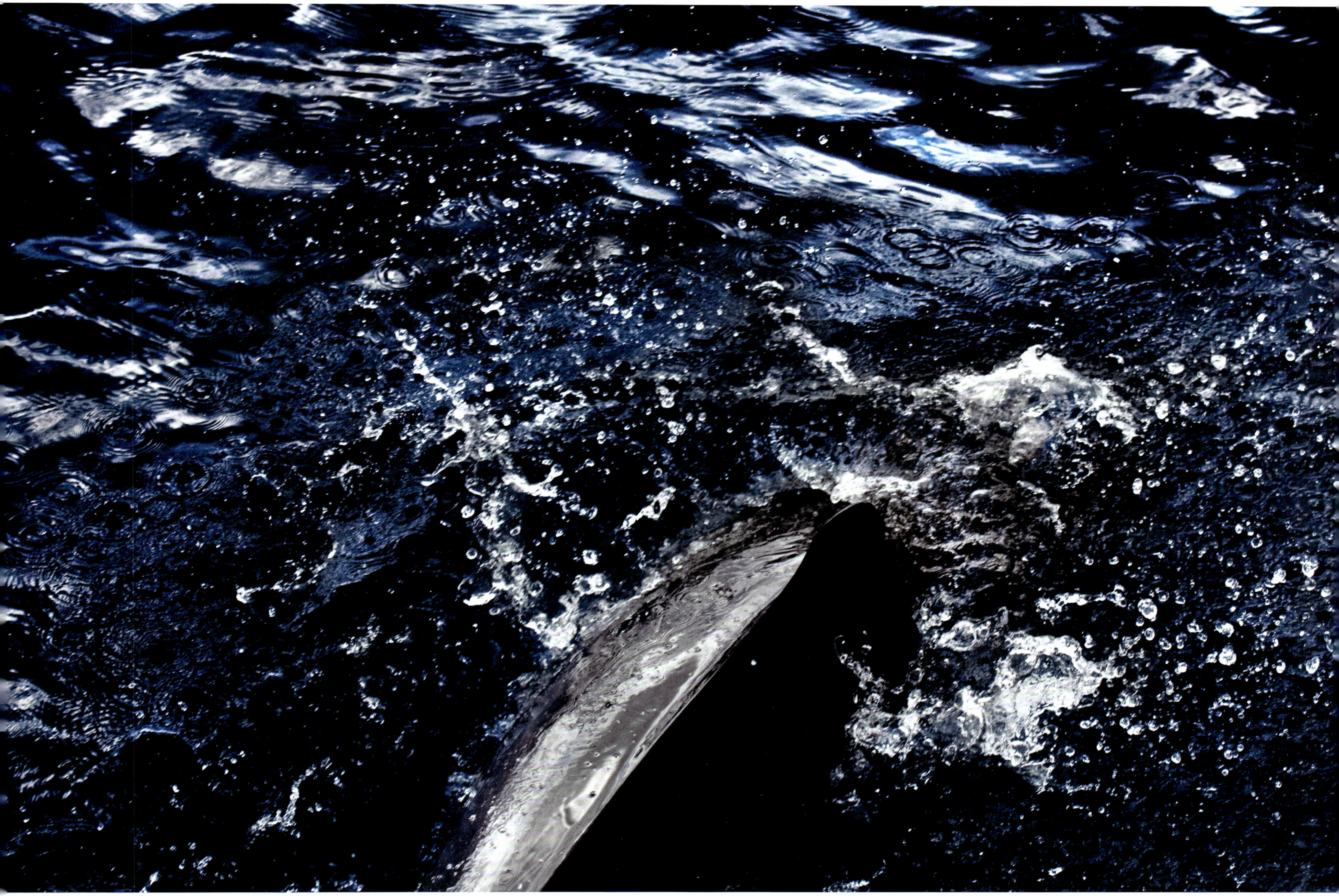

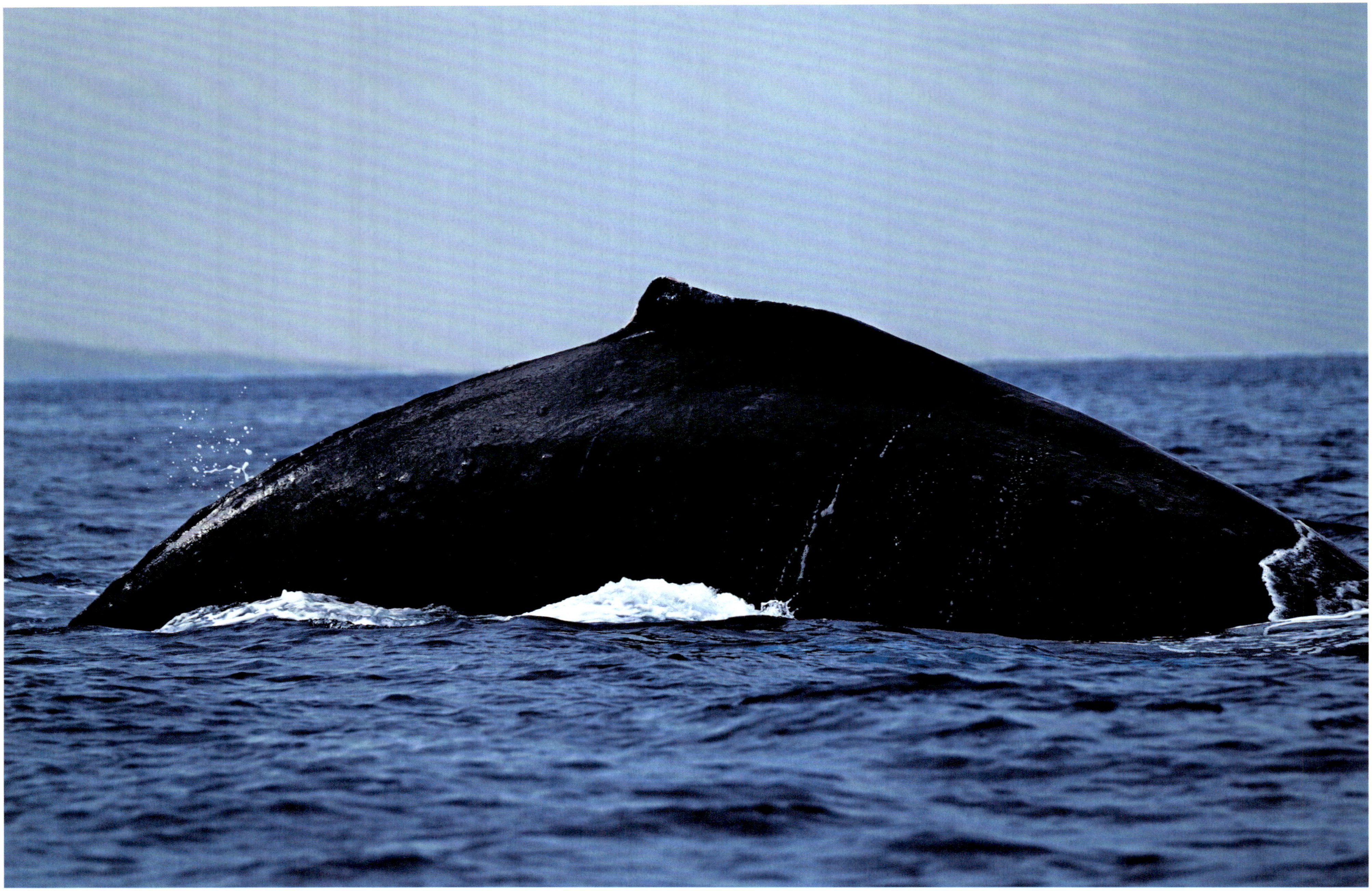

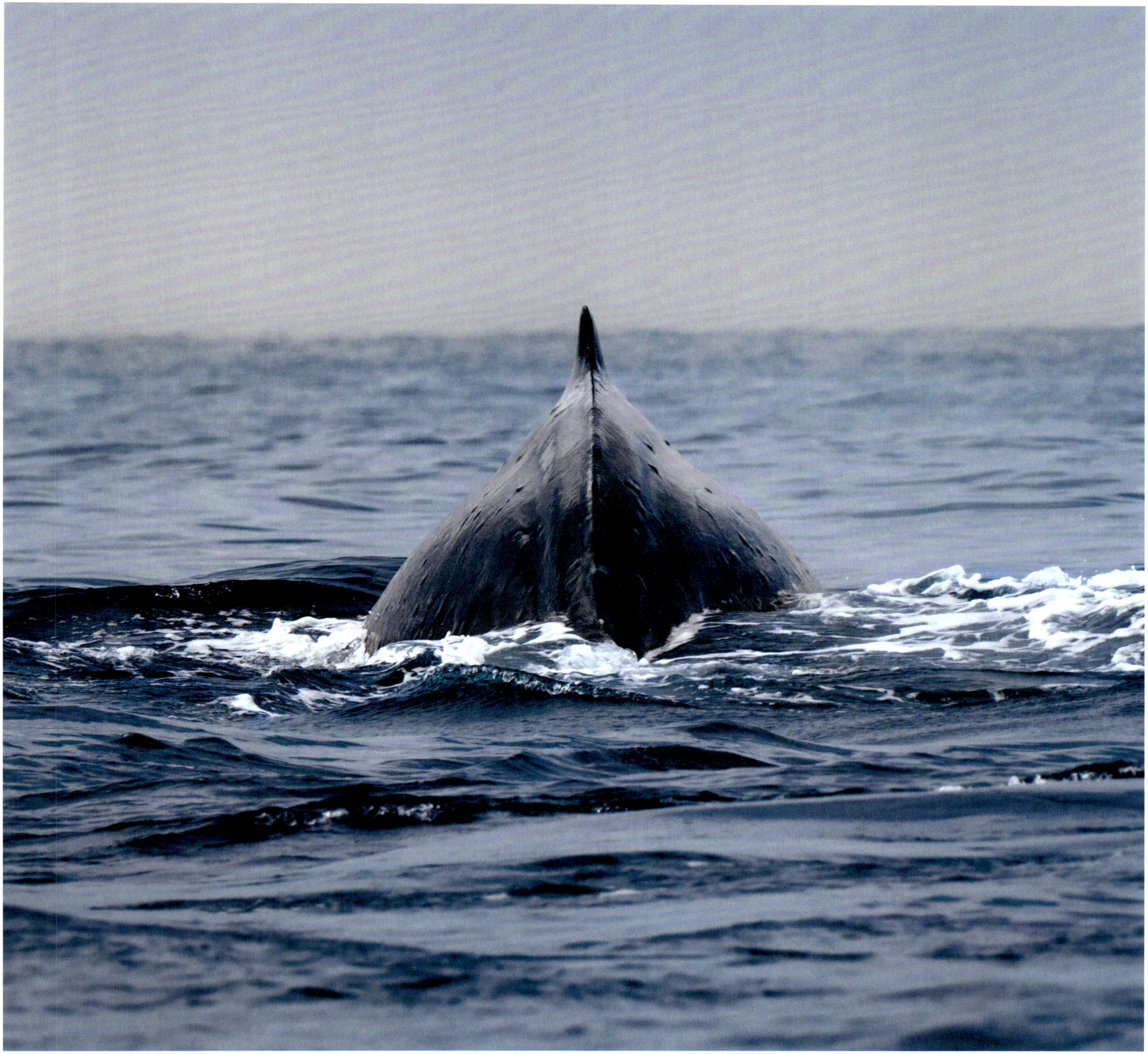

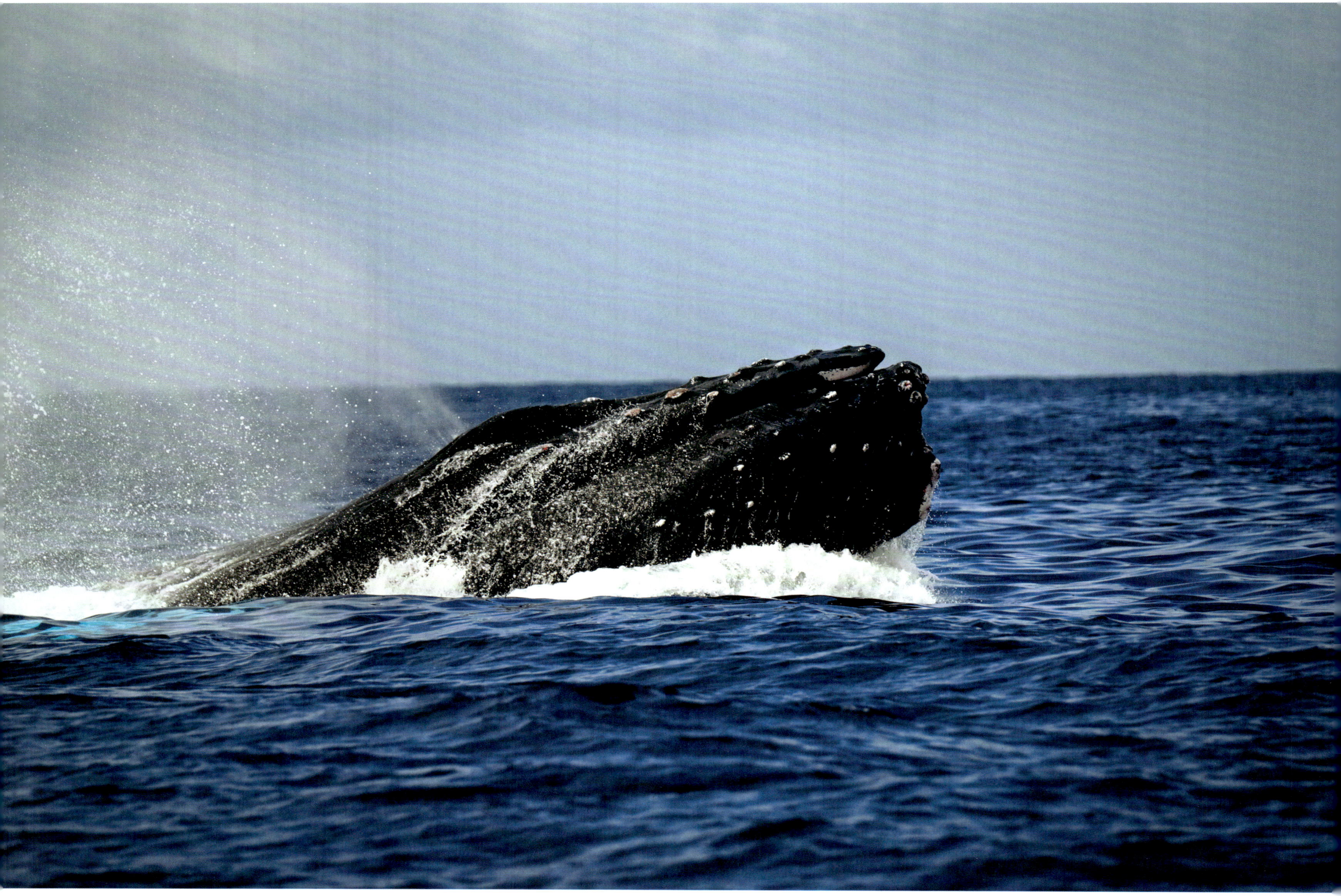

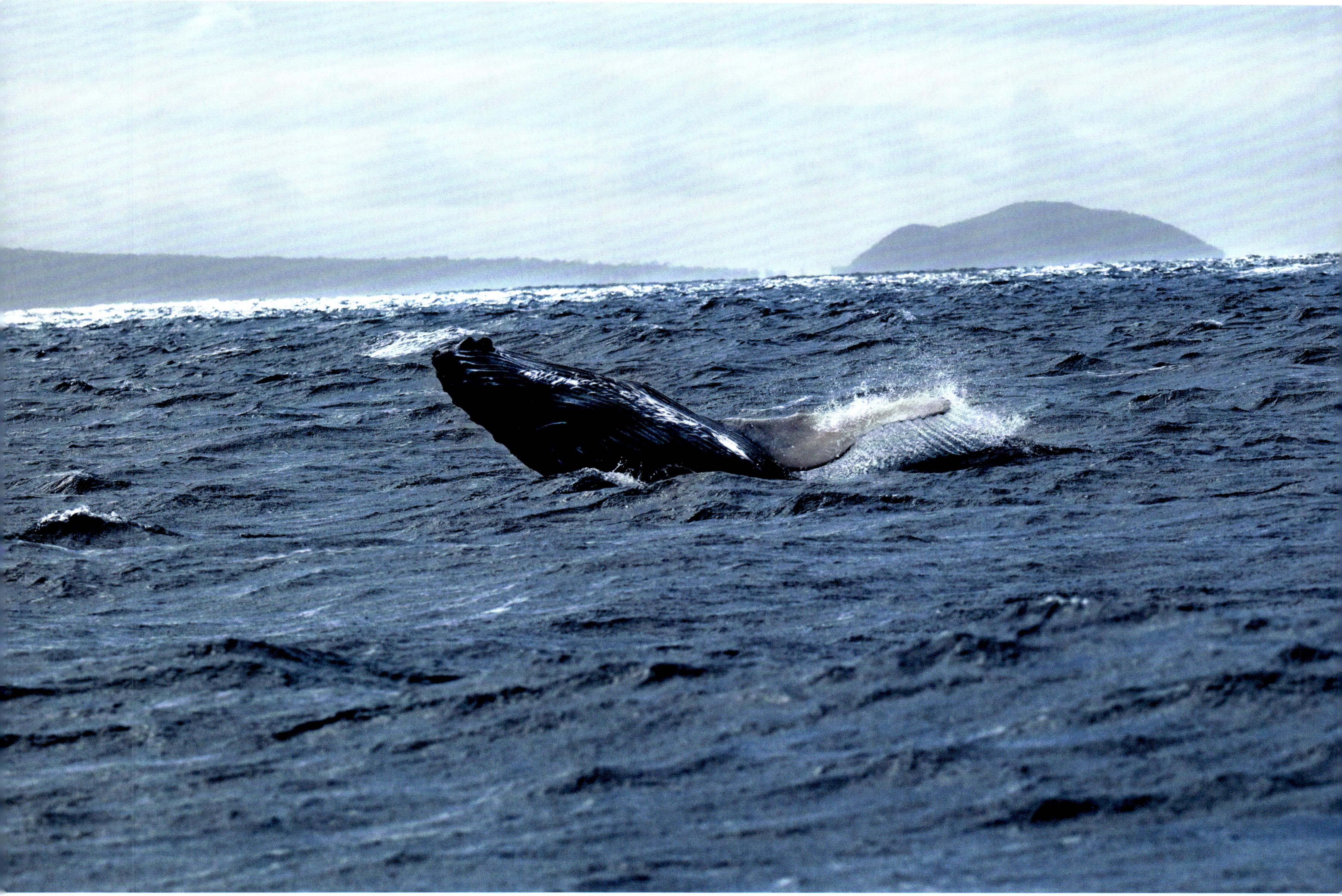

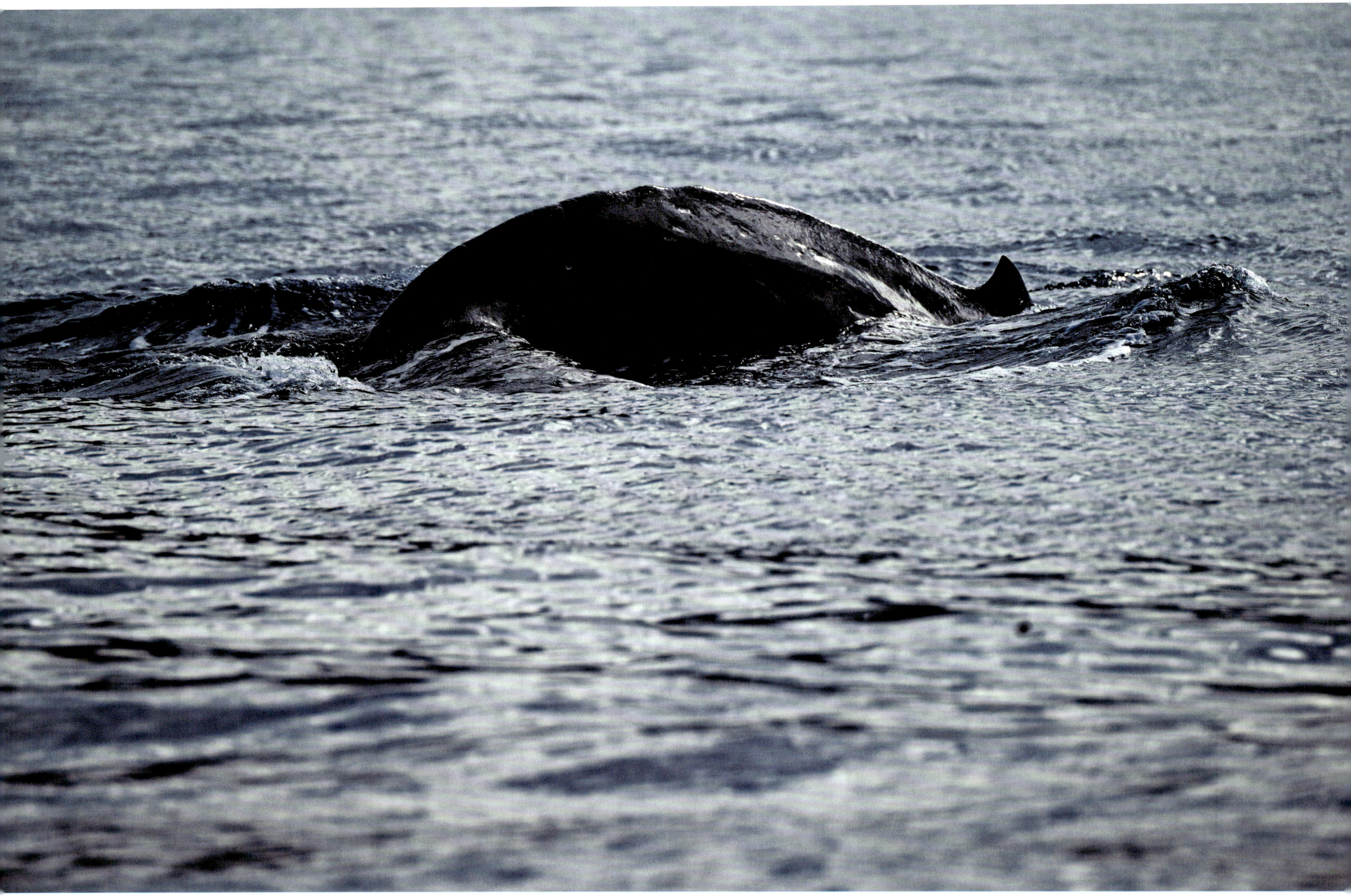

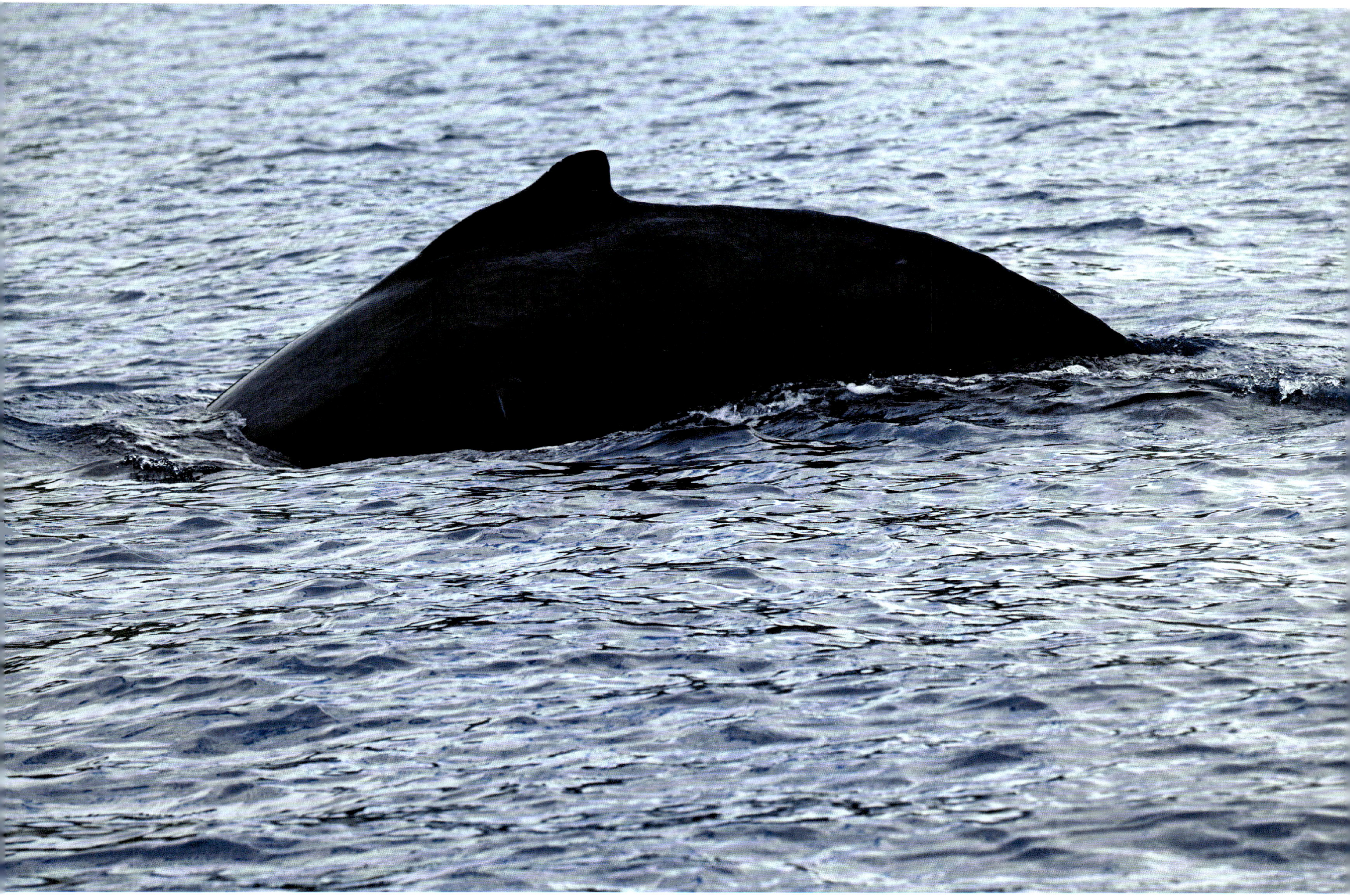

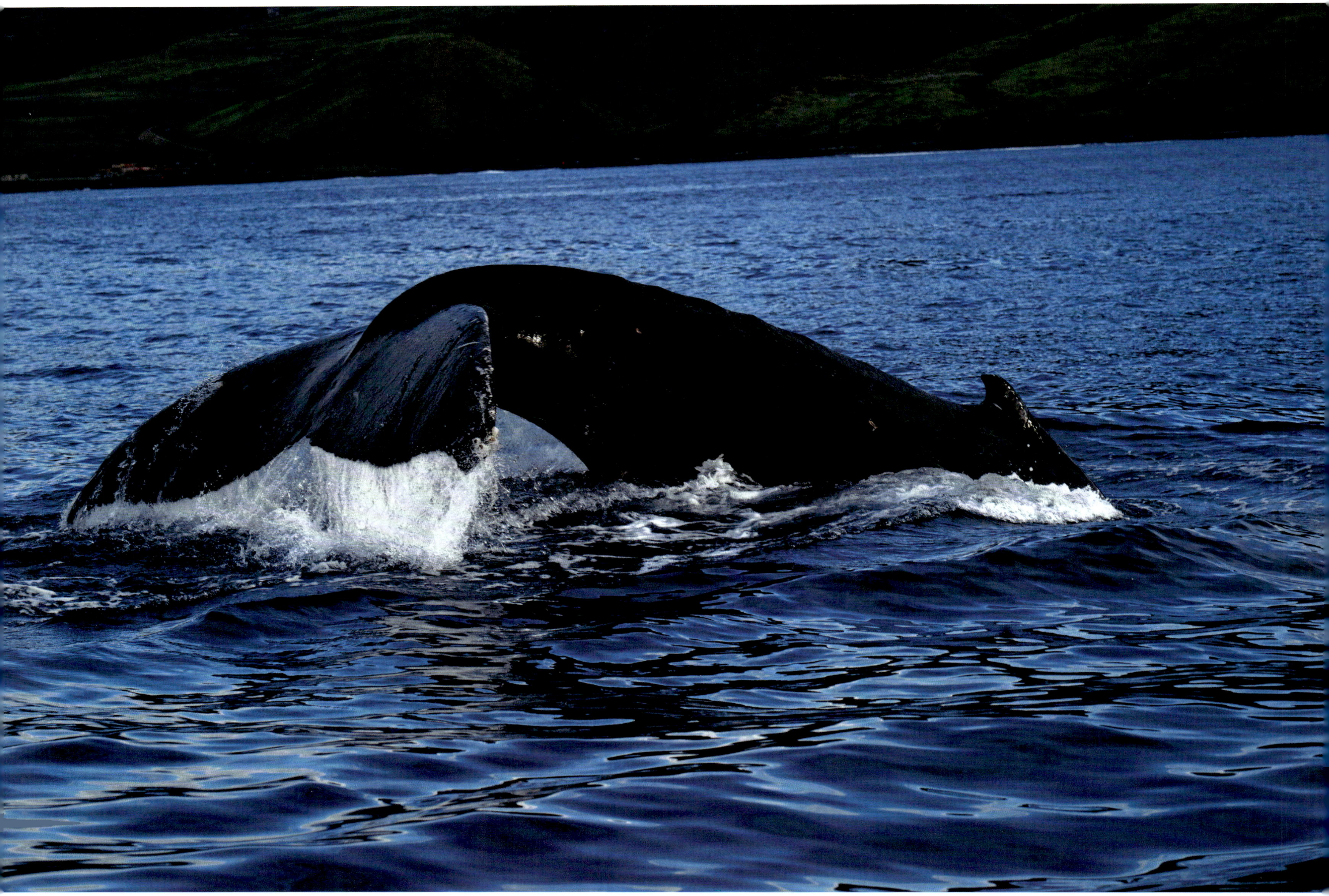

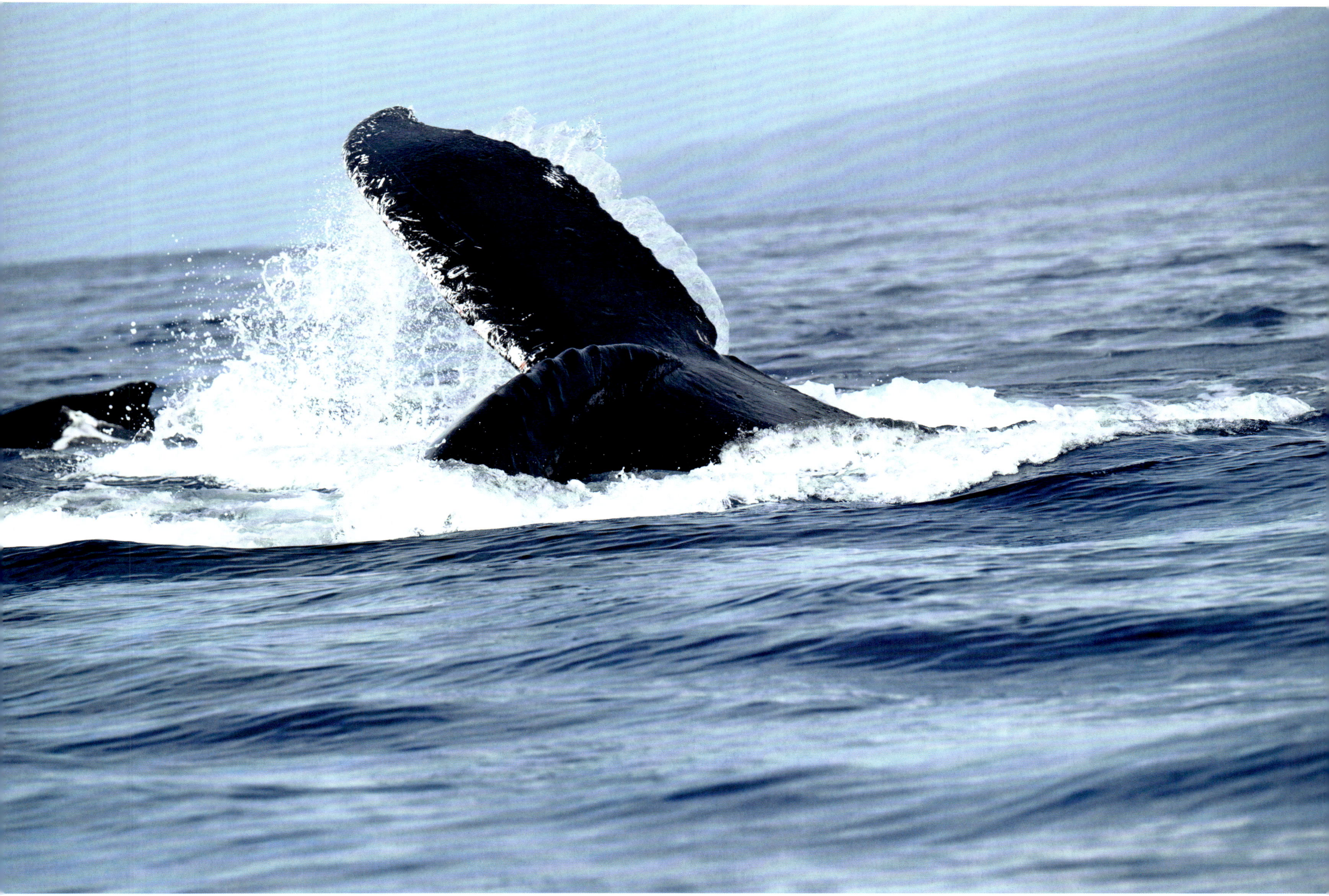

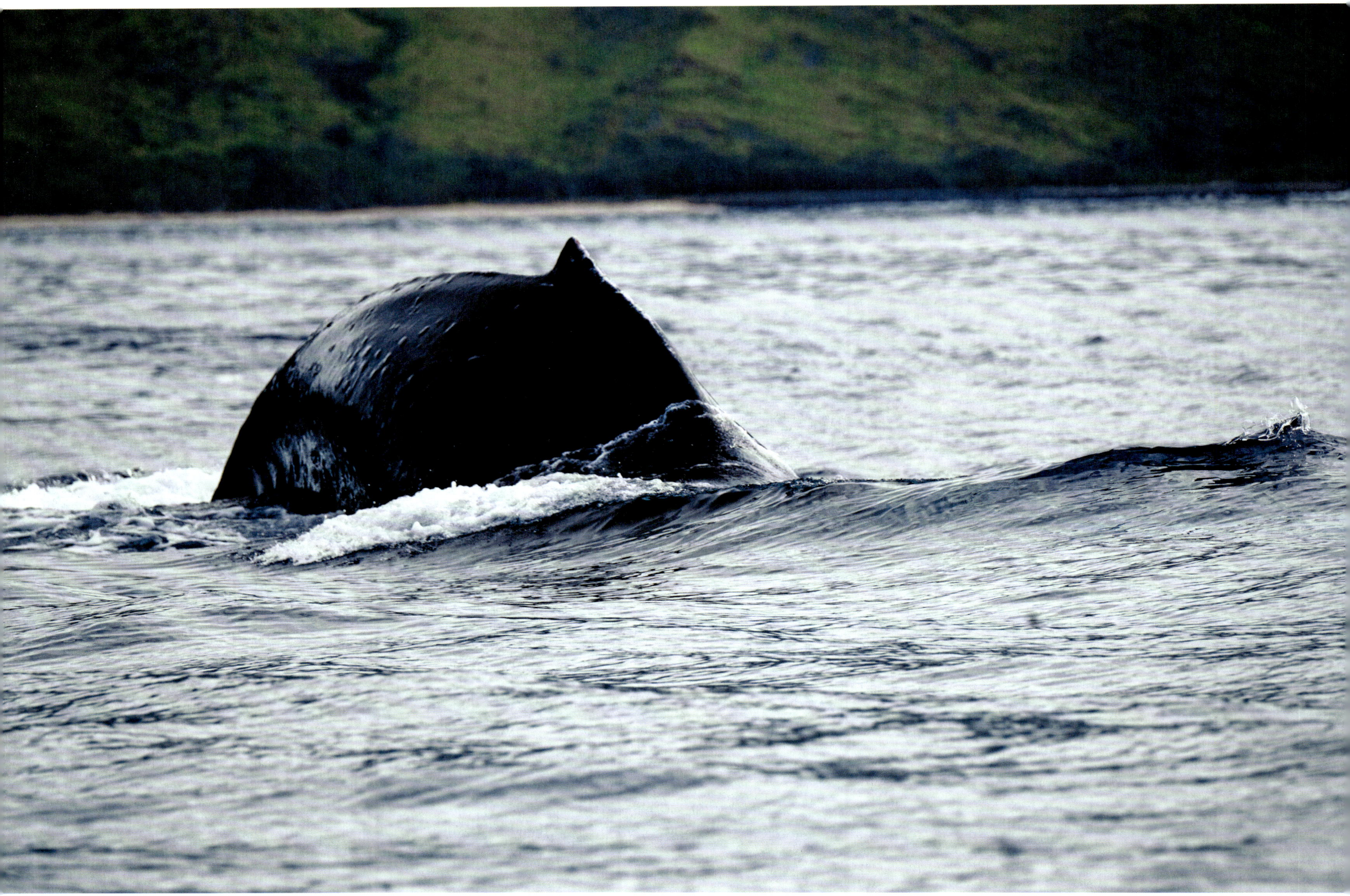

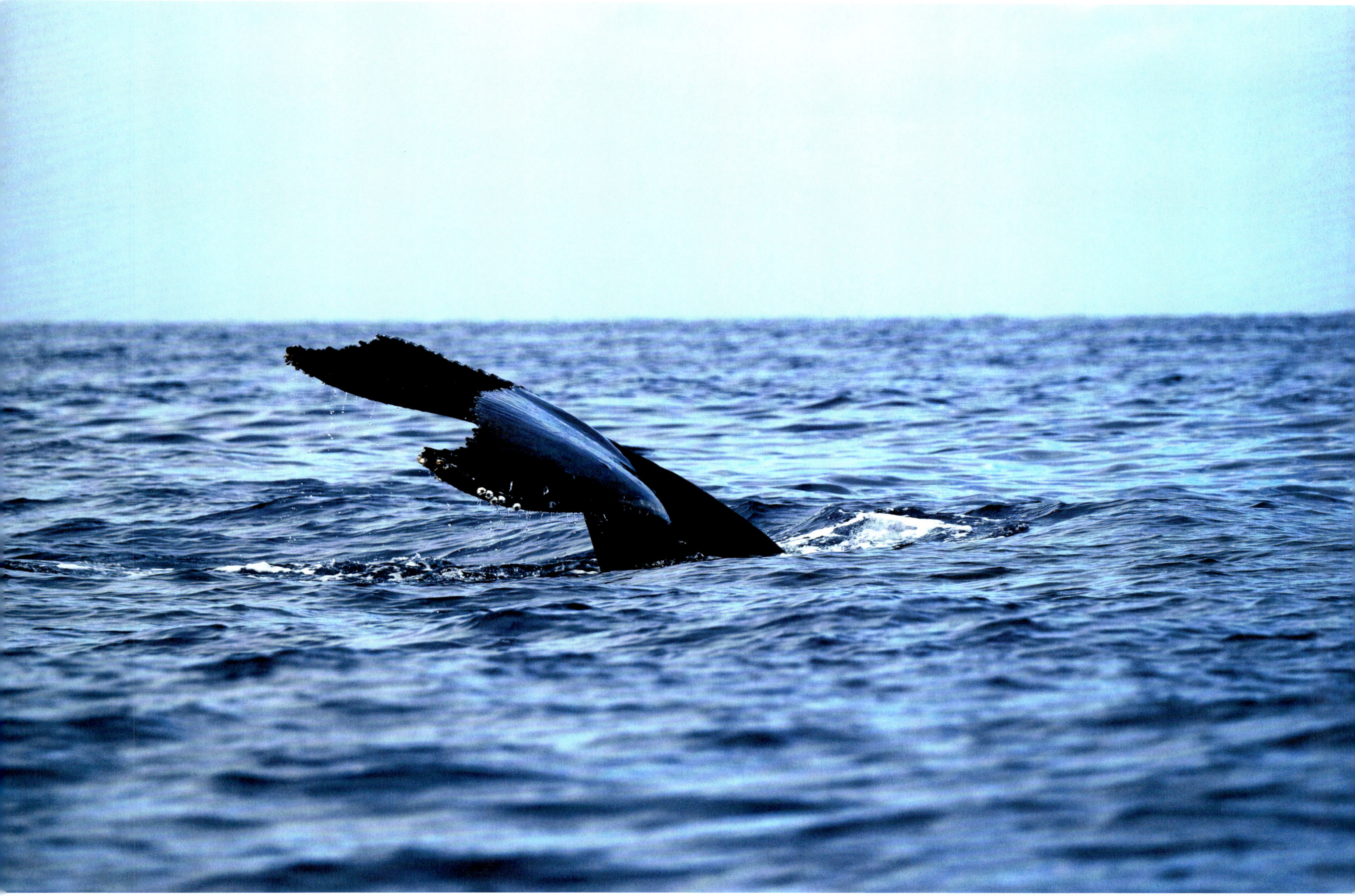

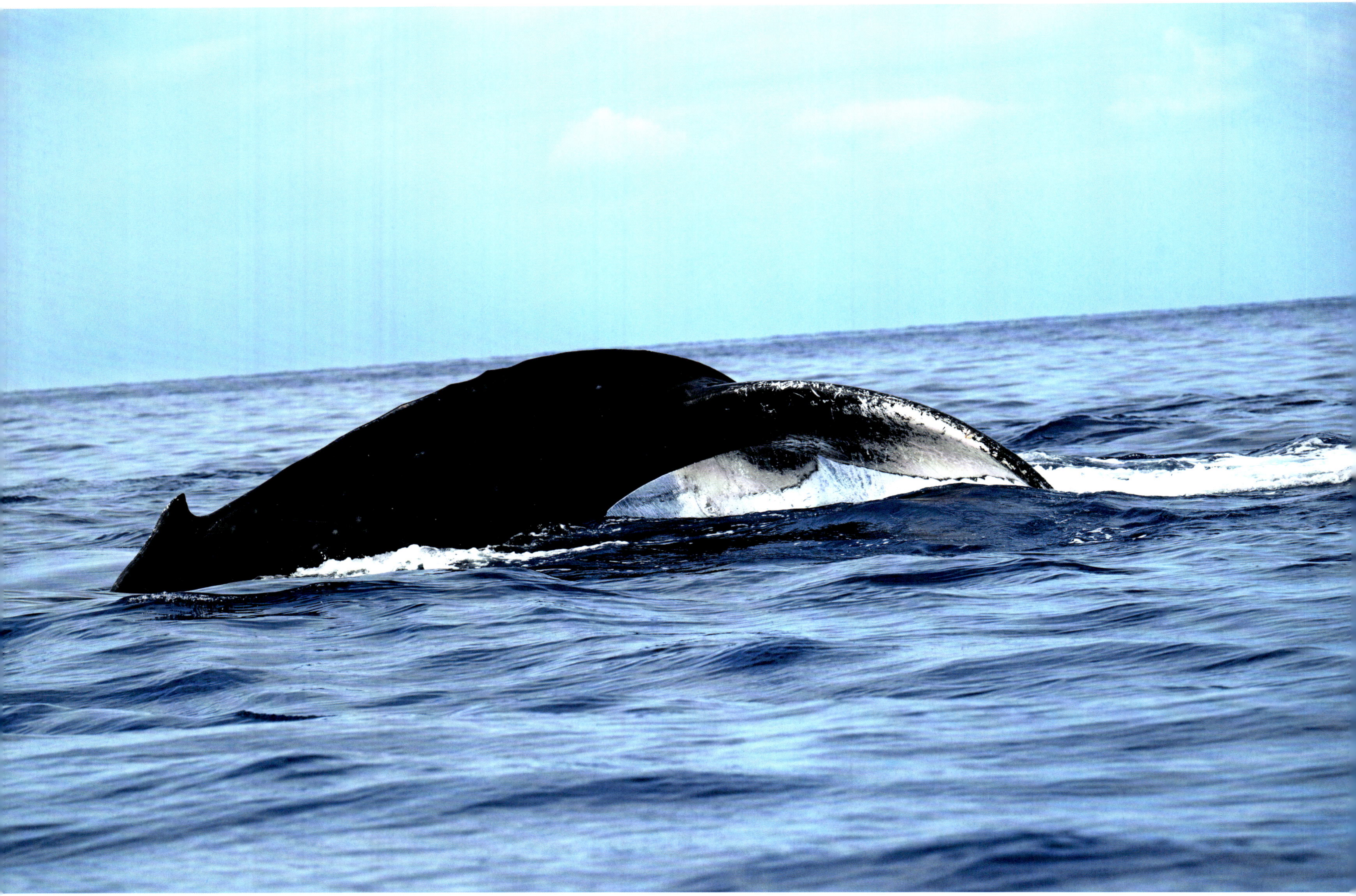

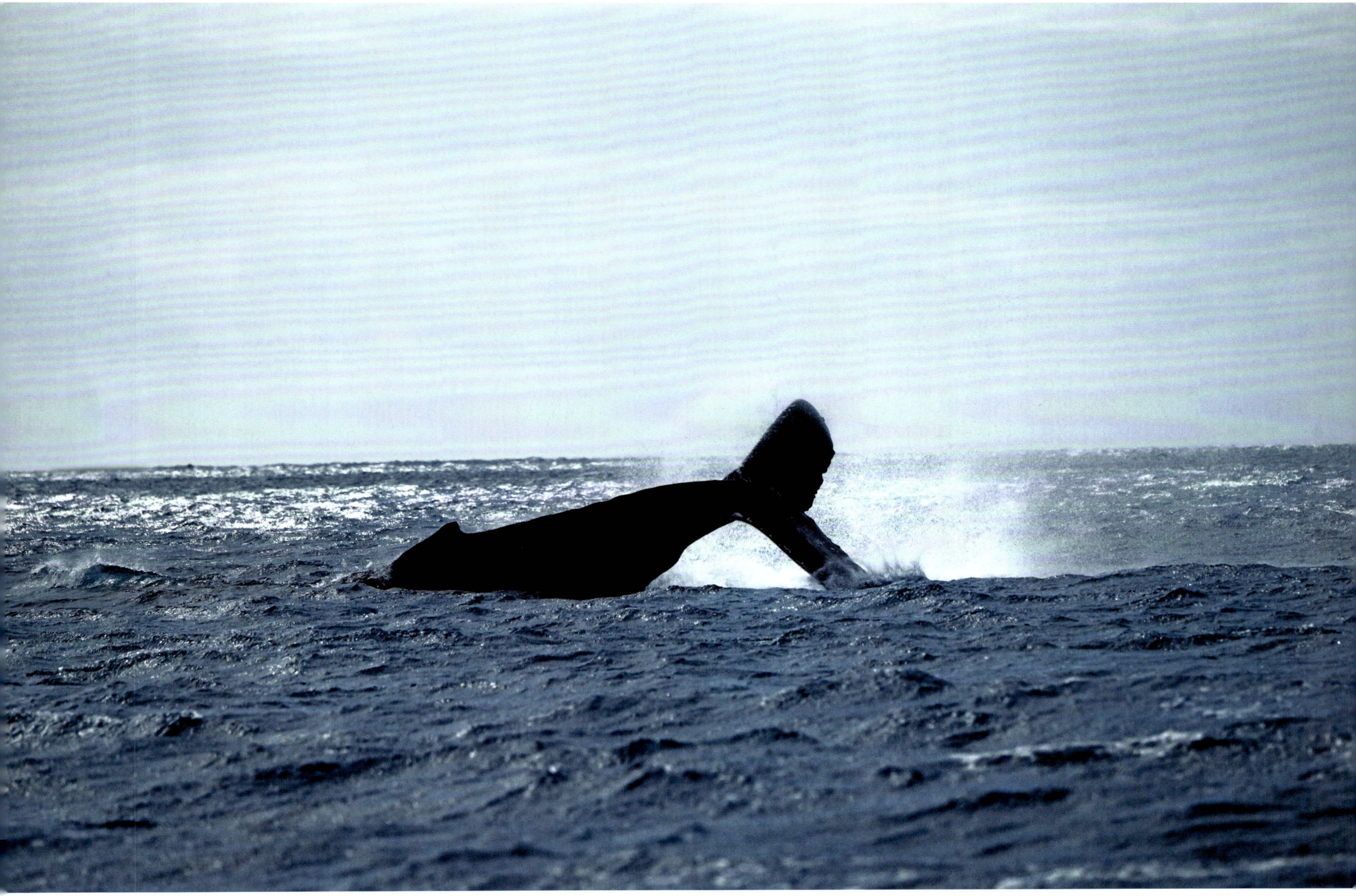

LASTING IMPACT

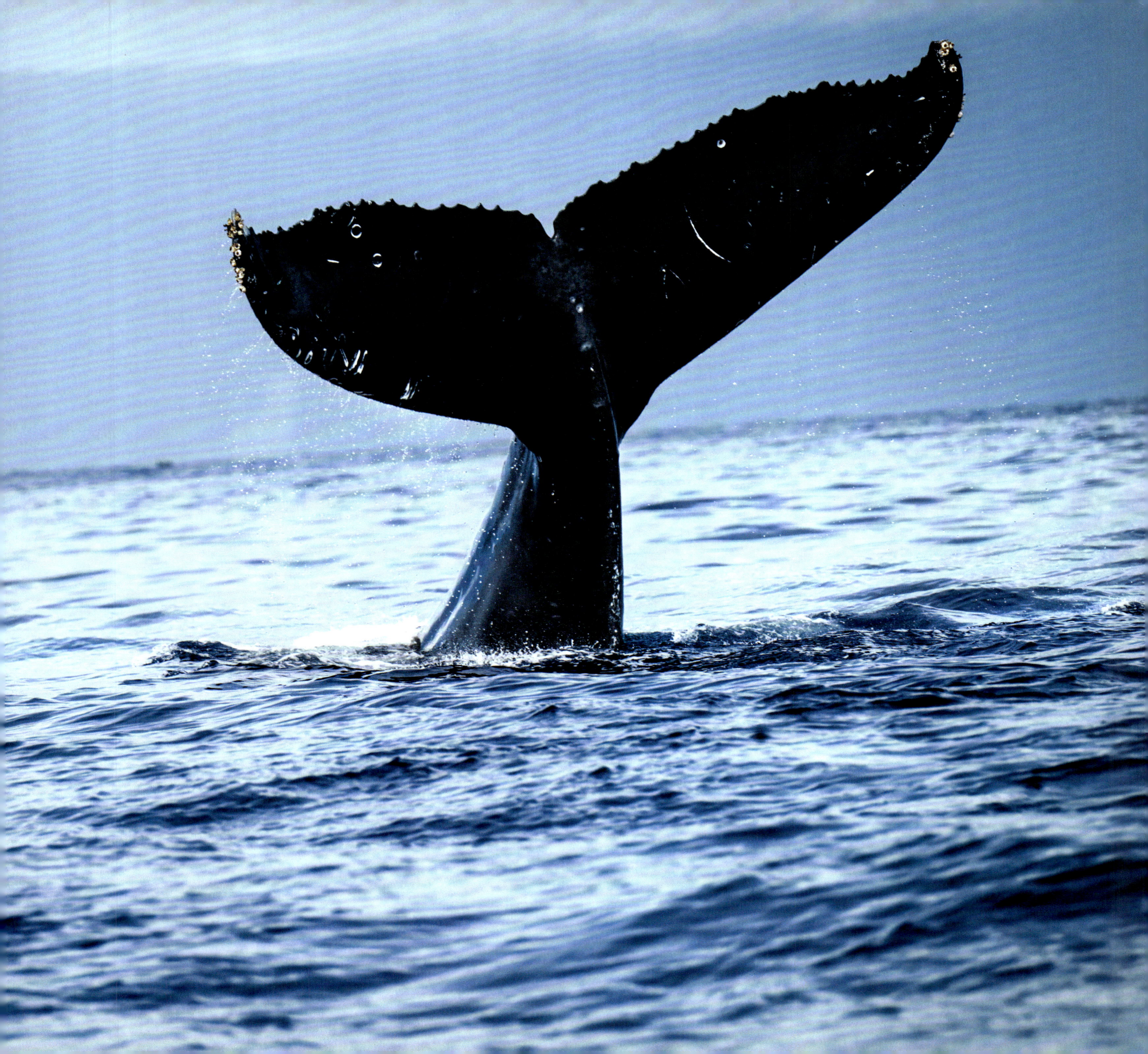

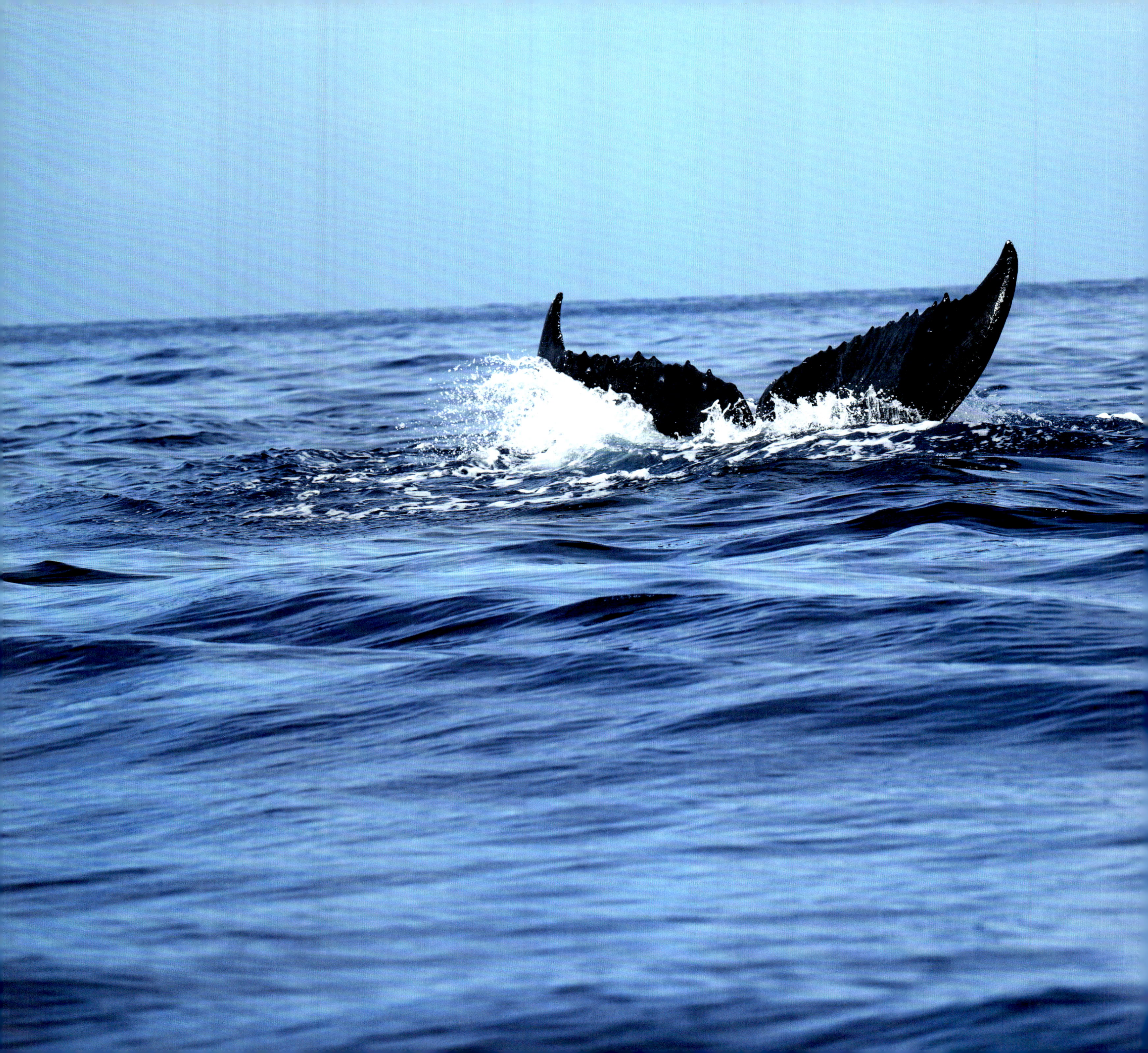

BECOMING A BULL FOR A MOMENT BEFORE
SLOWLY DISAPPEARING INTO THE ABYSS

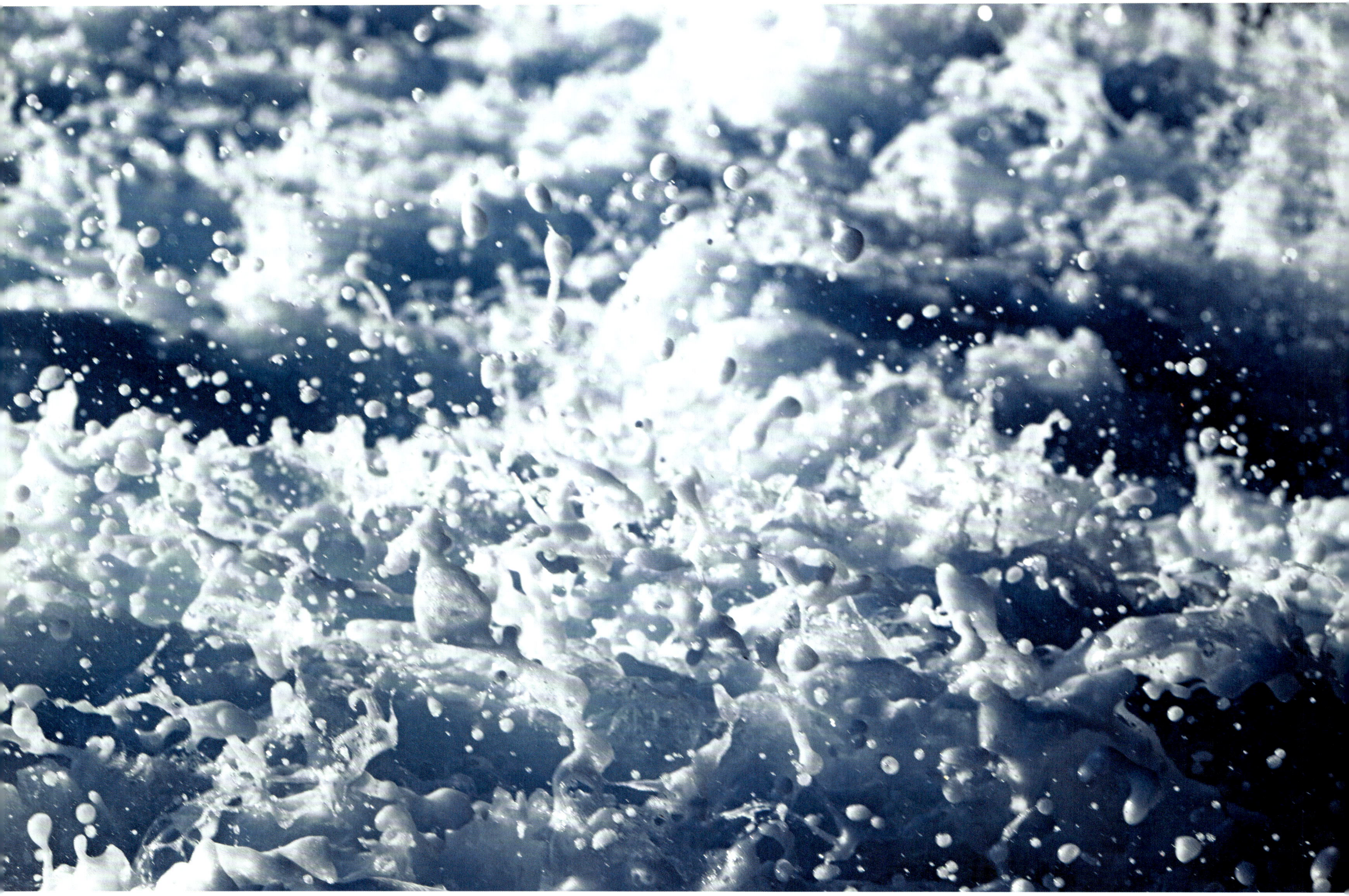

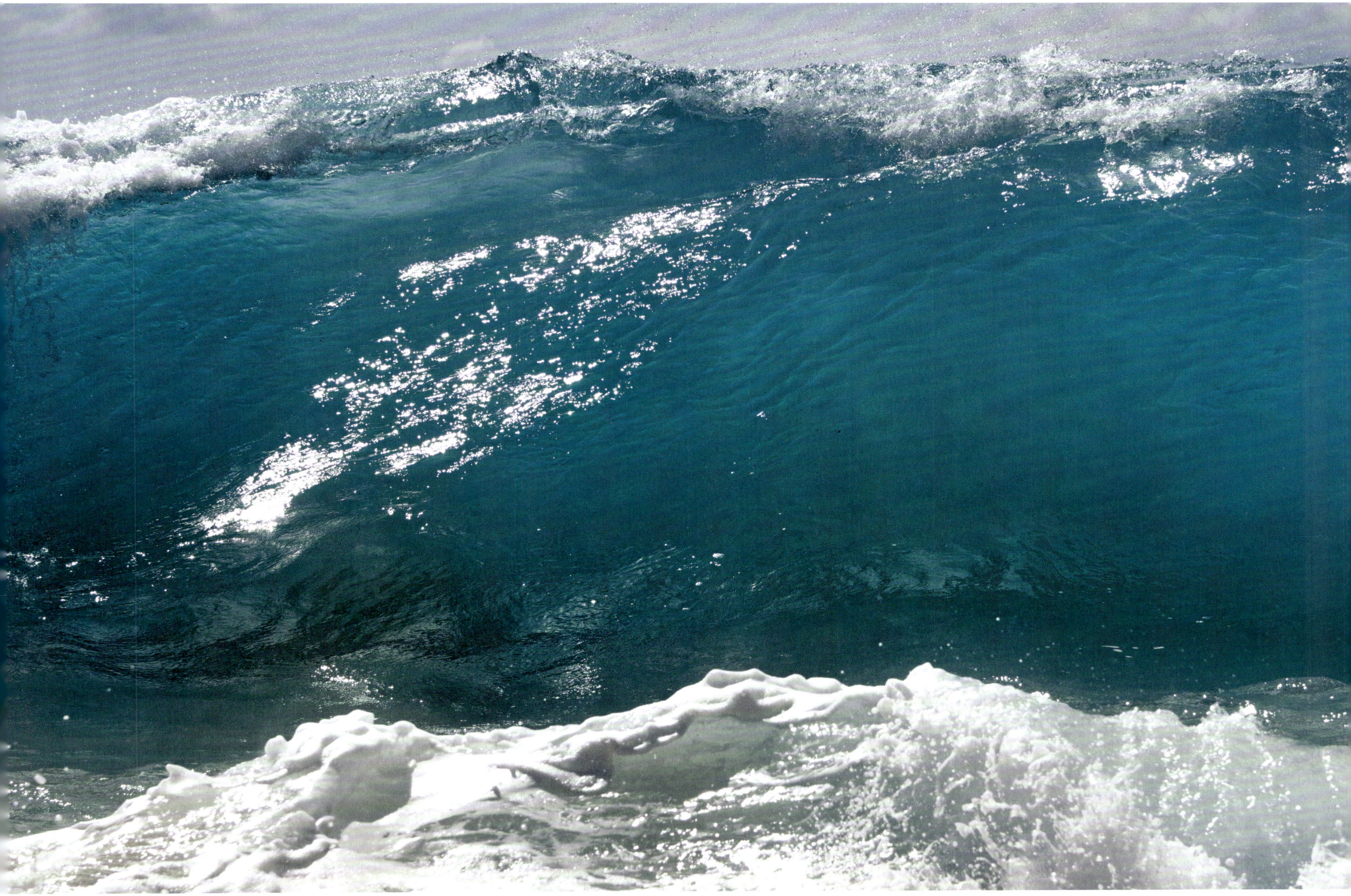

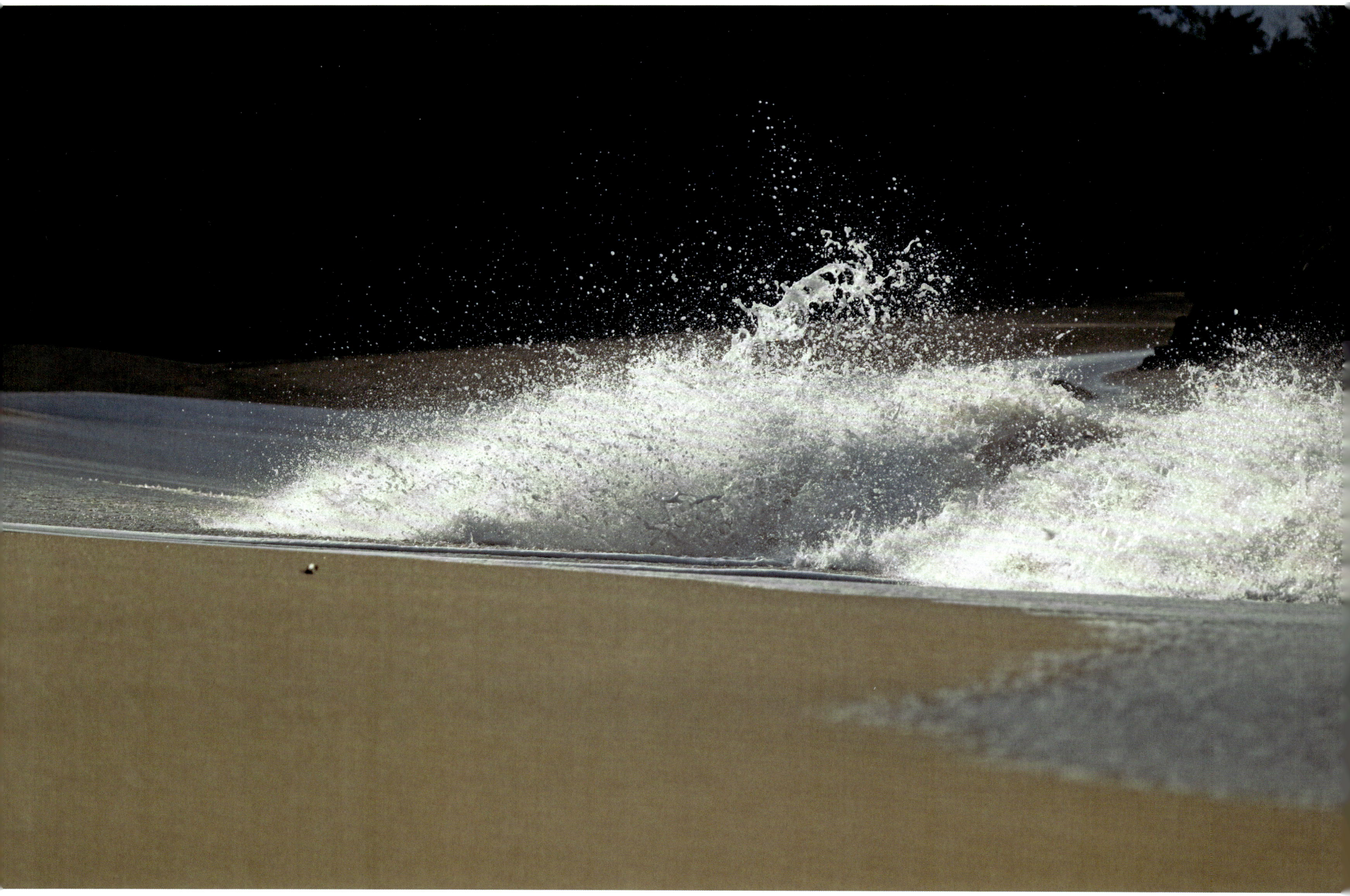

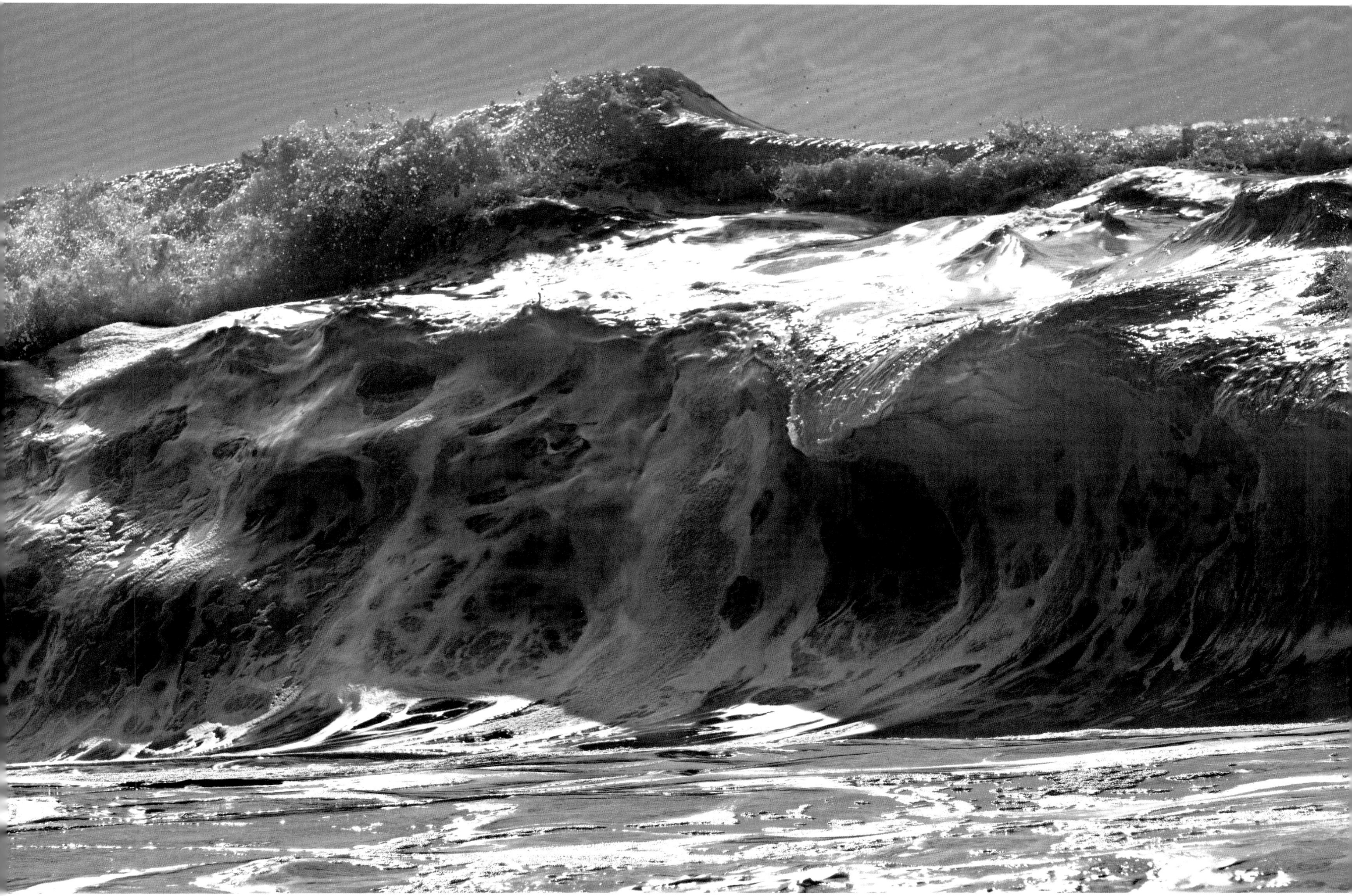

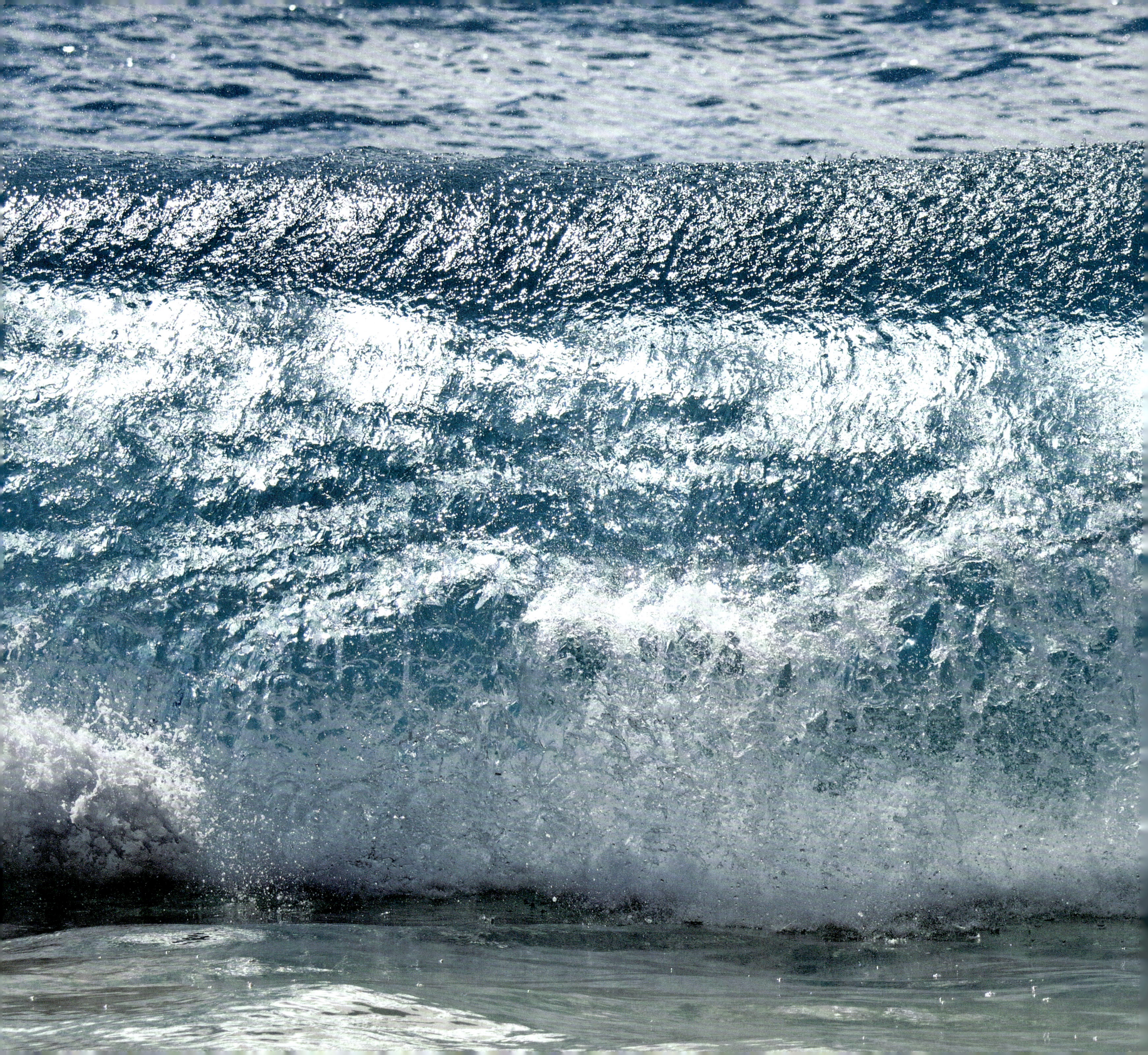

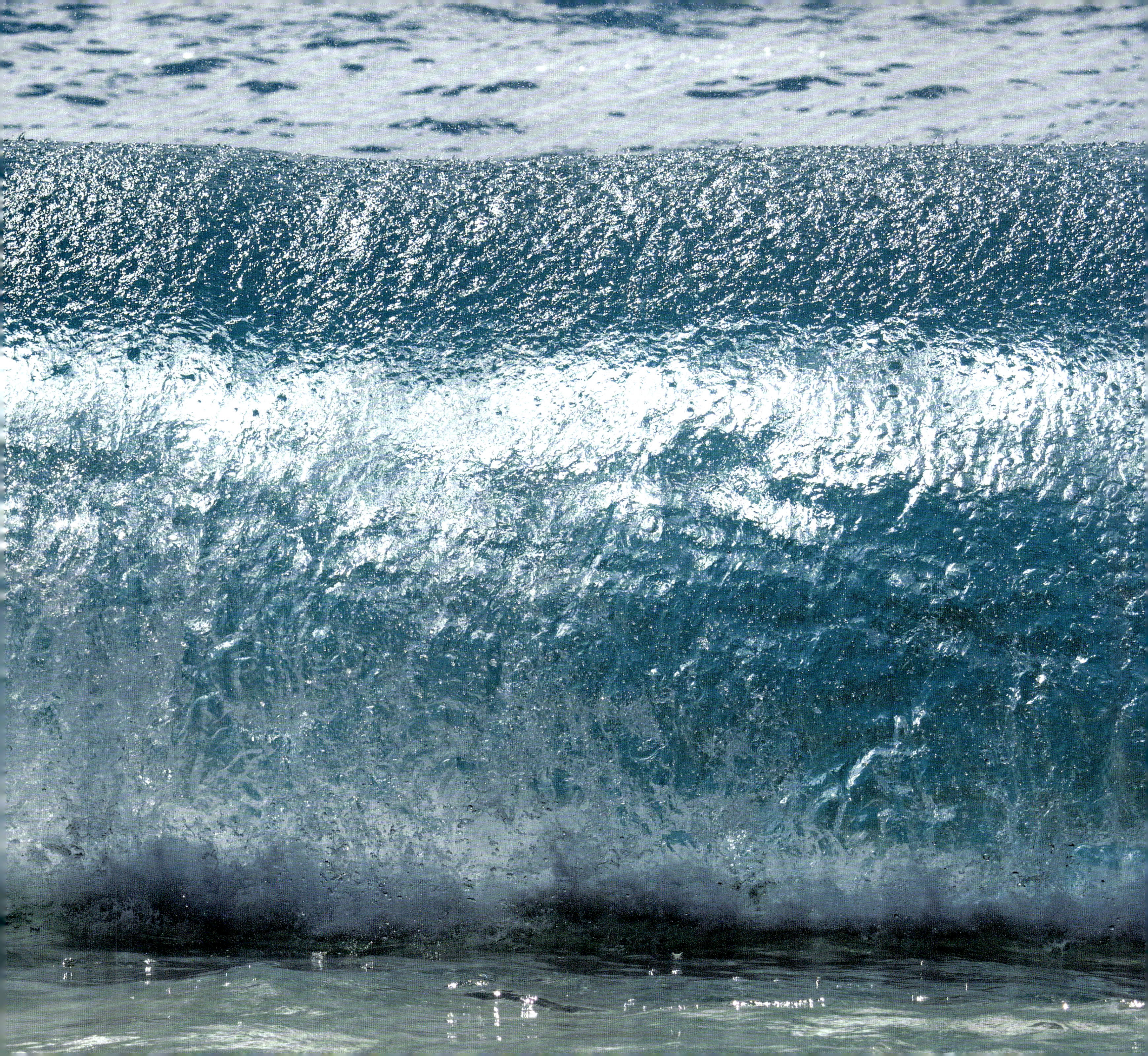

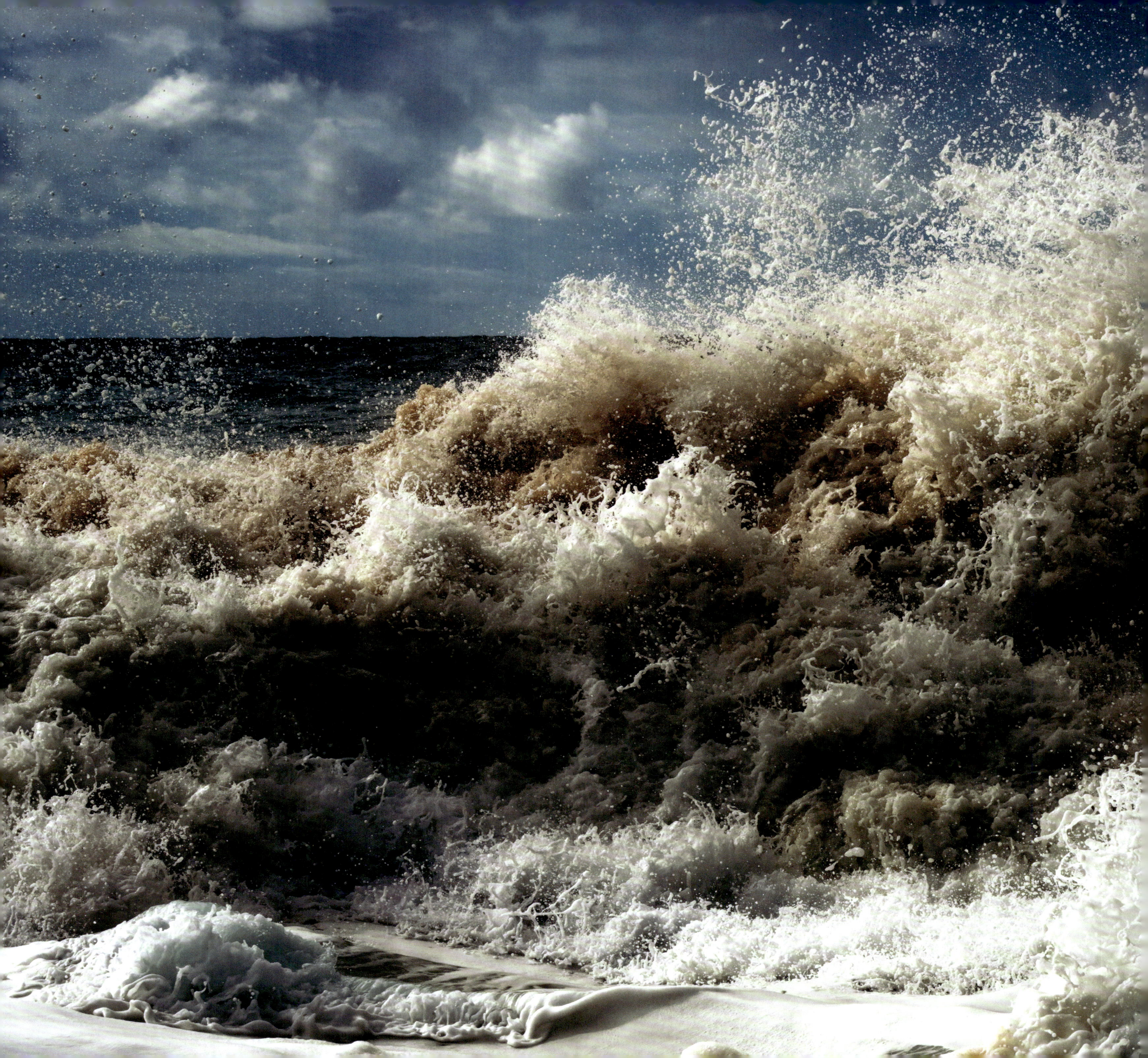

61

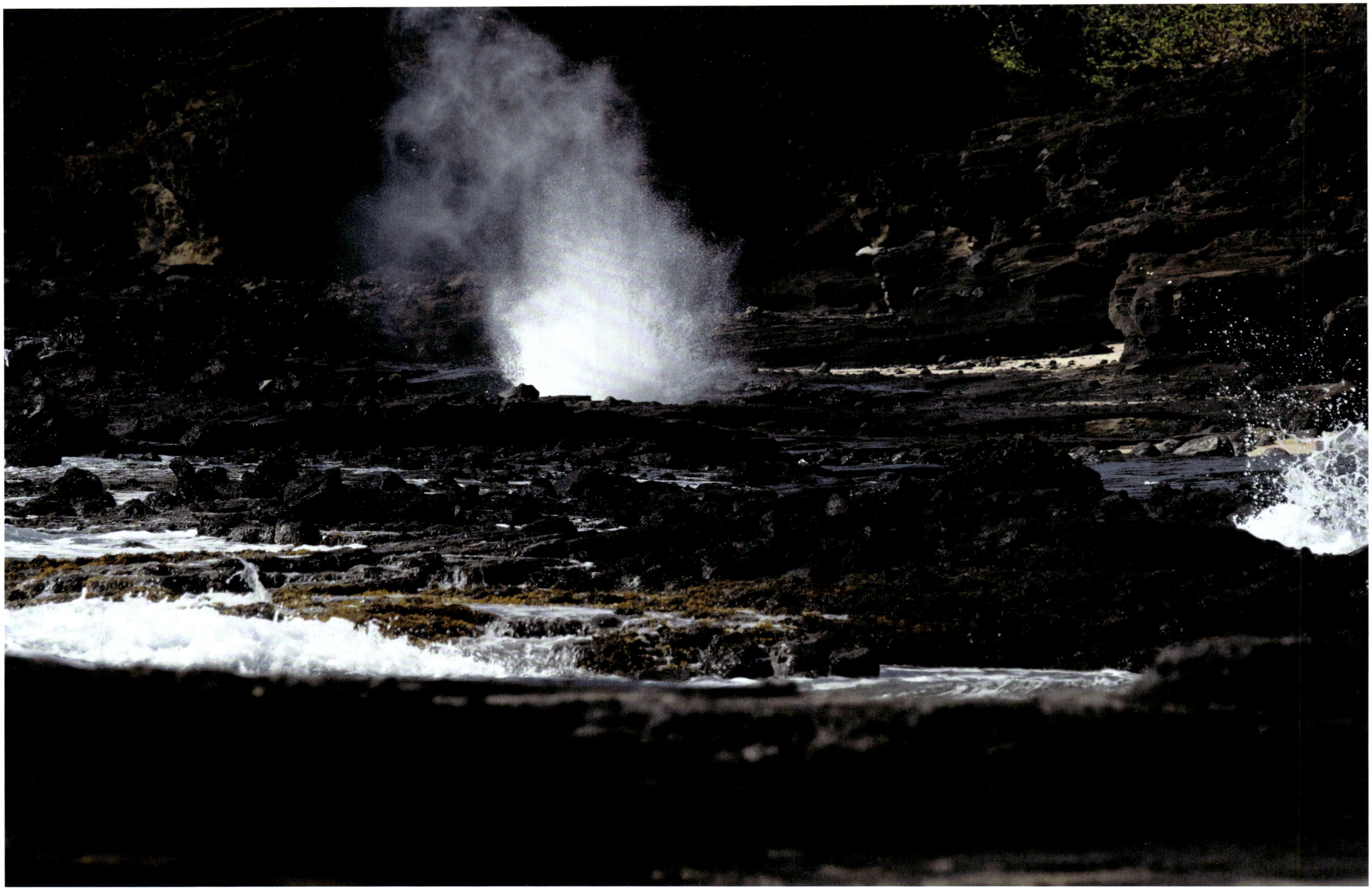

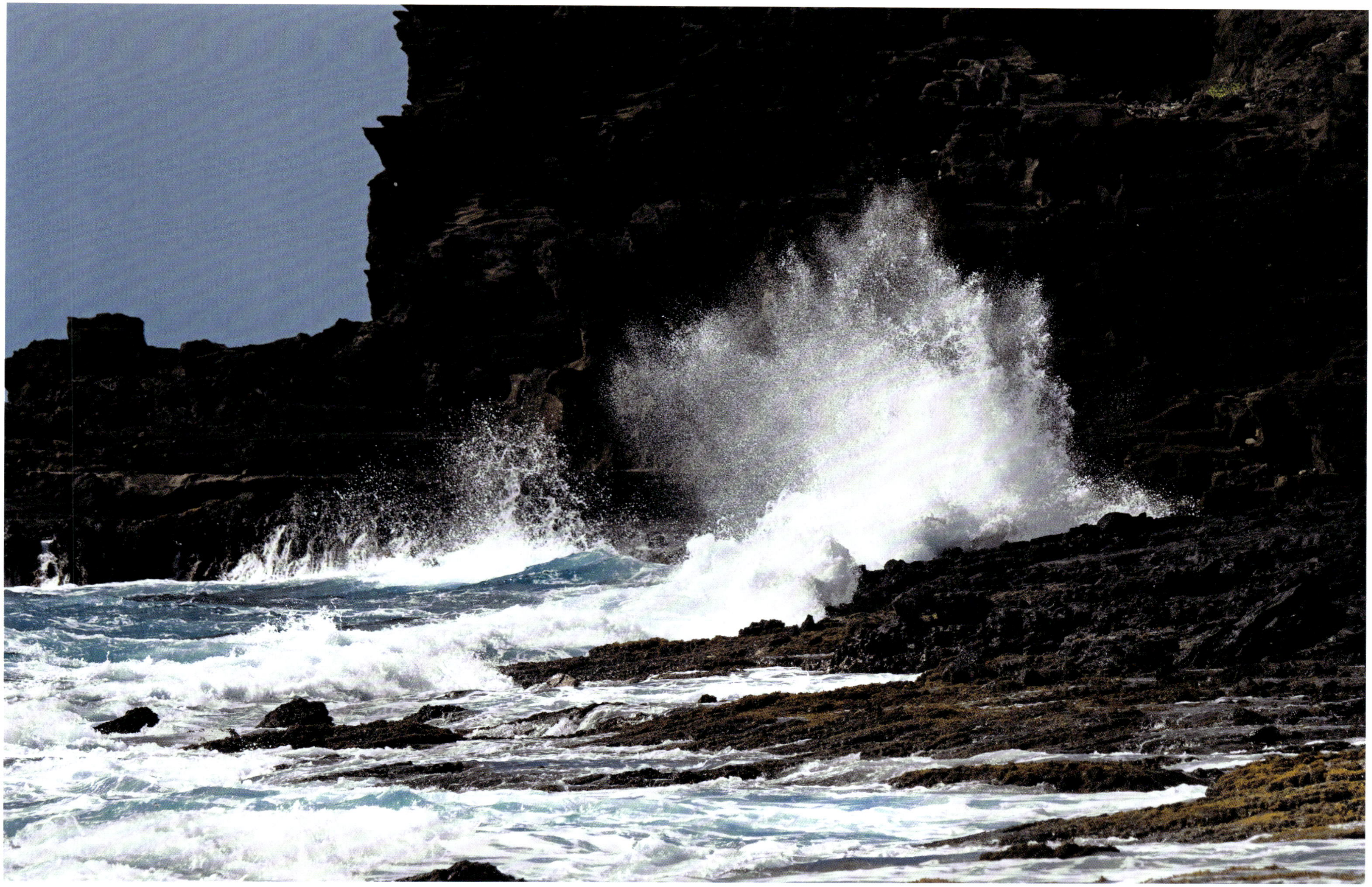

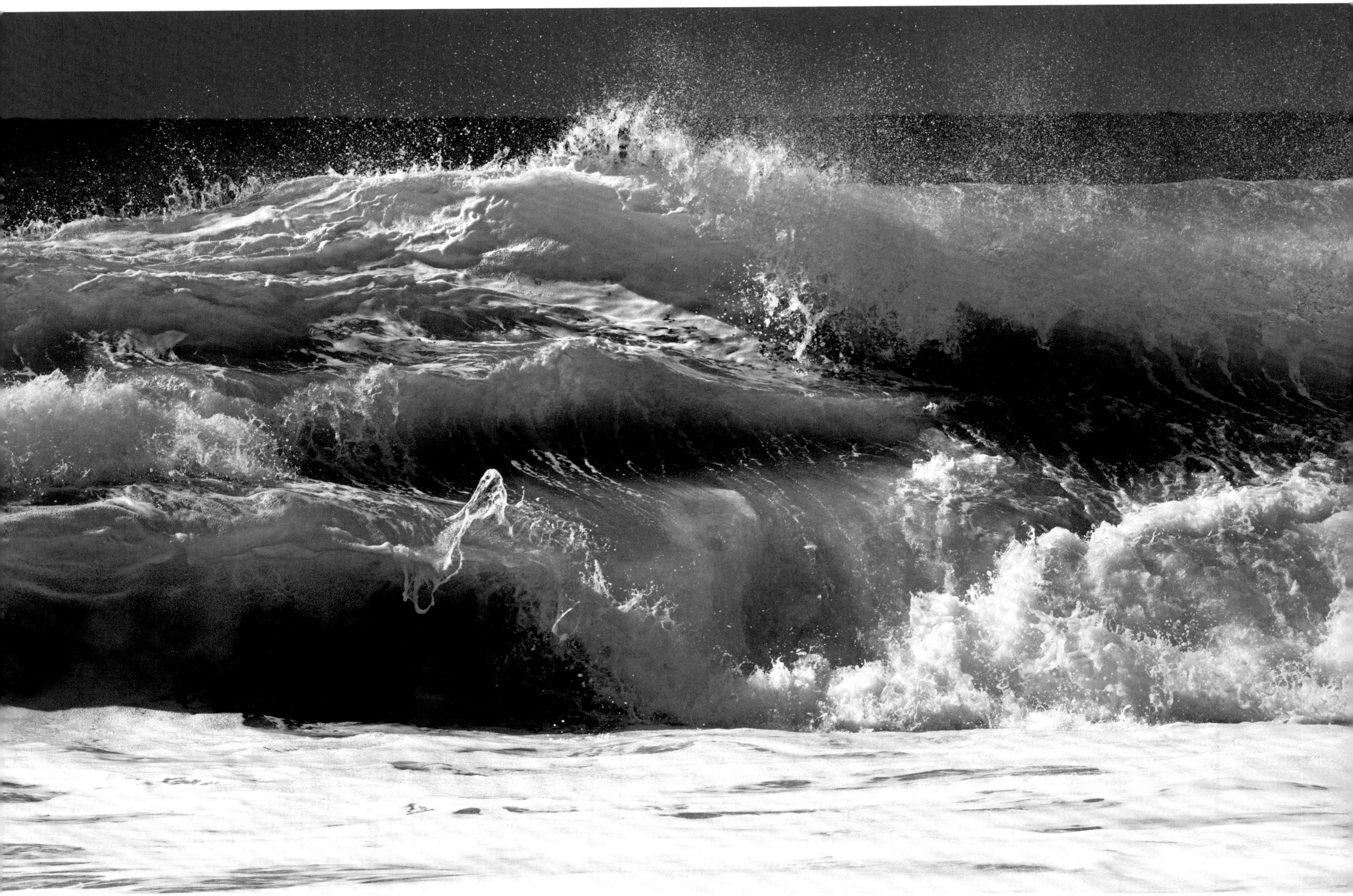

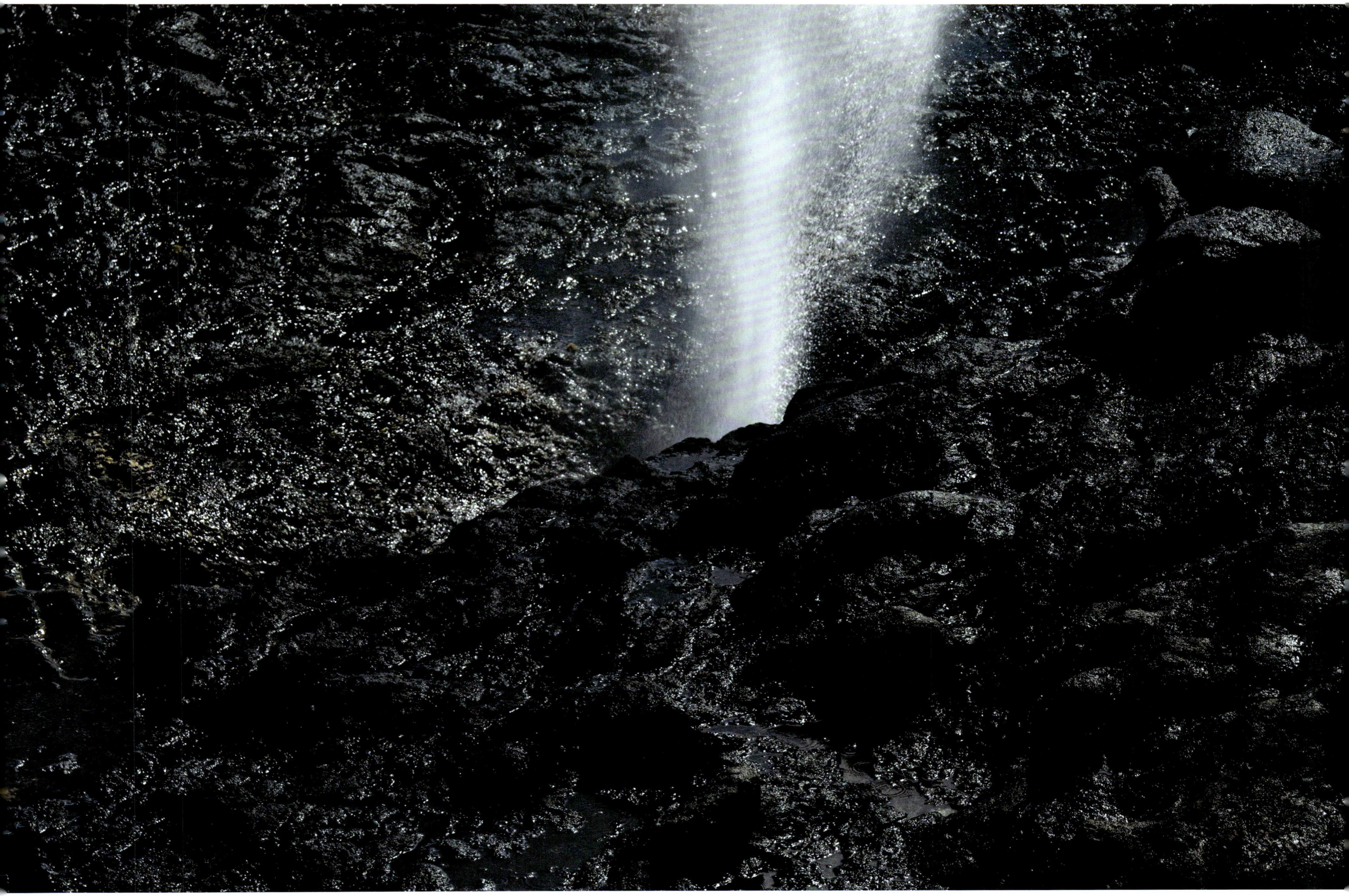

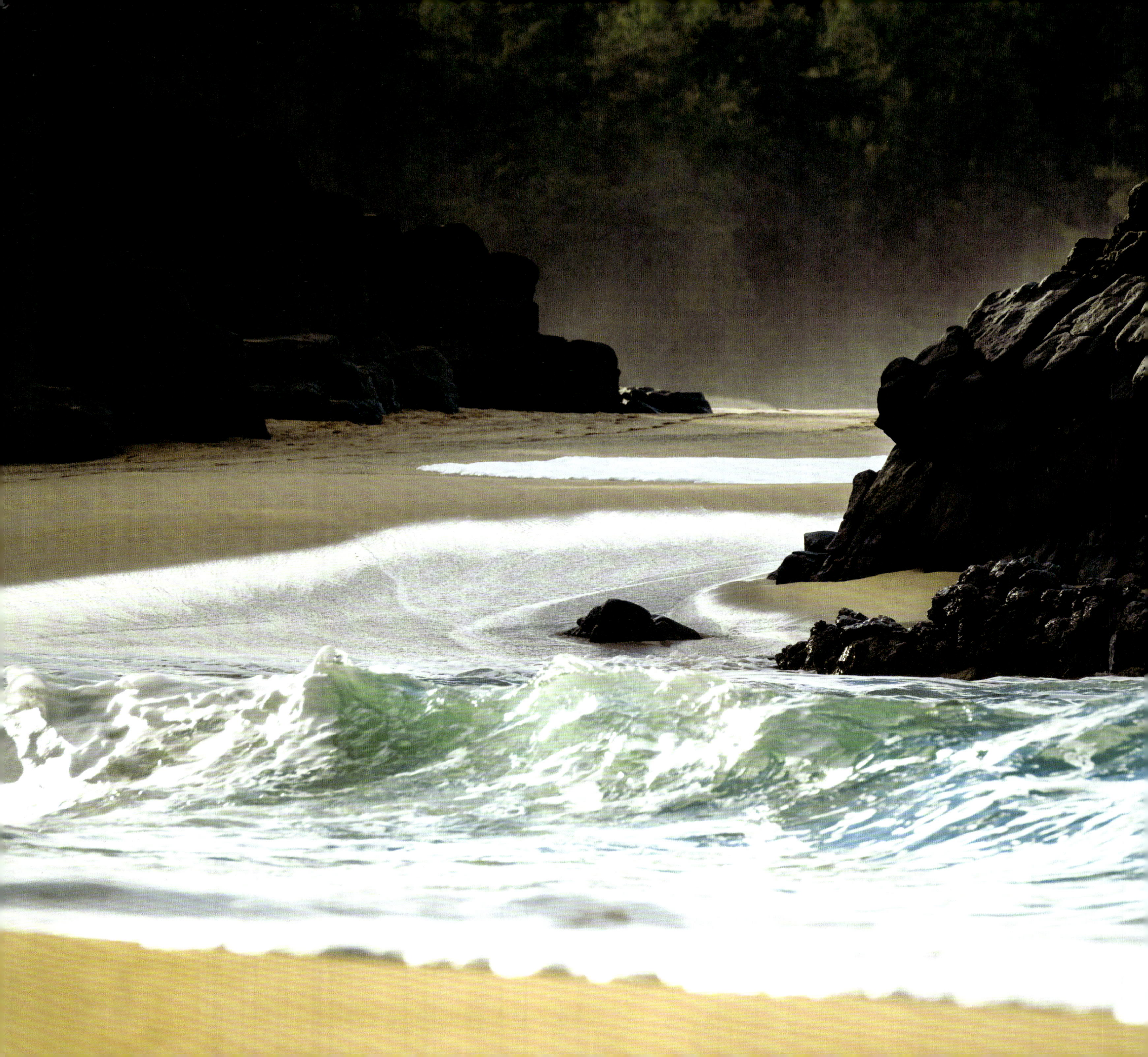

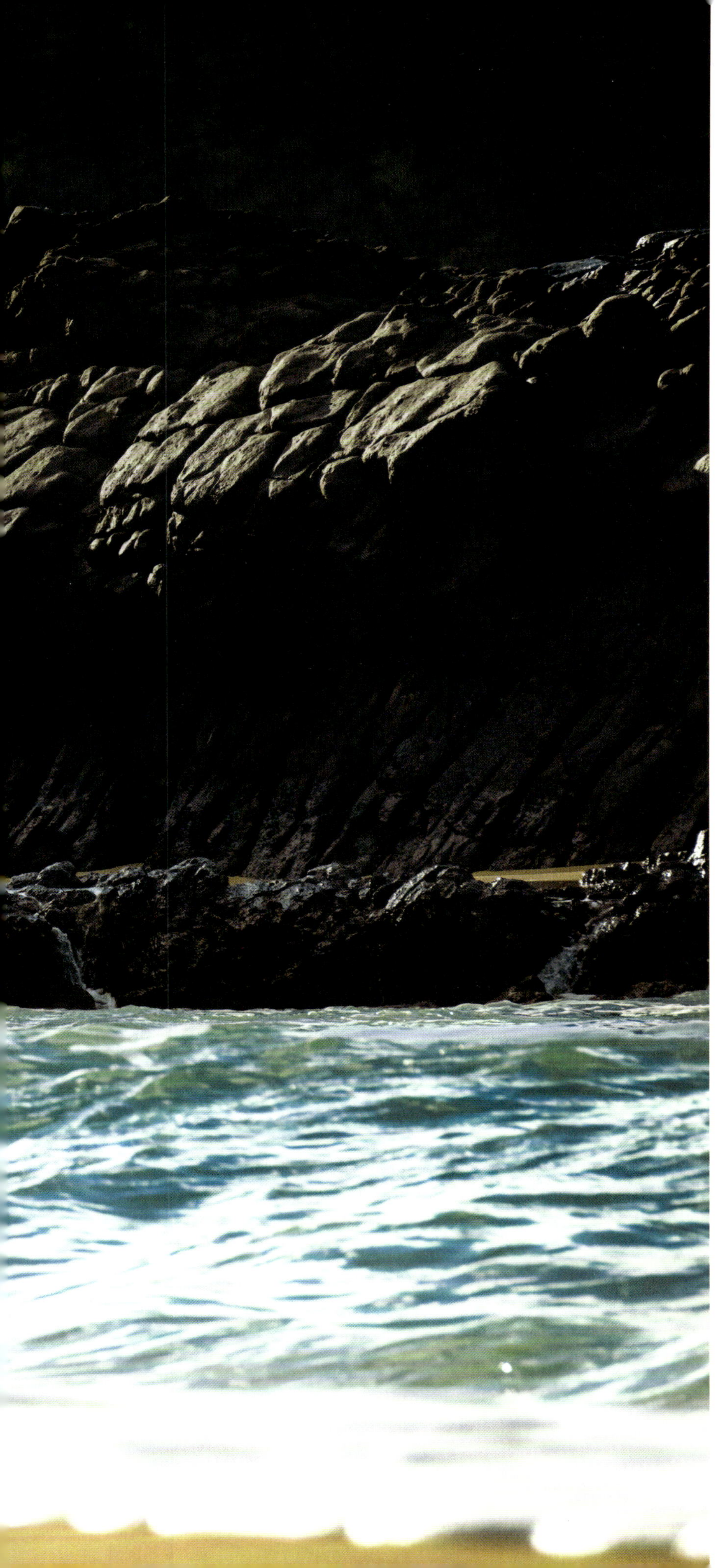

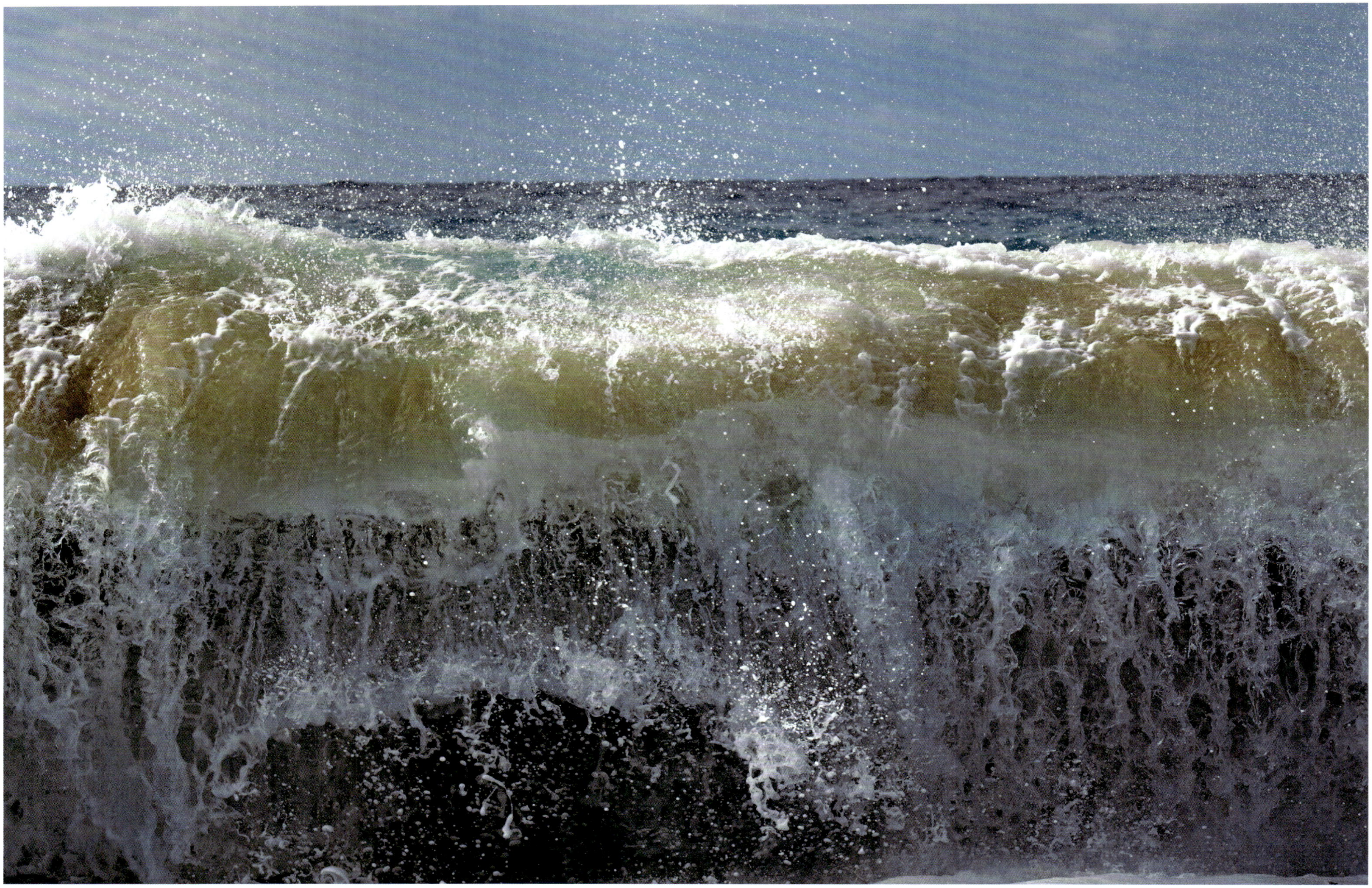

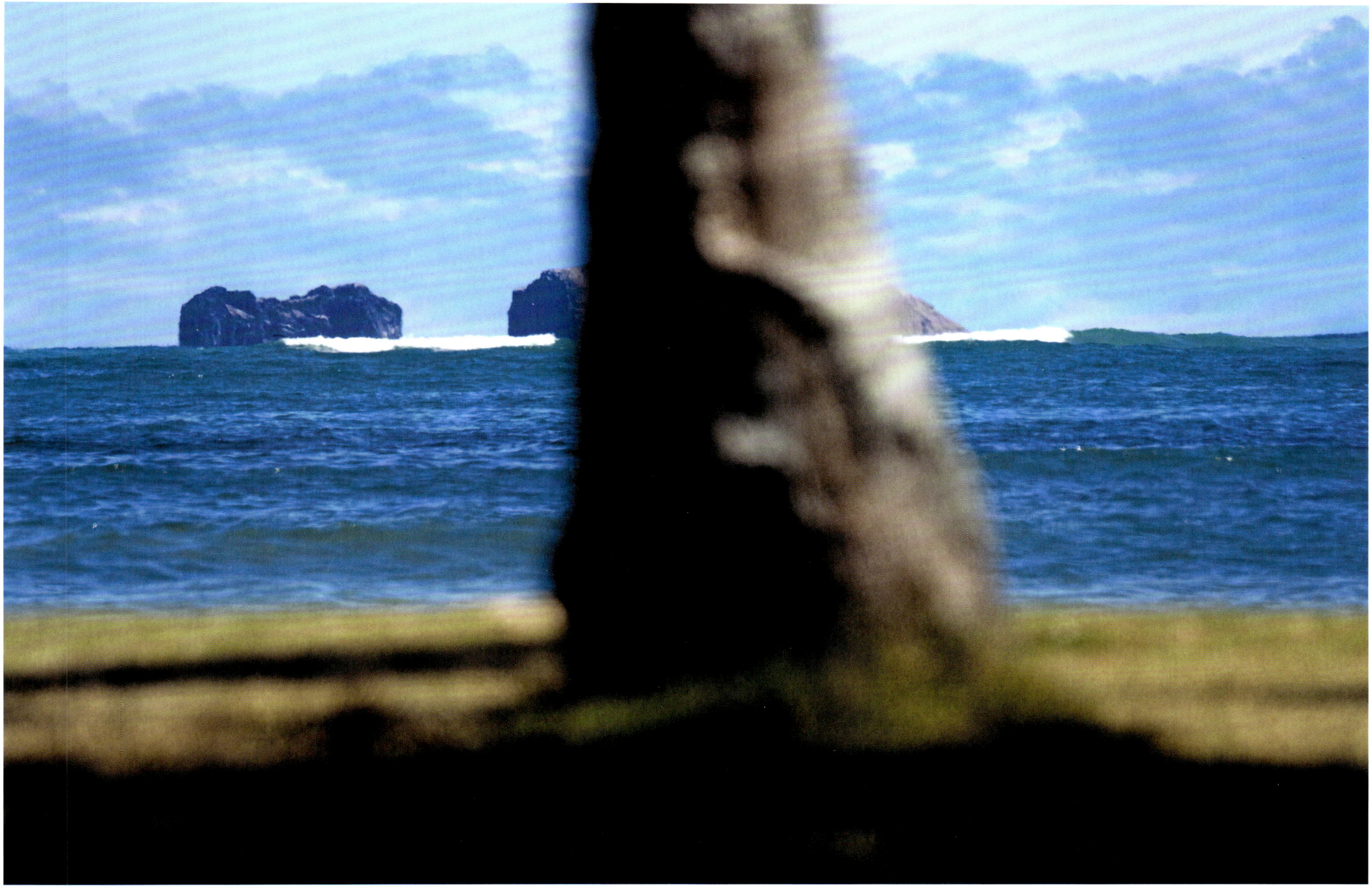

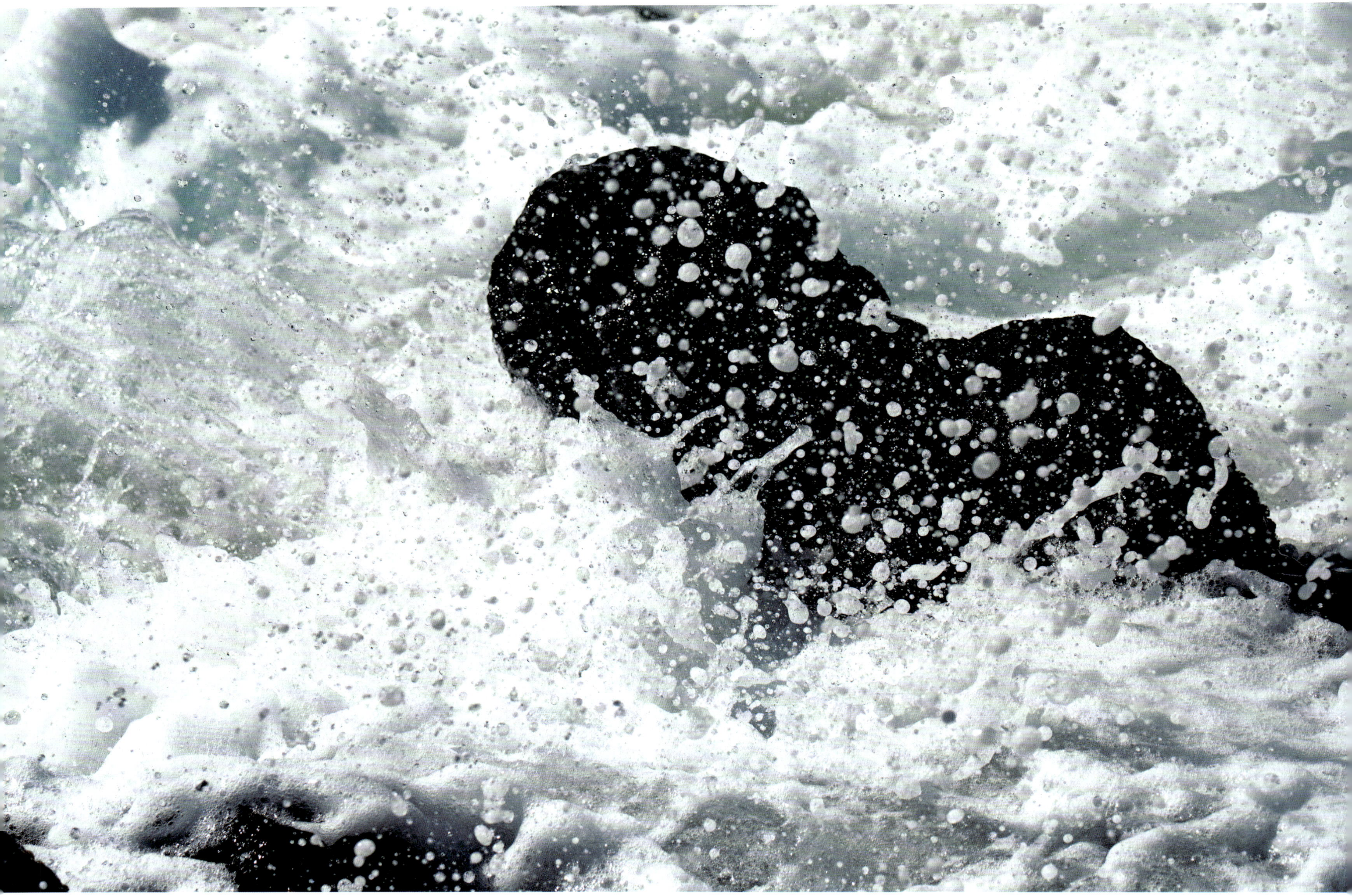

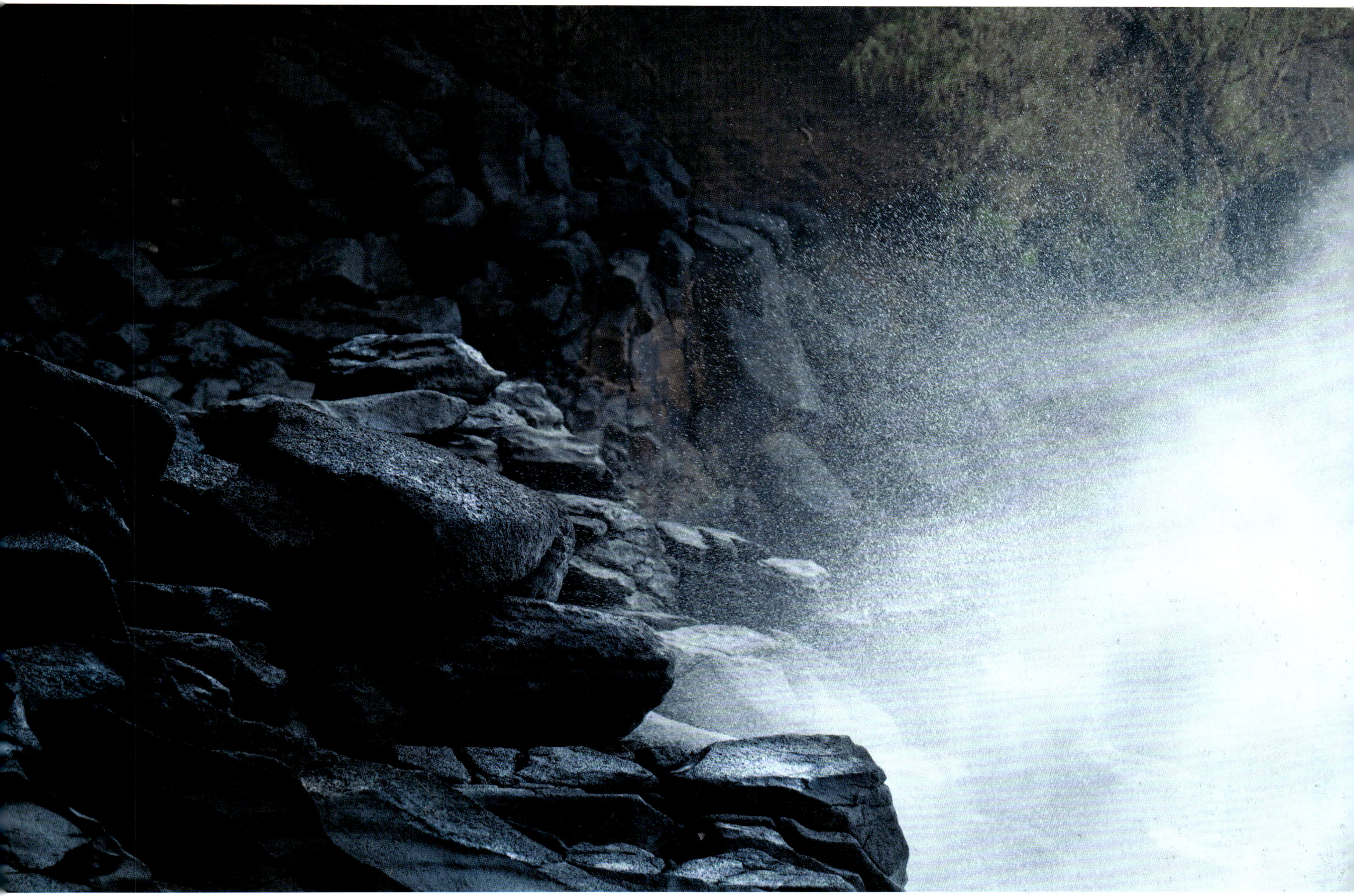

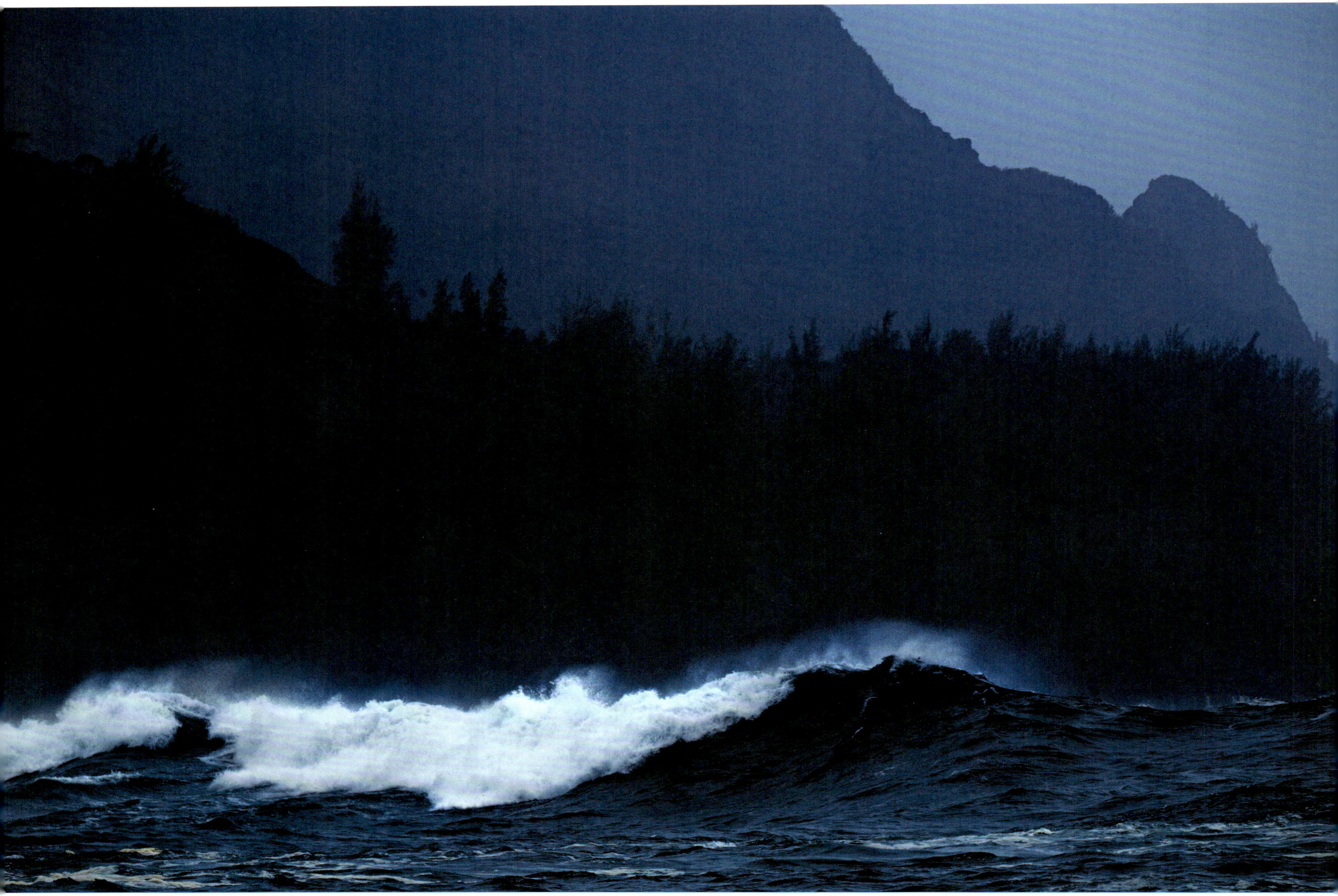

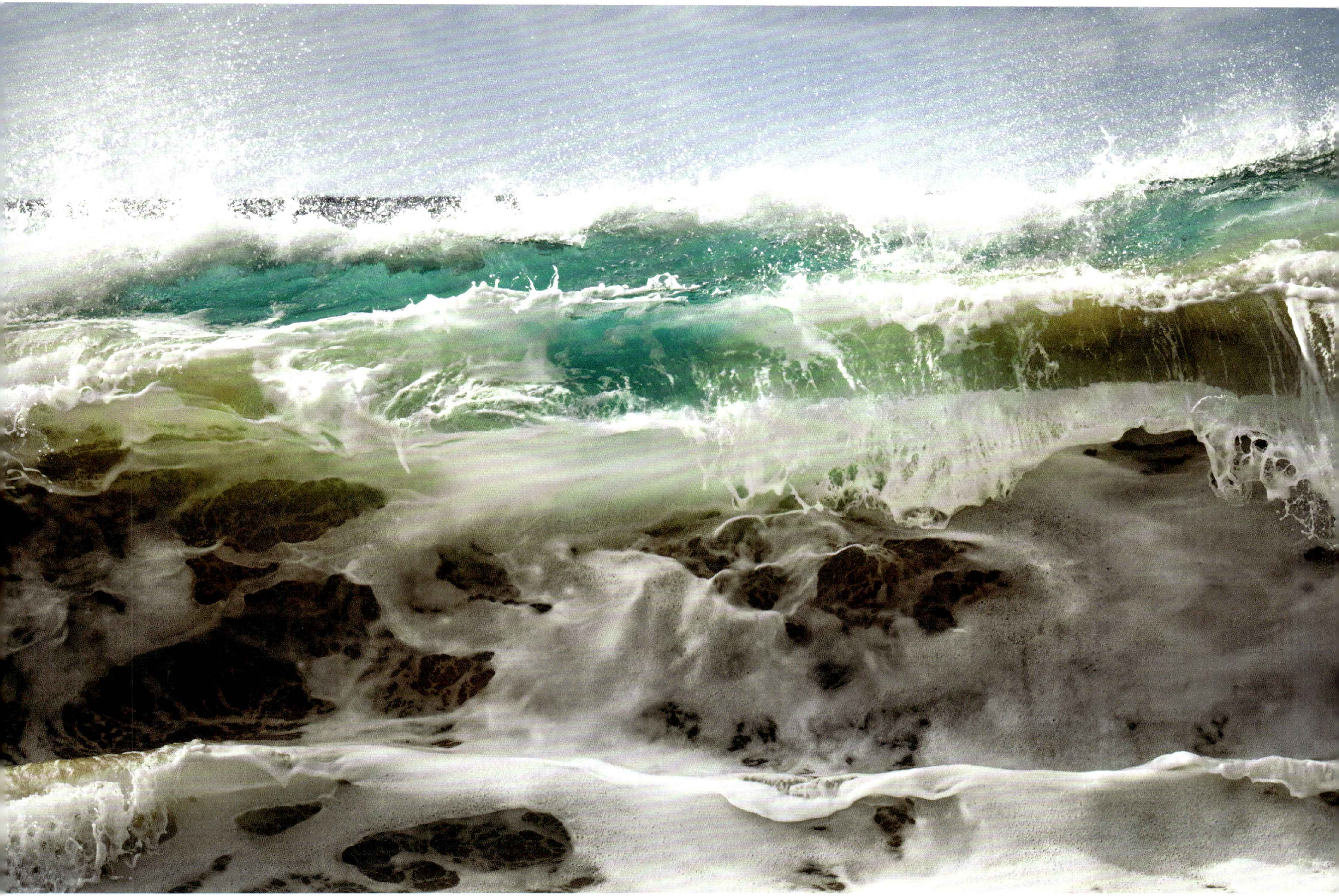

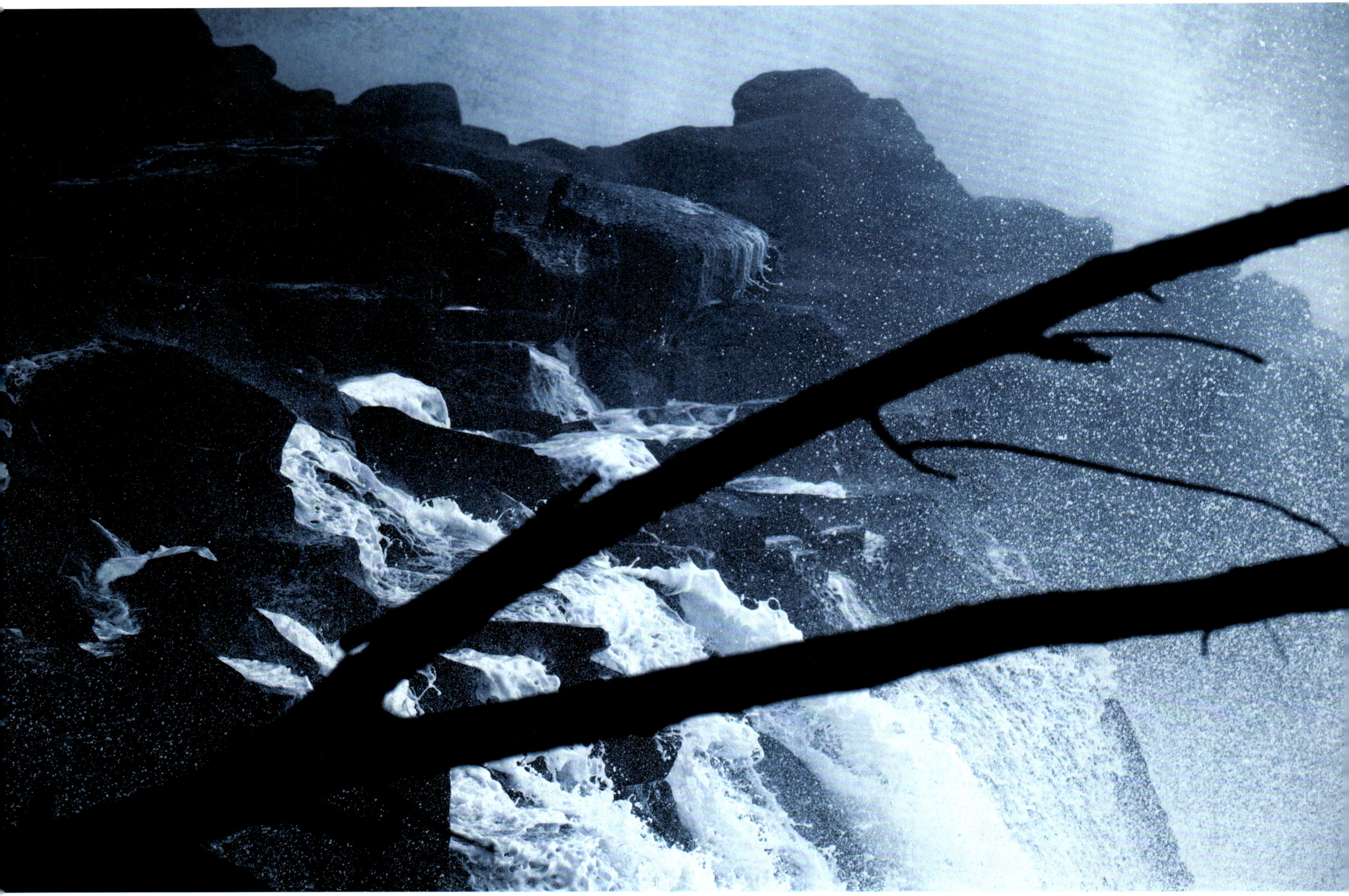

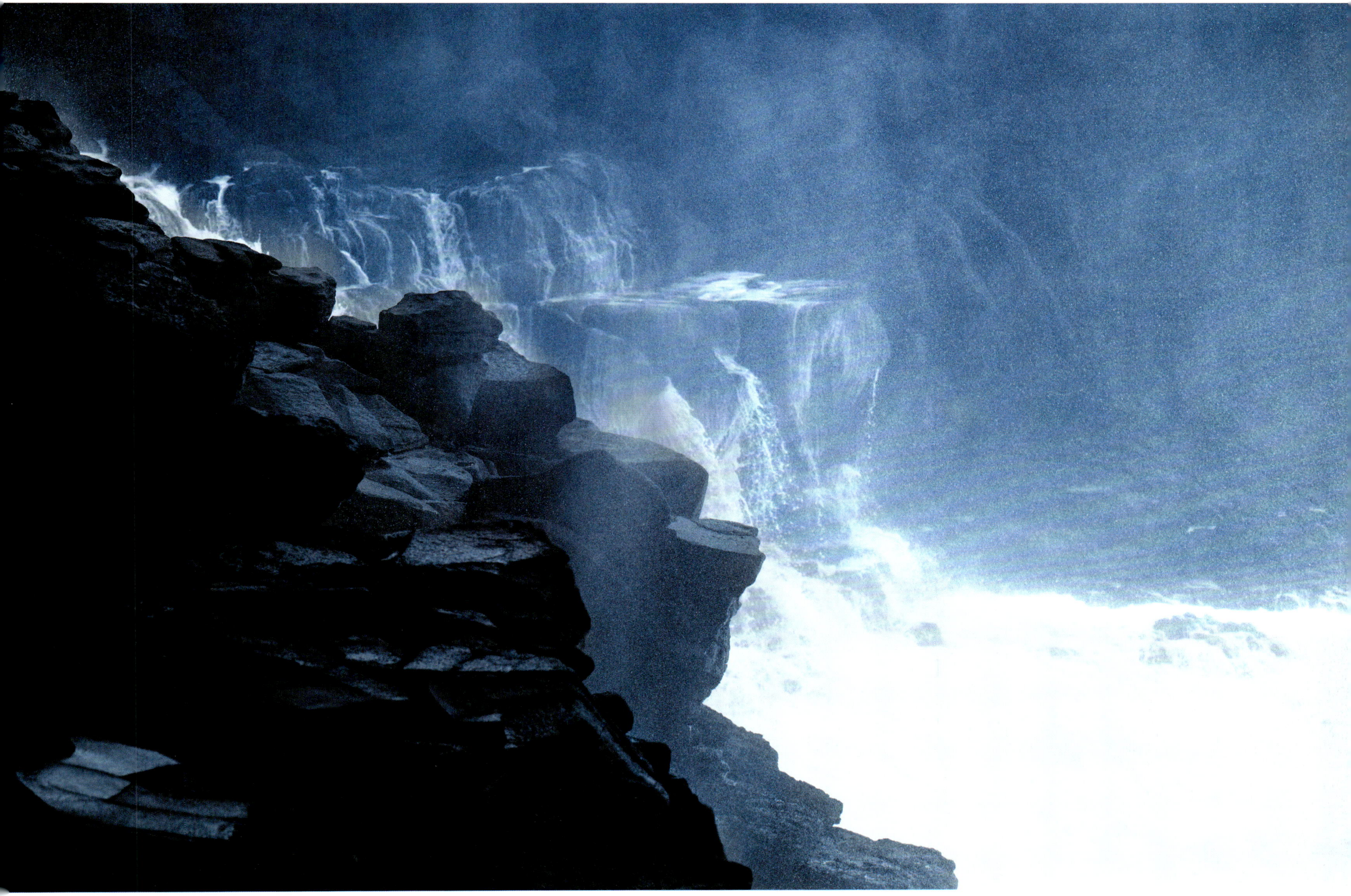

THE VERY ESSENCE OF THE MARBLE

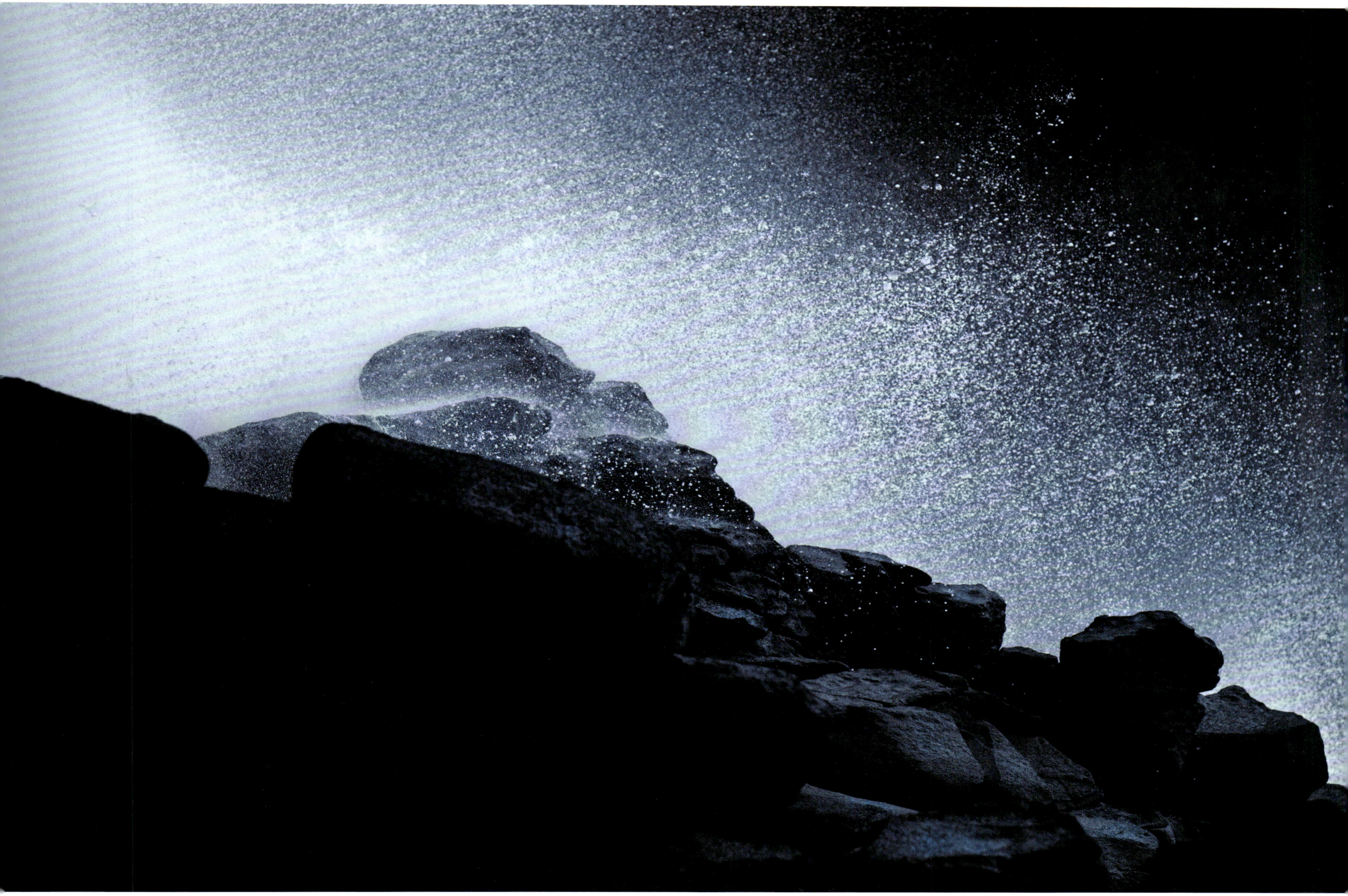

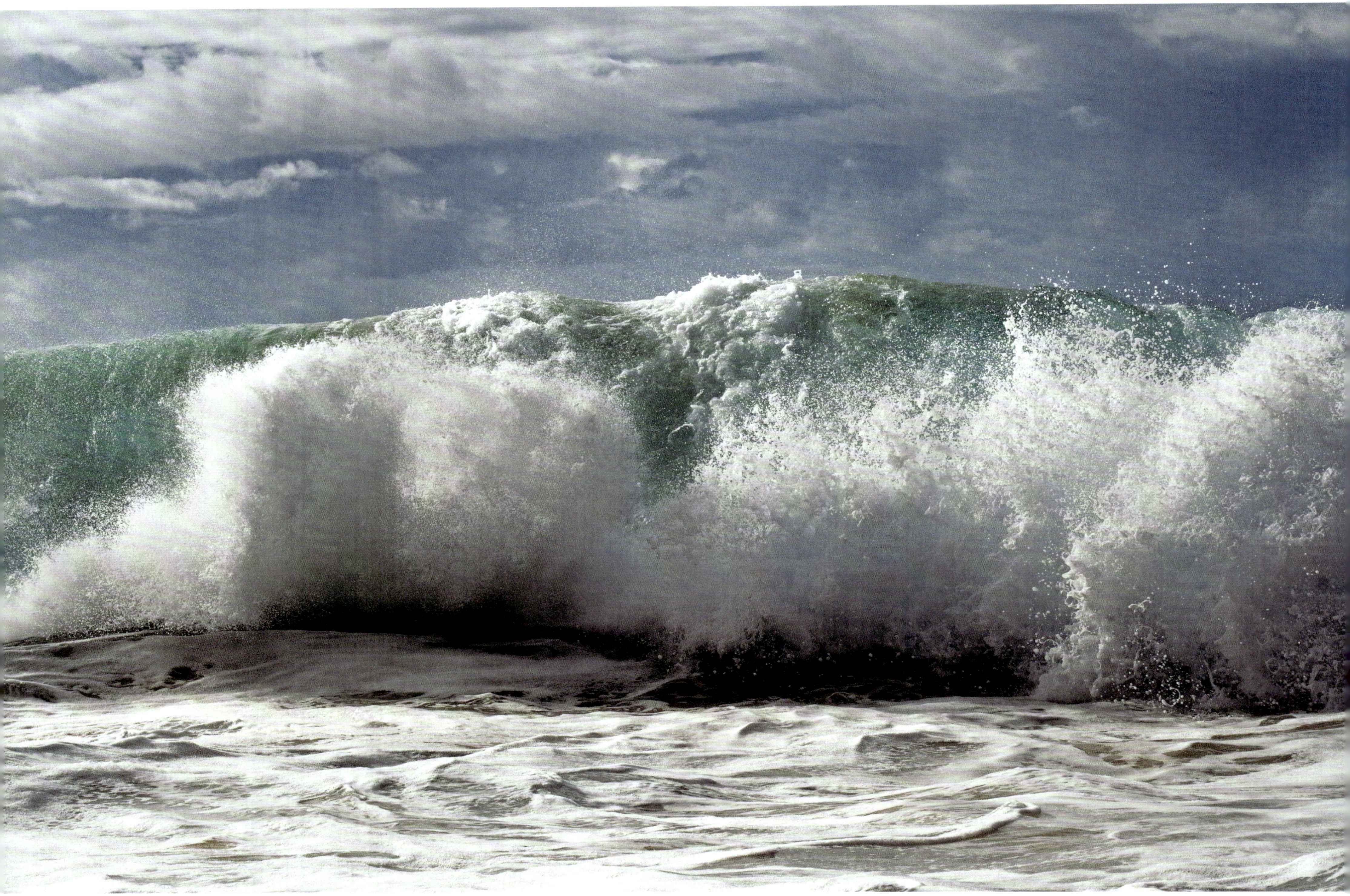

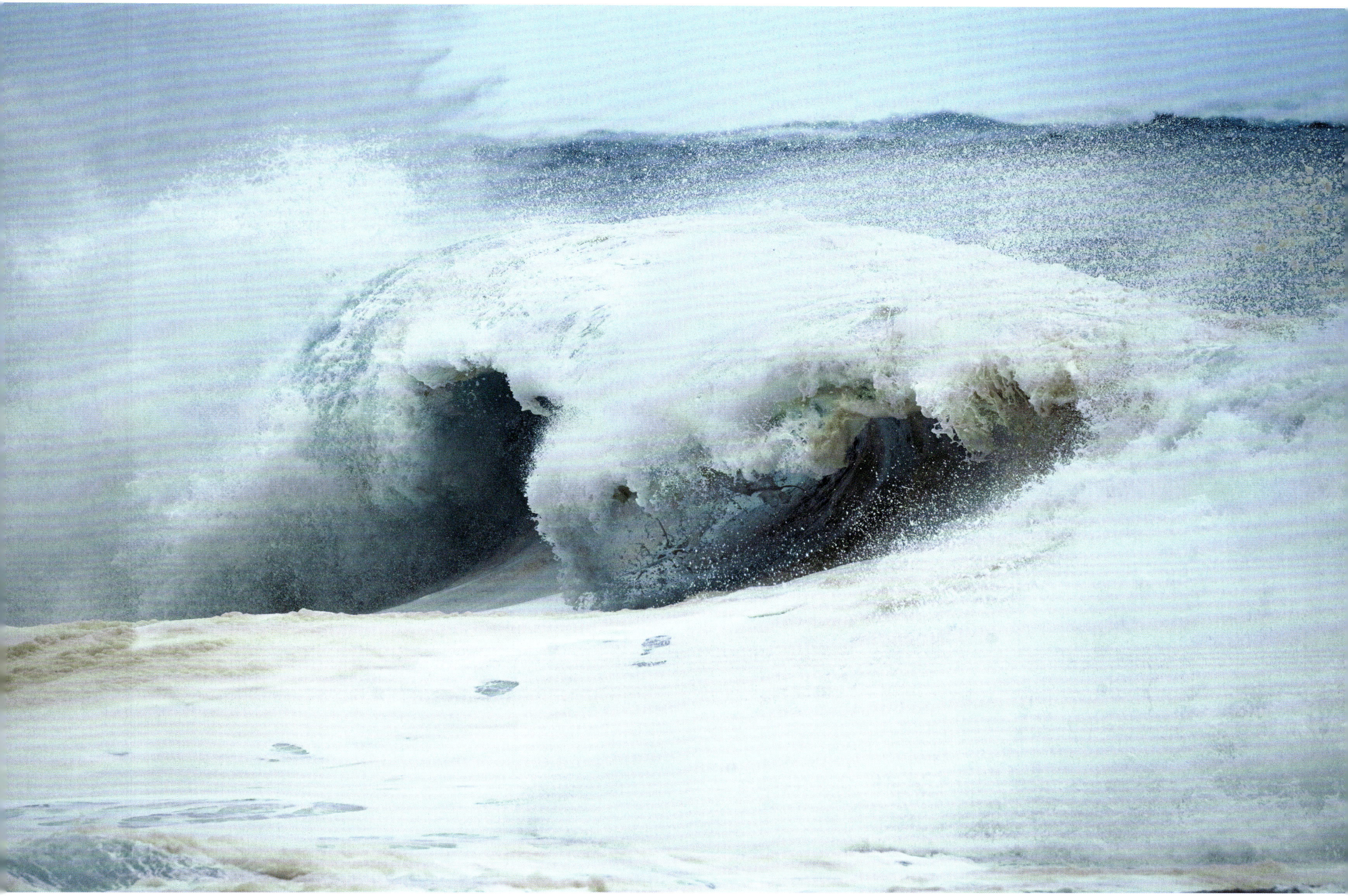

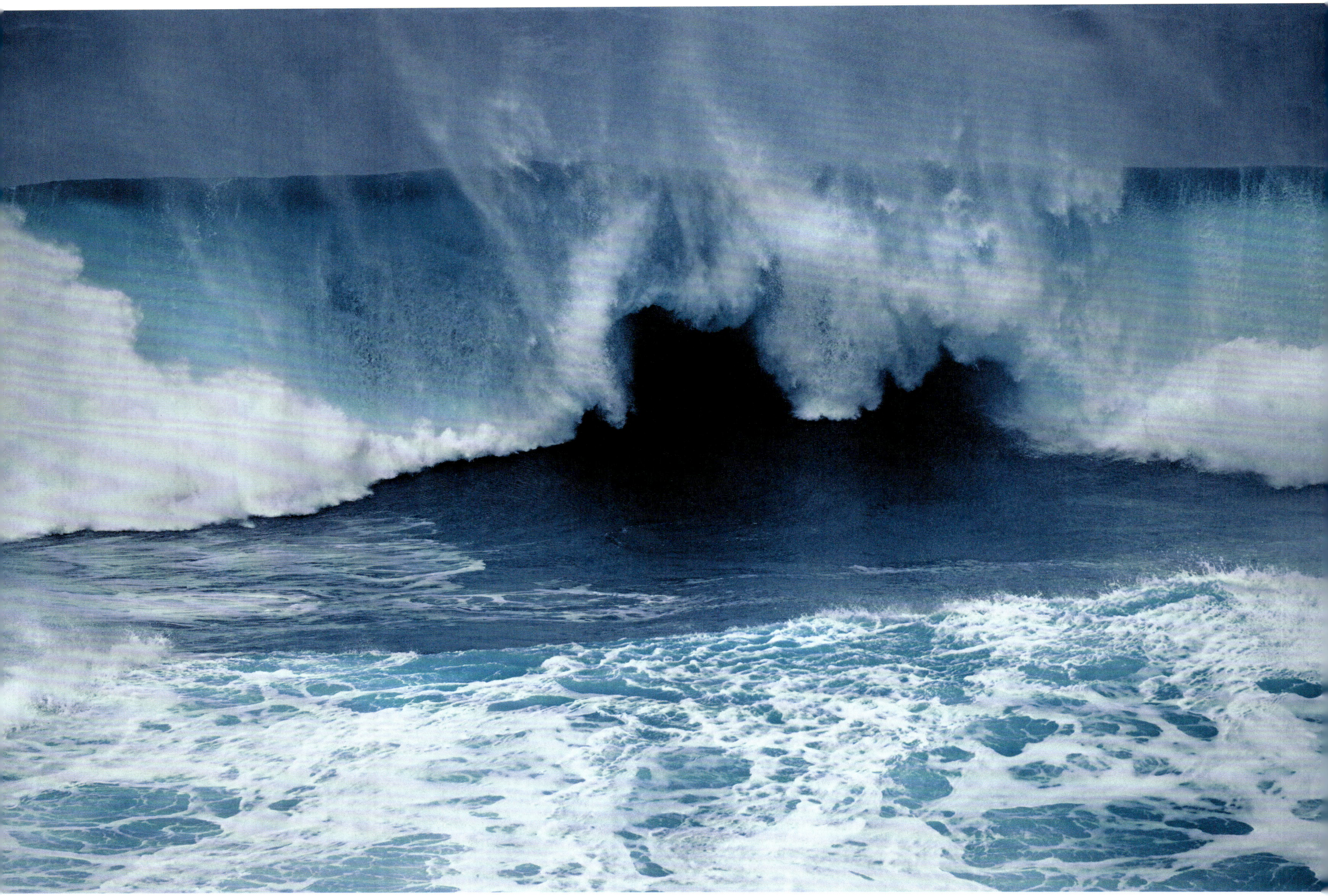

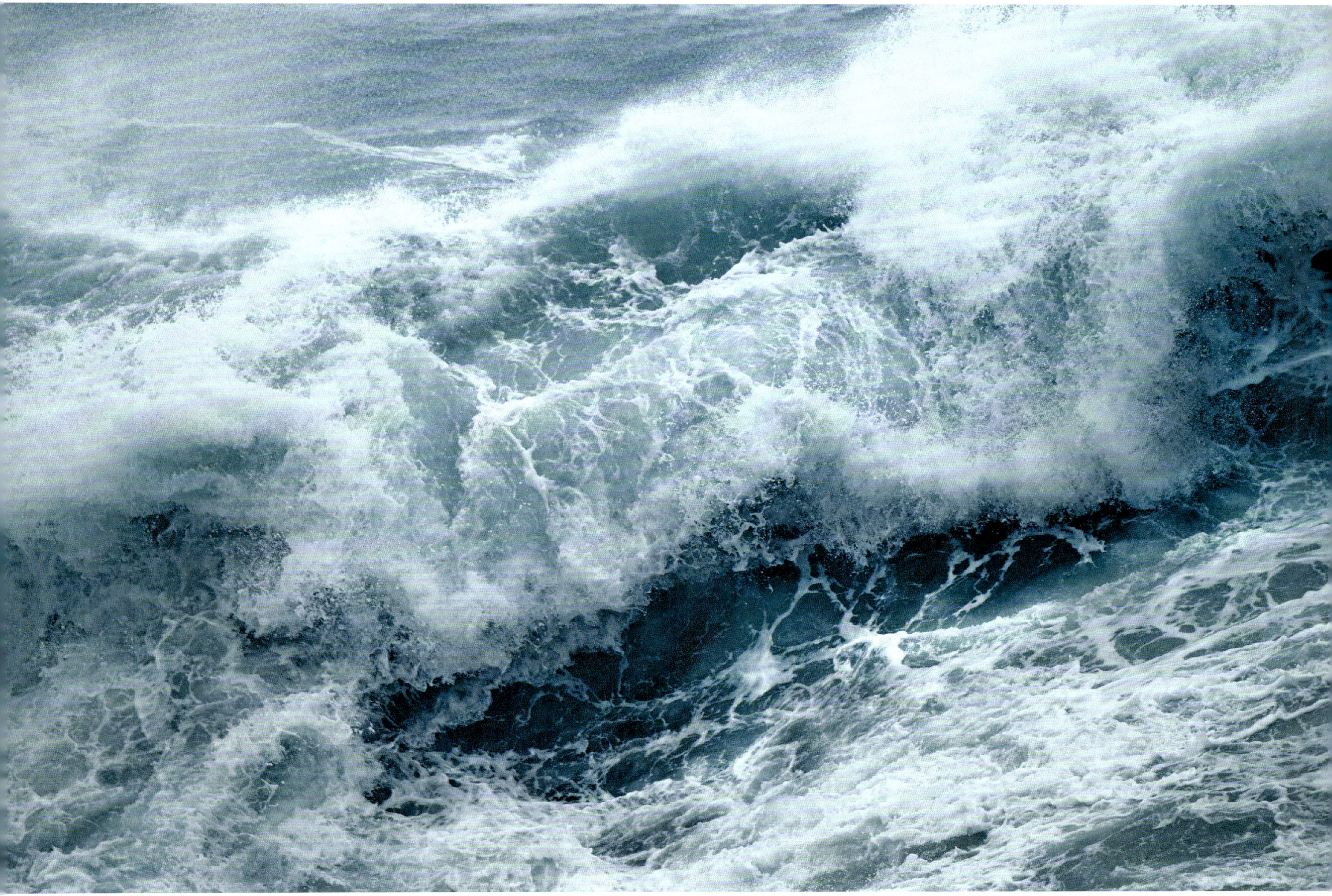

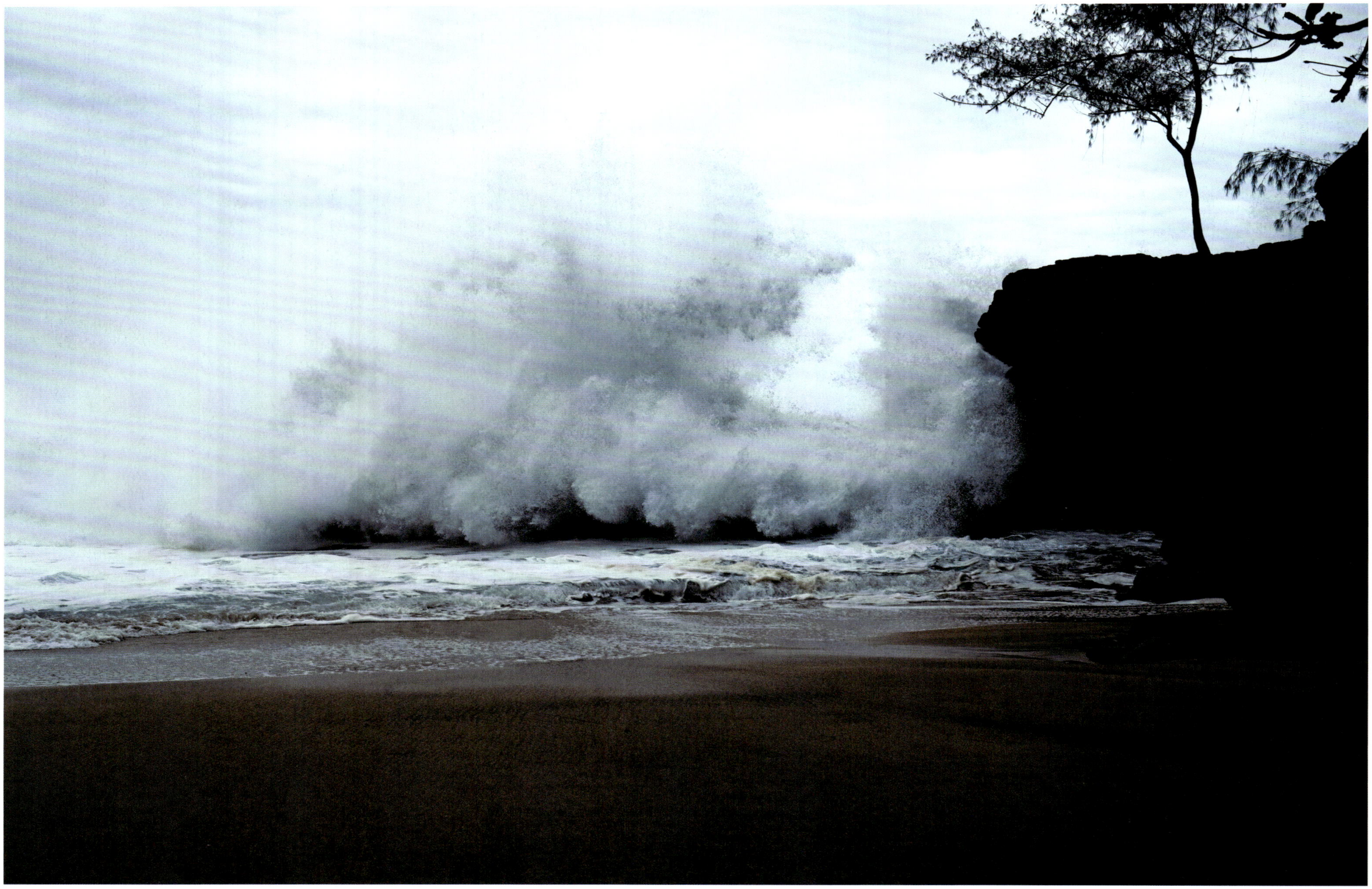

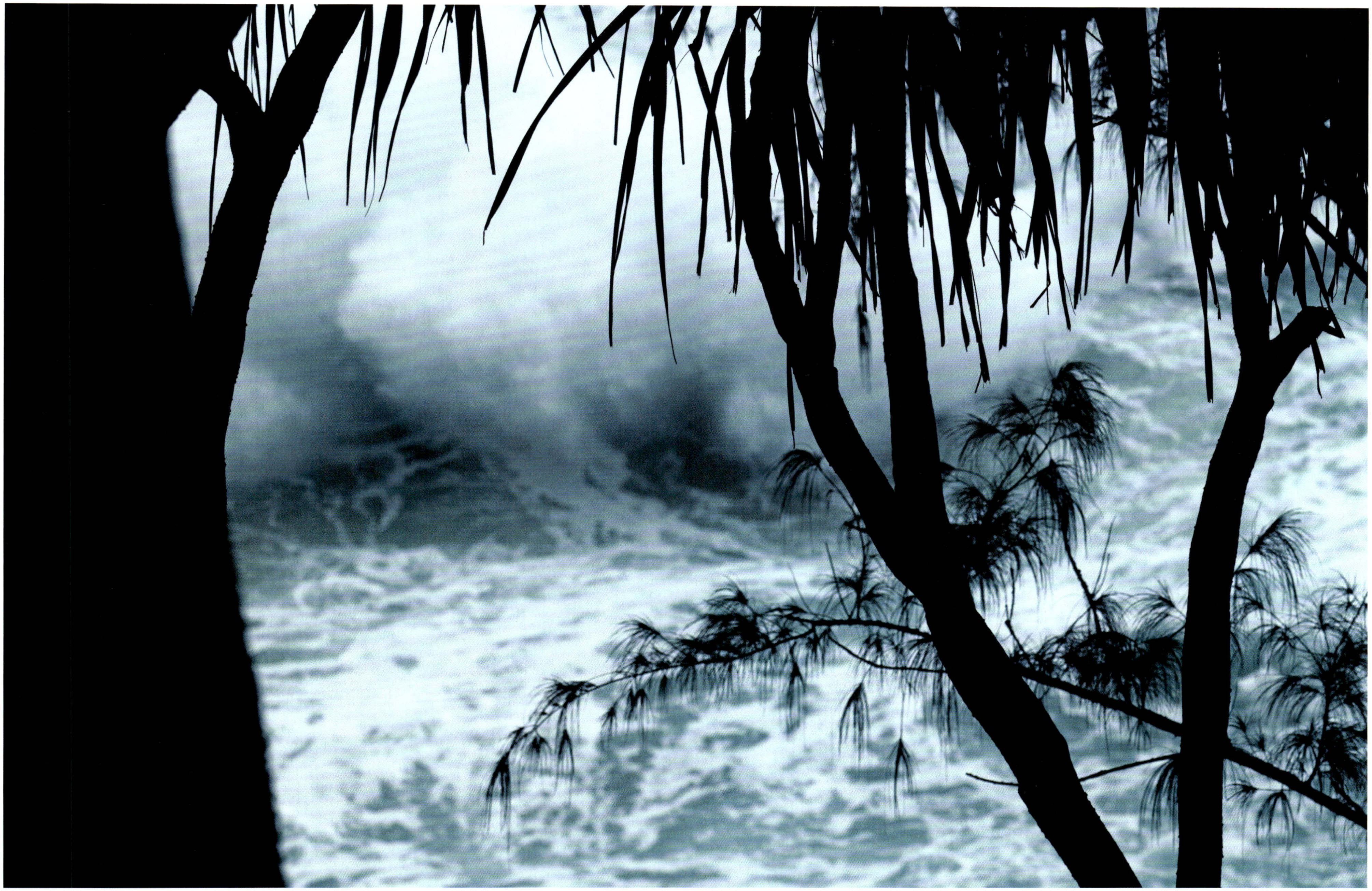

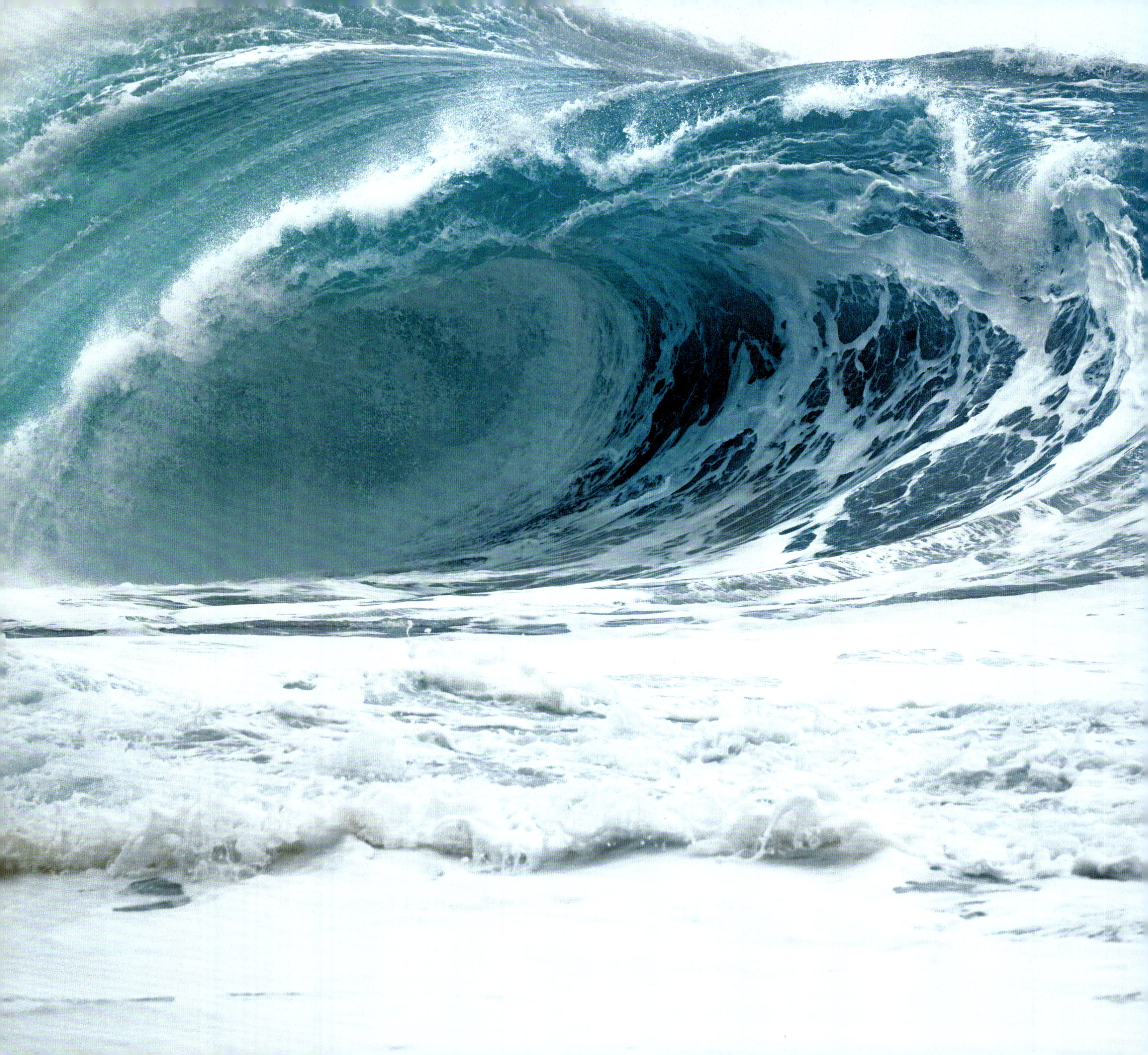

AND THE WAVES STILL KEEP THEIR SECRETS INSIDE

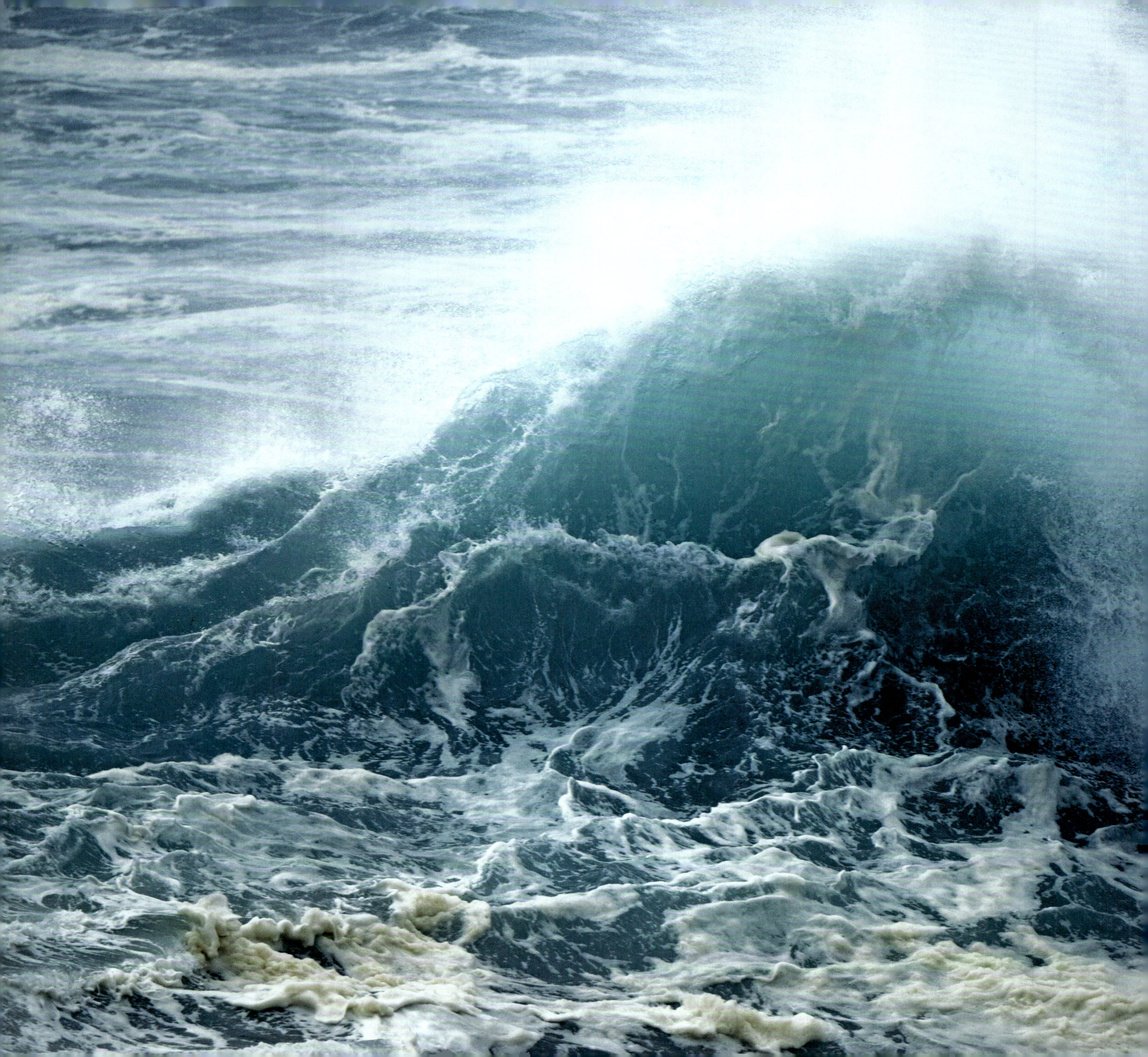

87

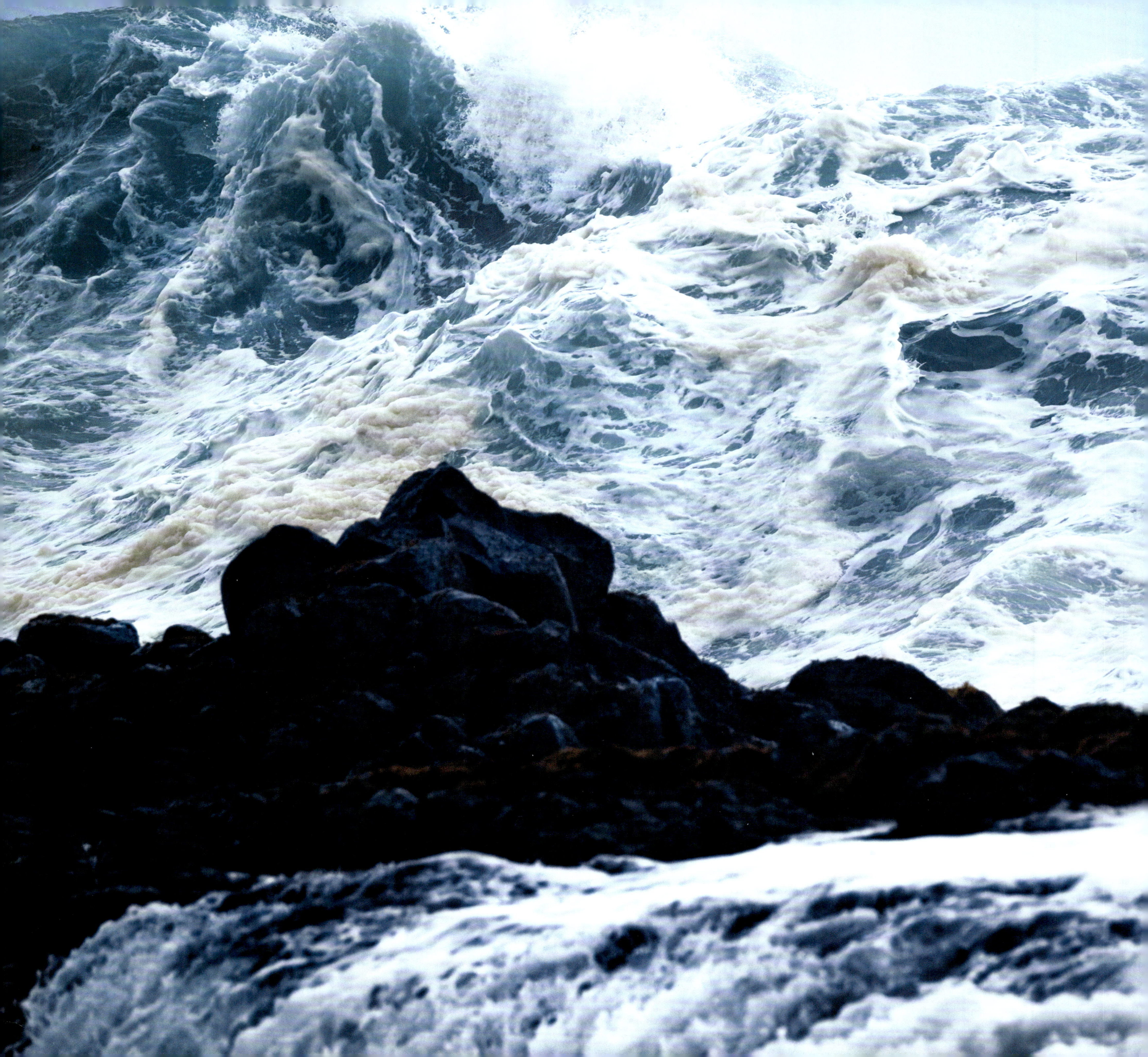

THE LAST TOUCH OF ENERGY

I ALMOST SAW SPARKS

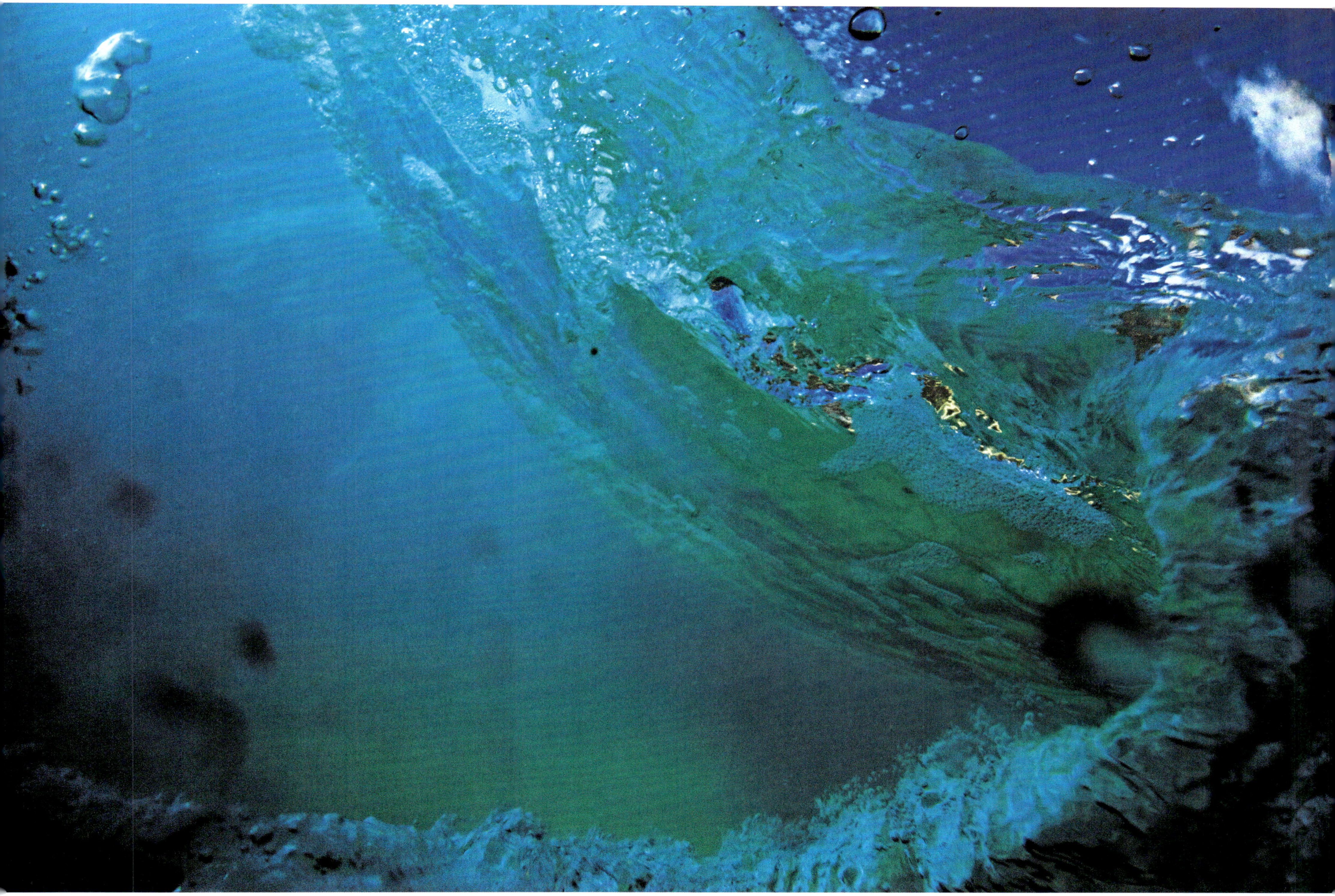

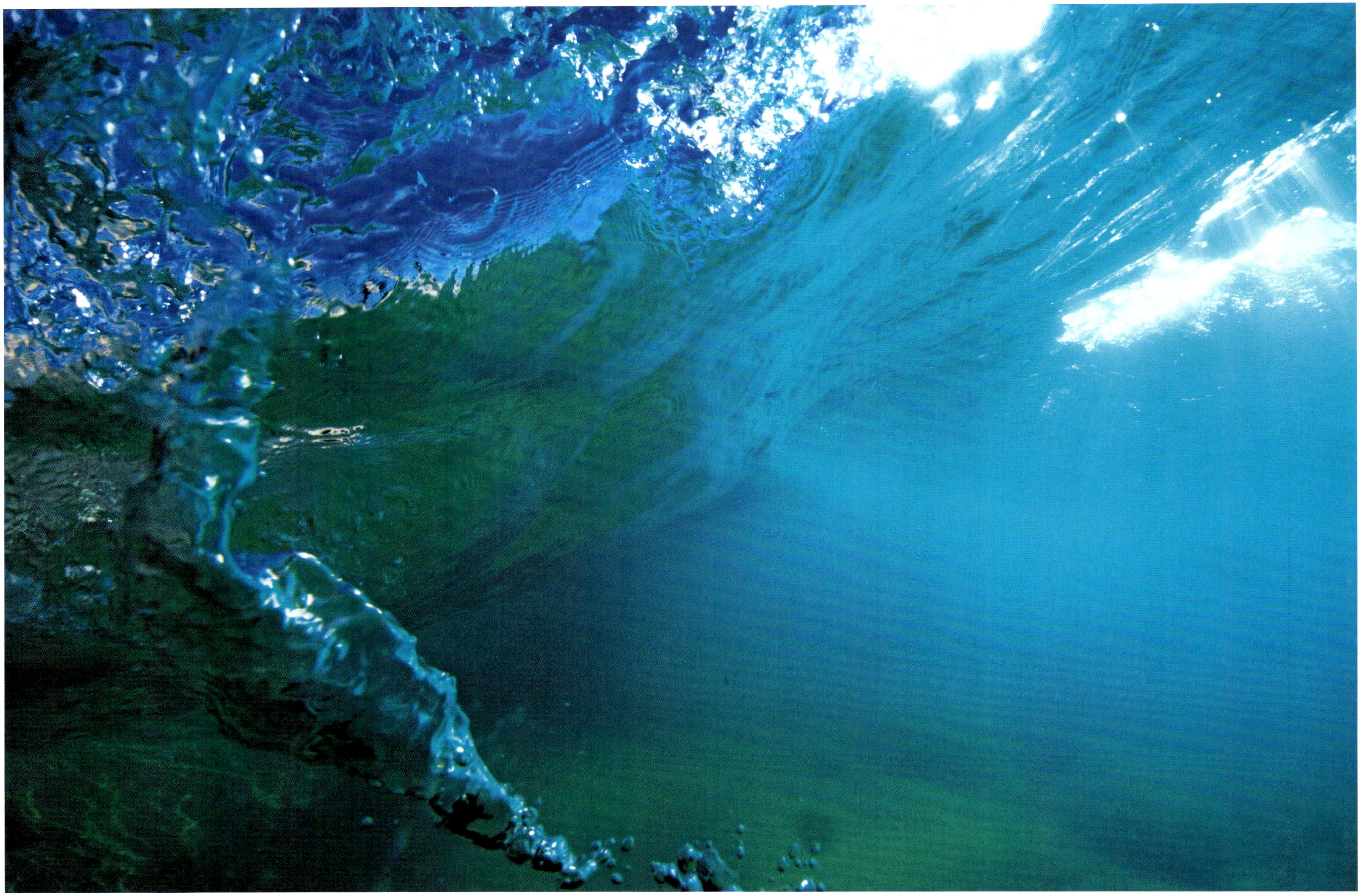

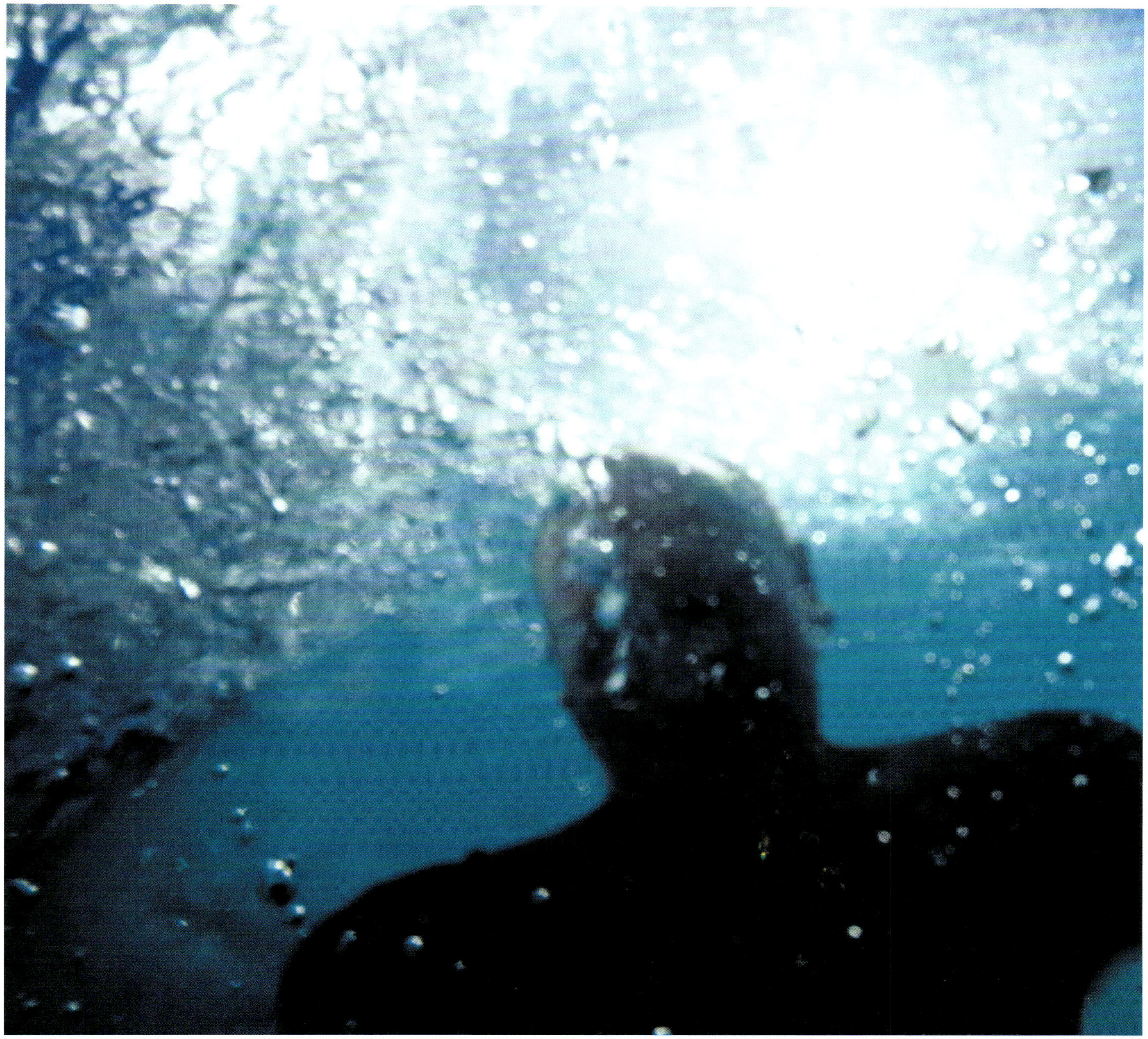

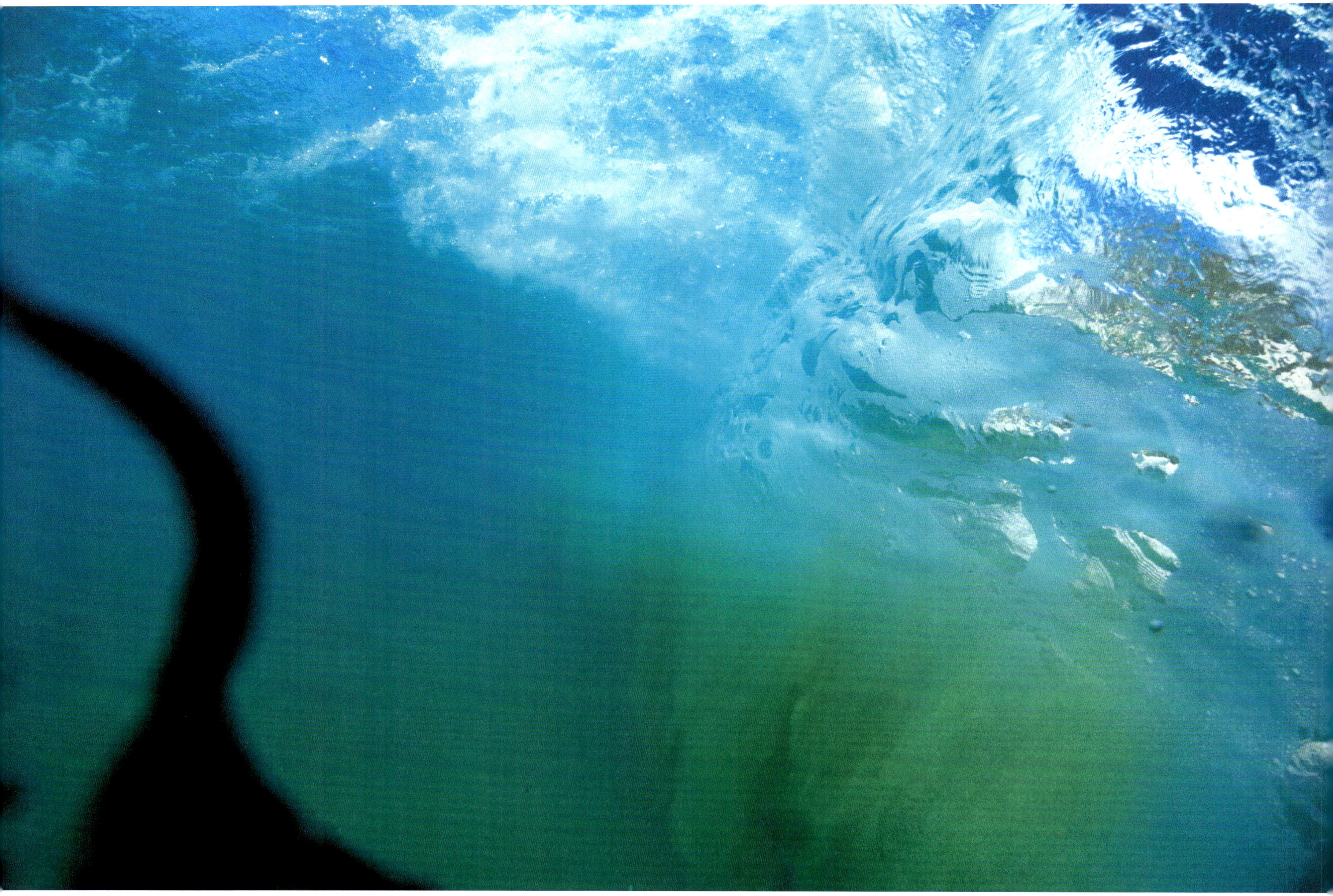

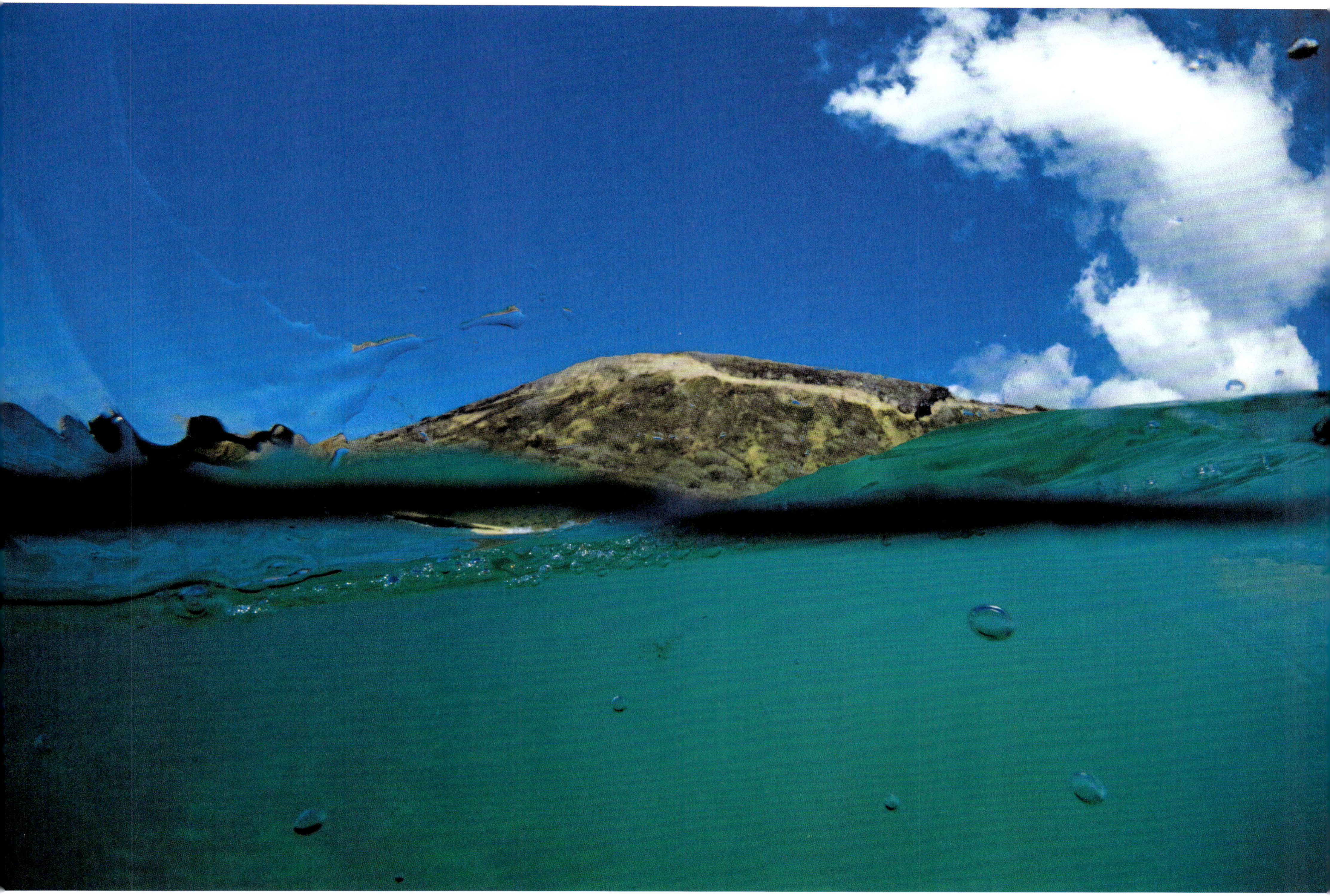

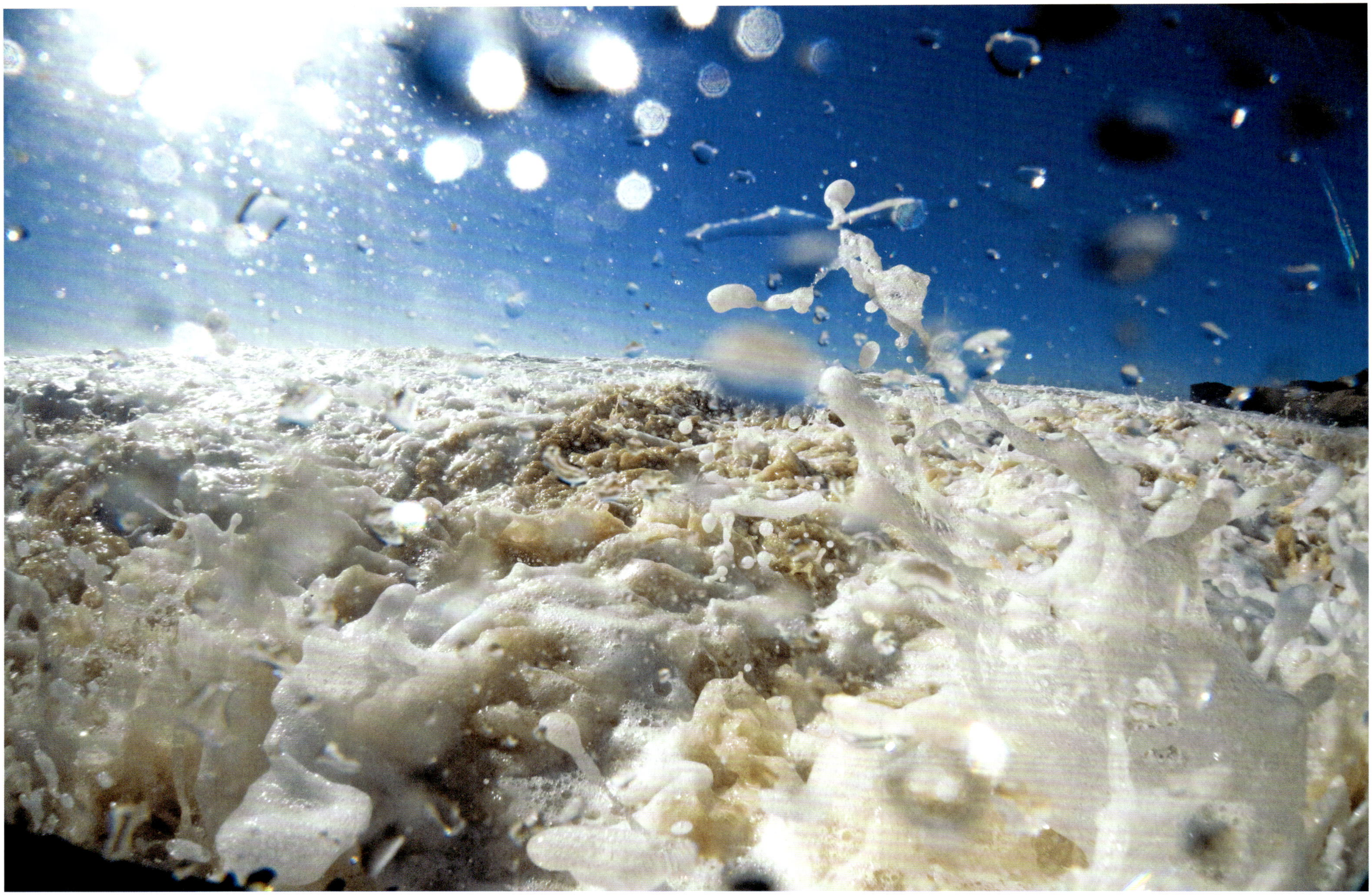

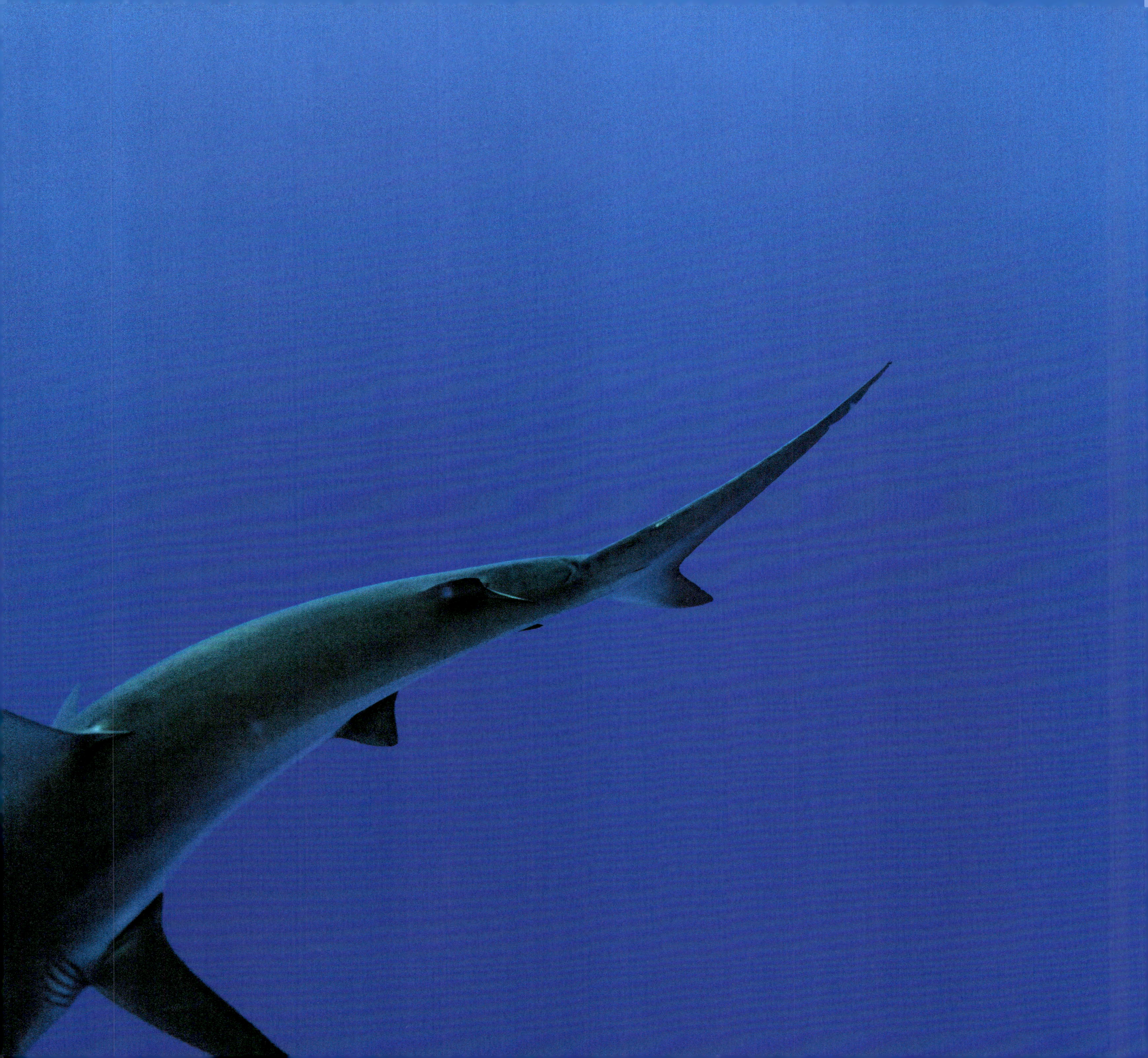

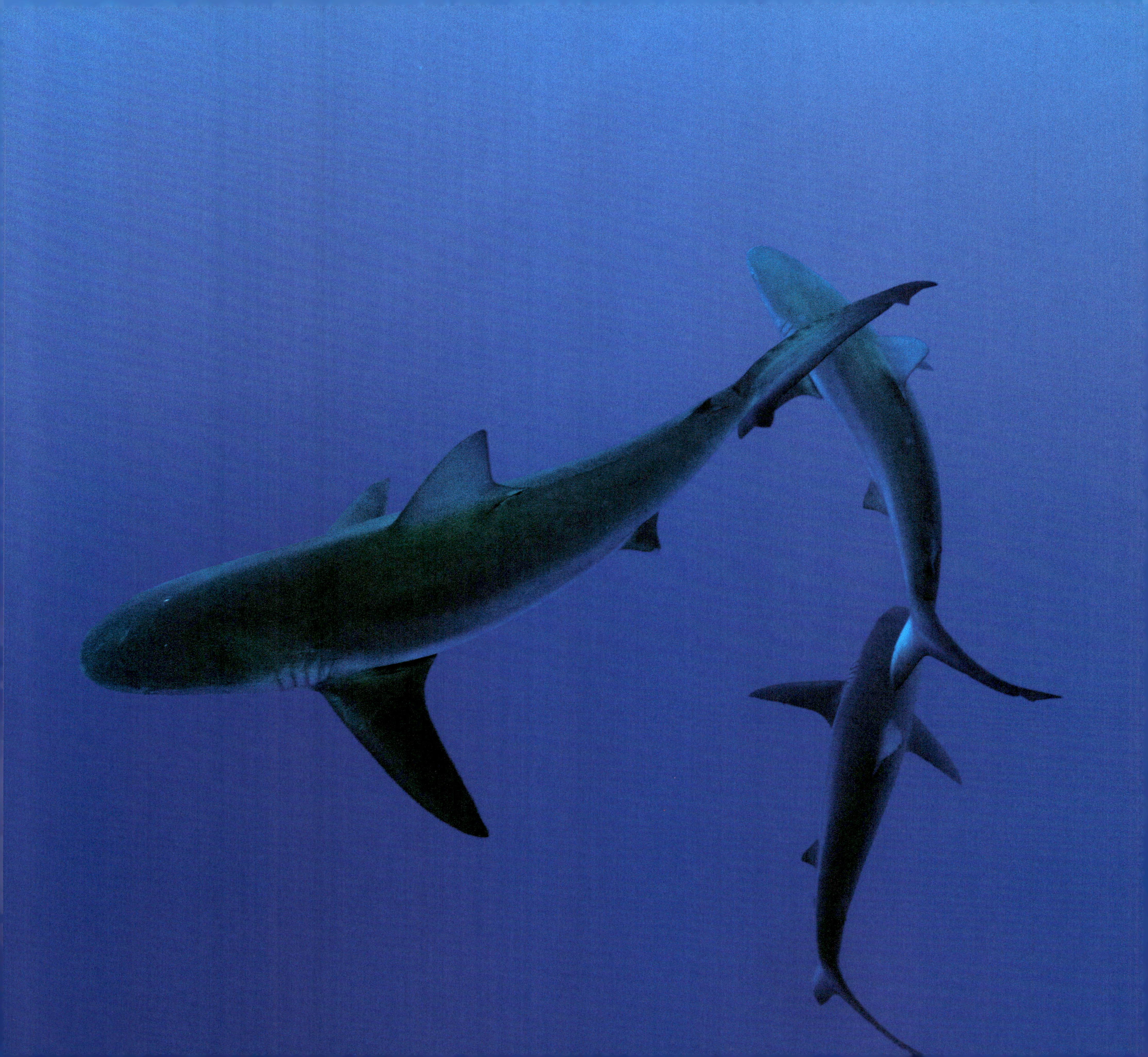

"DON'T MESS WITH MY WORLD"

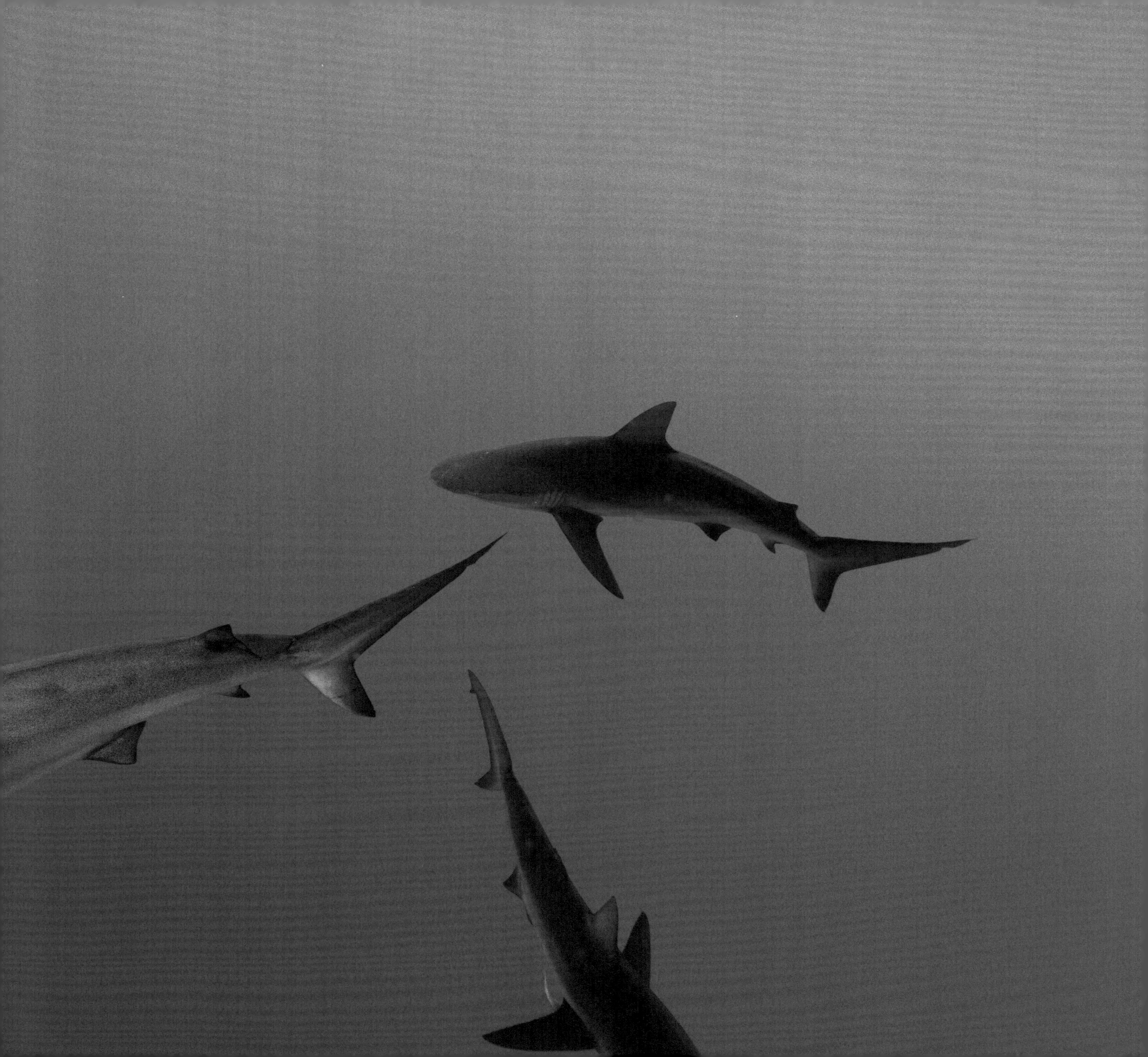

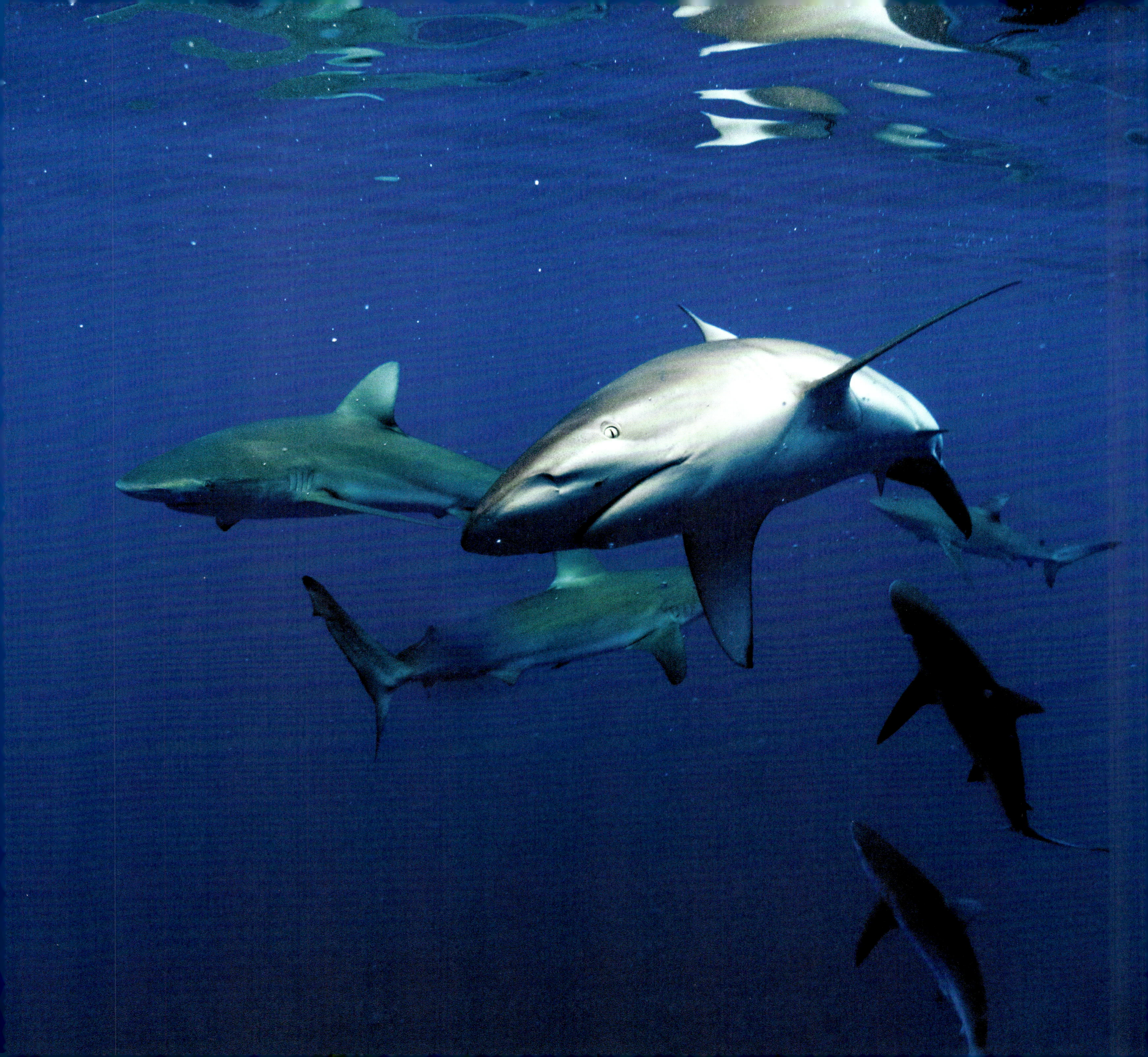

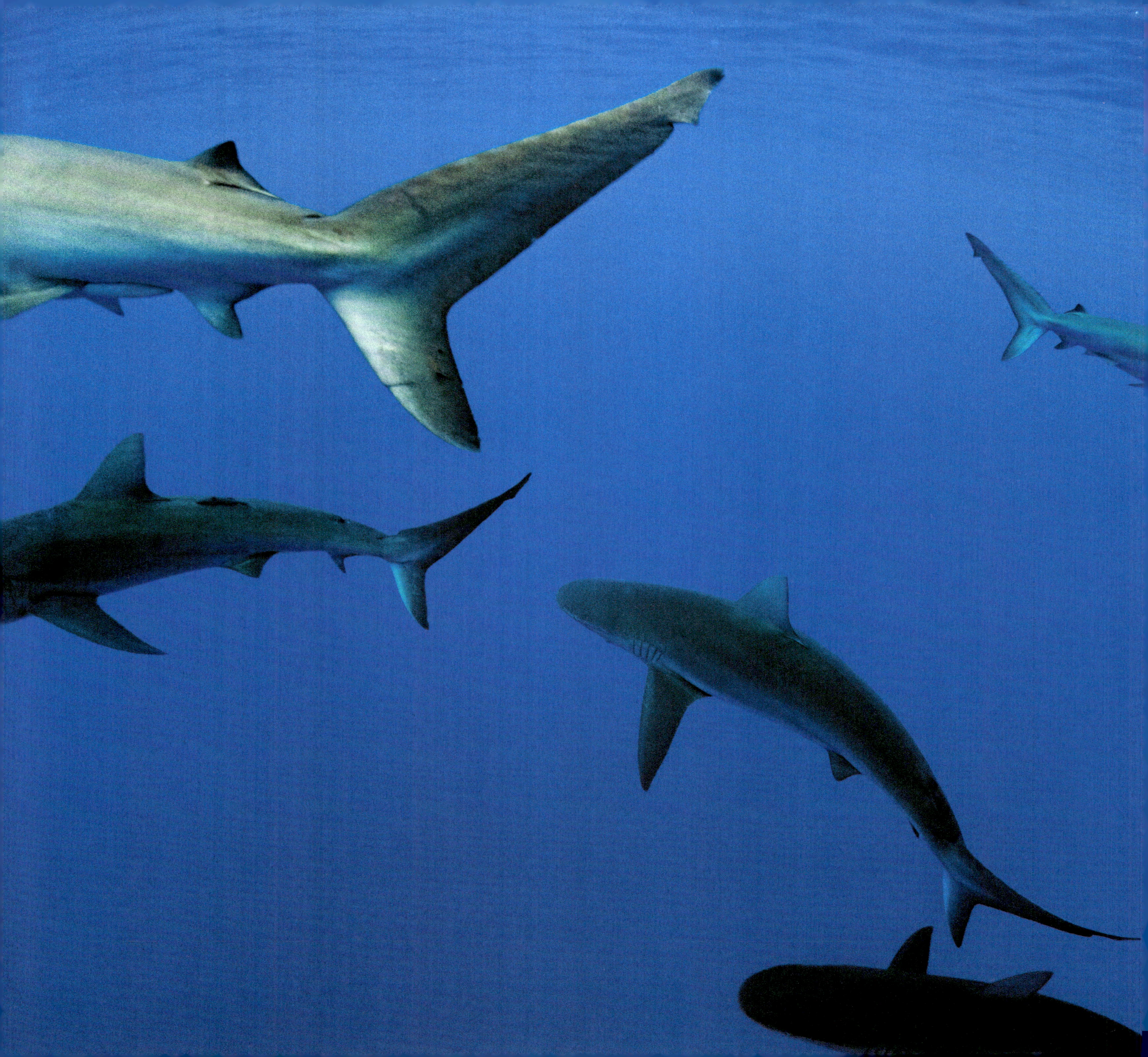

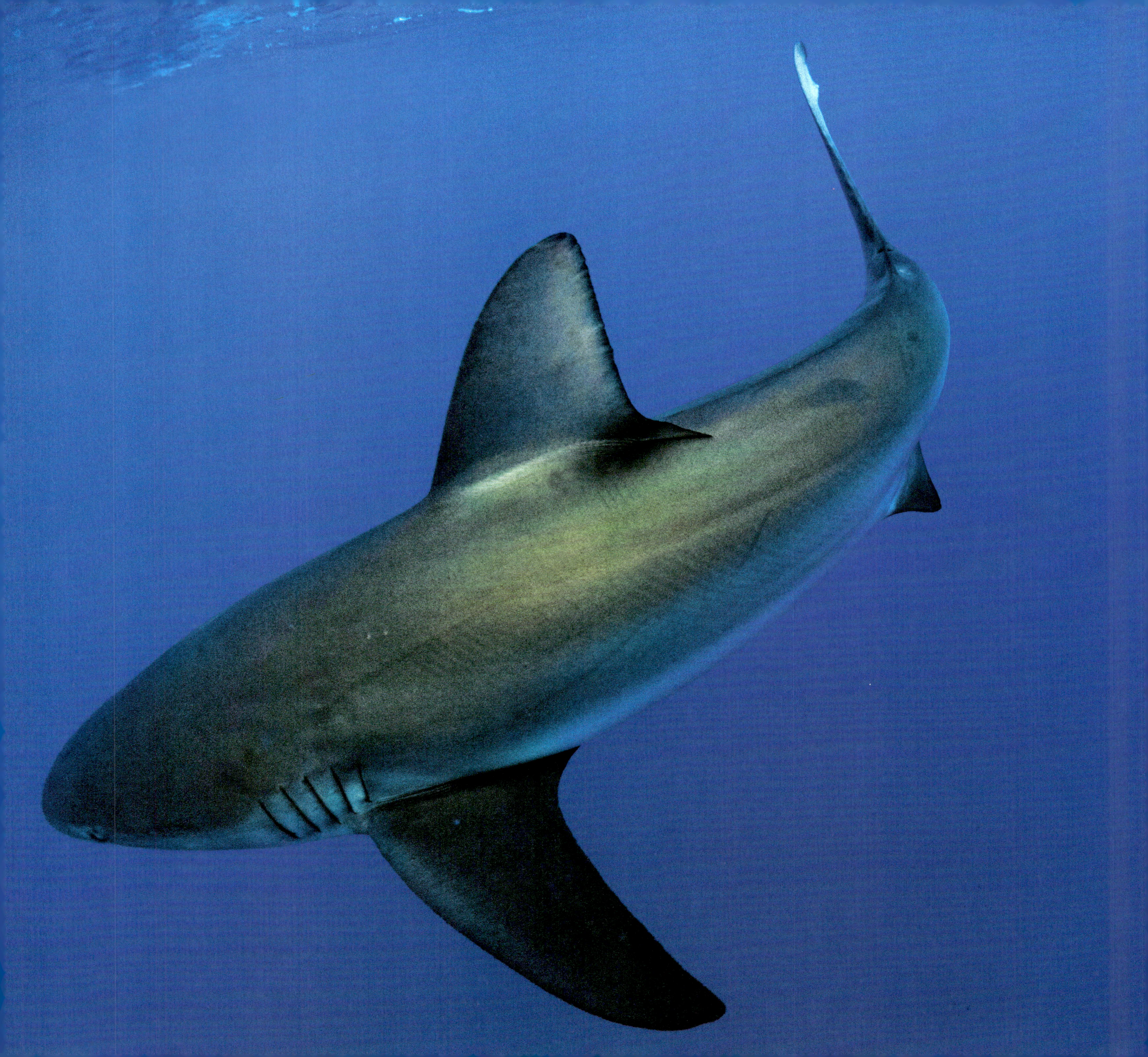

TO UNDERSTAND SHARKS YOU NEED TO BECOME ONE

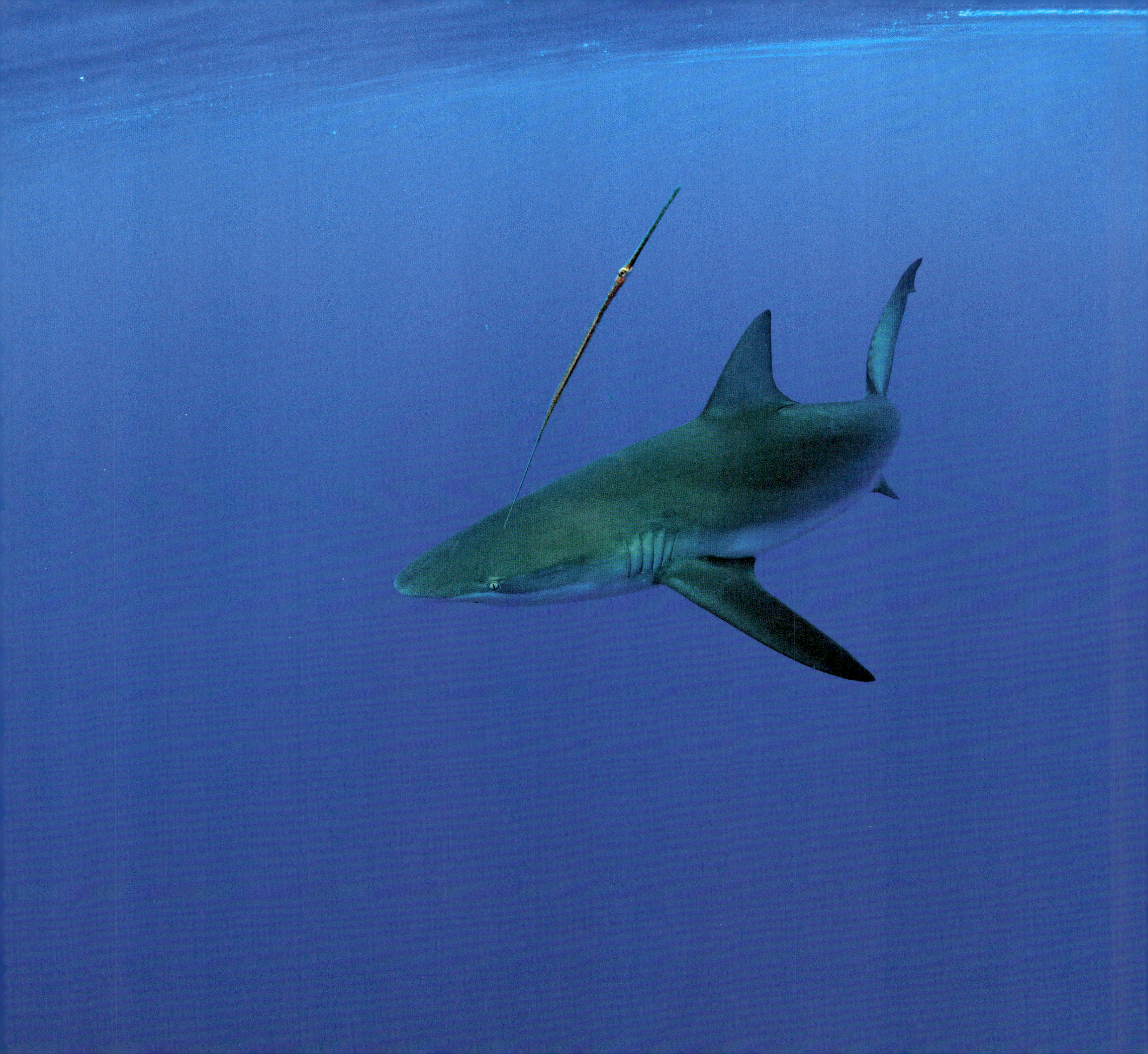

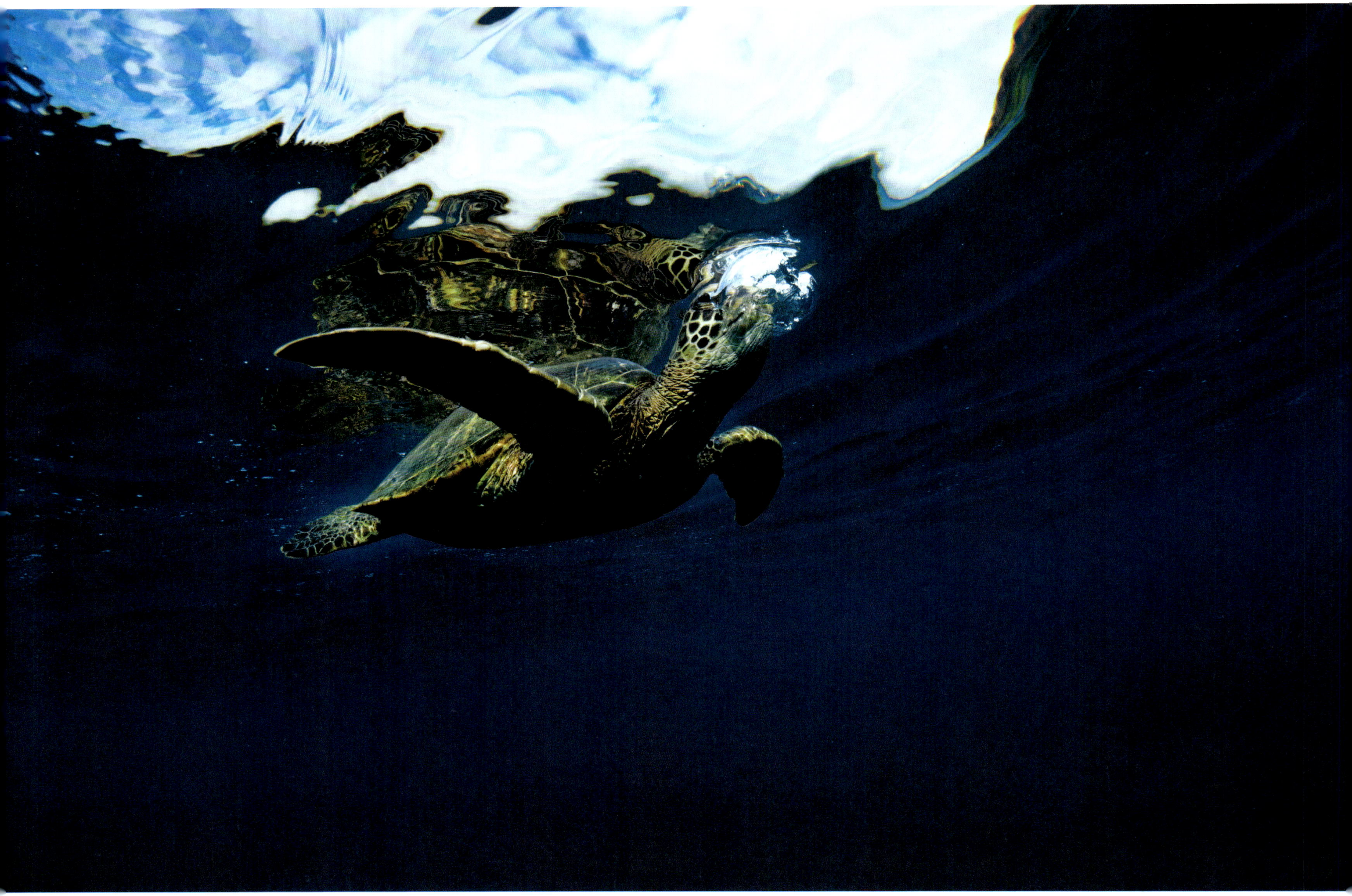

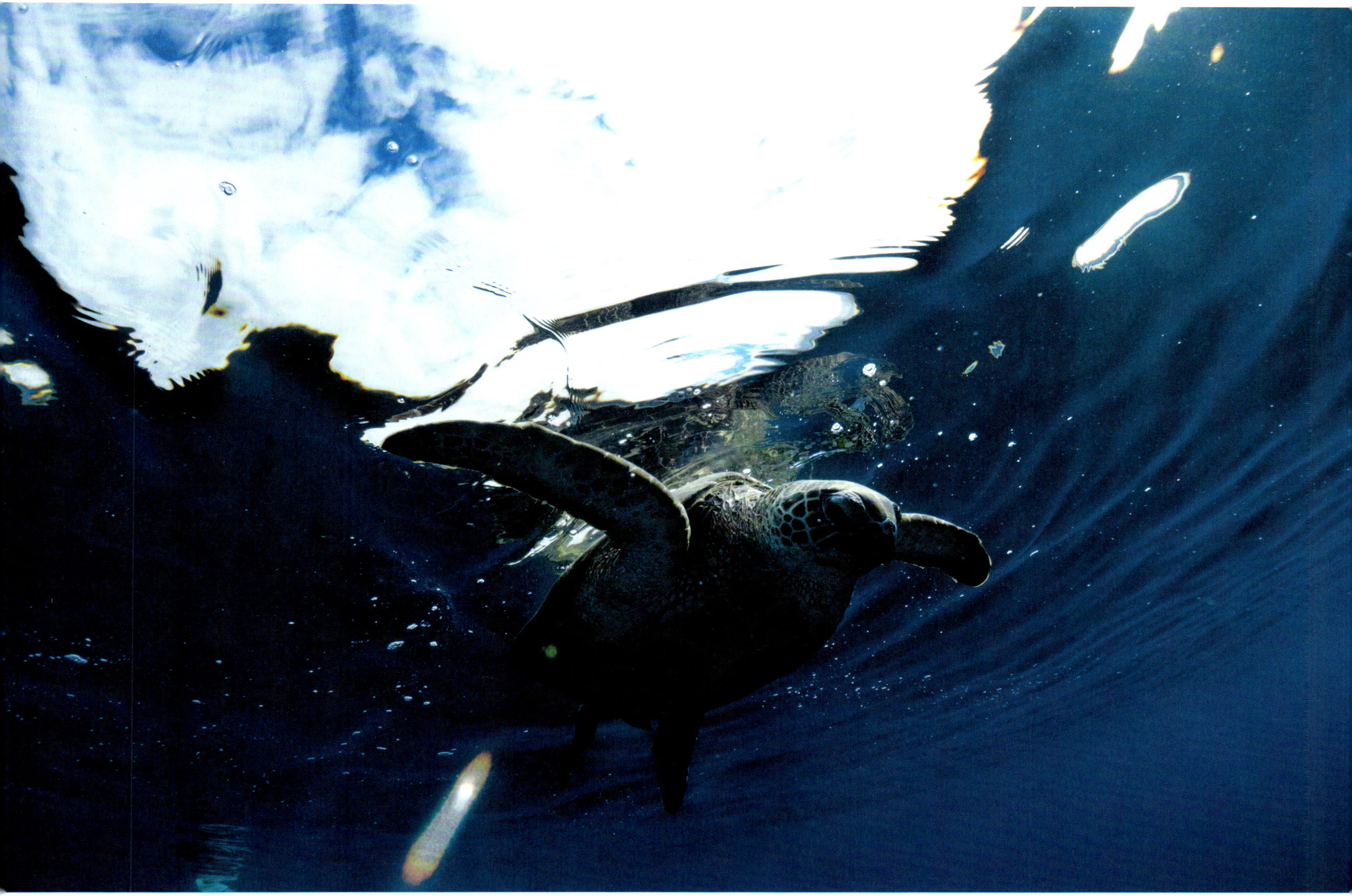

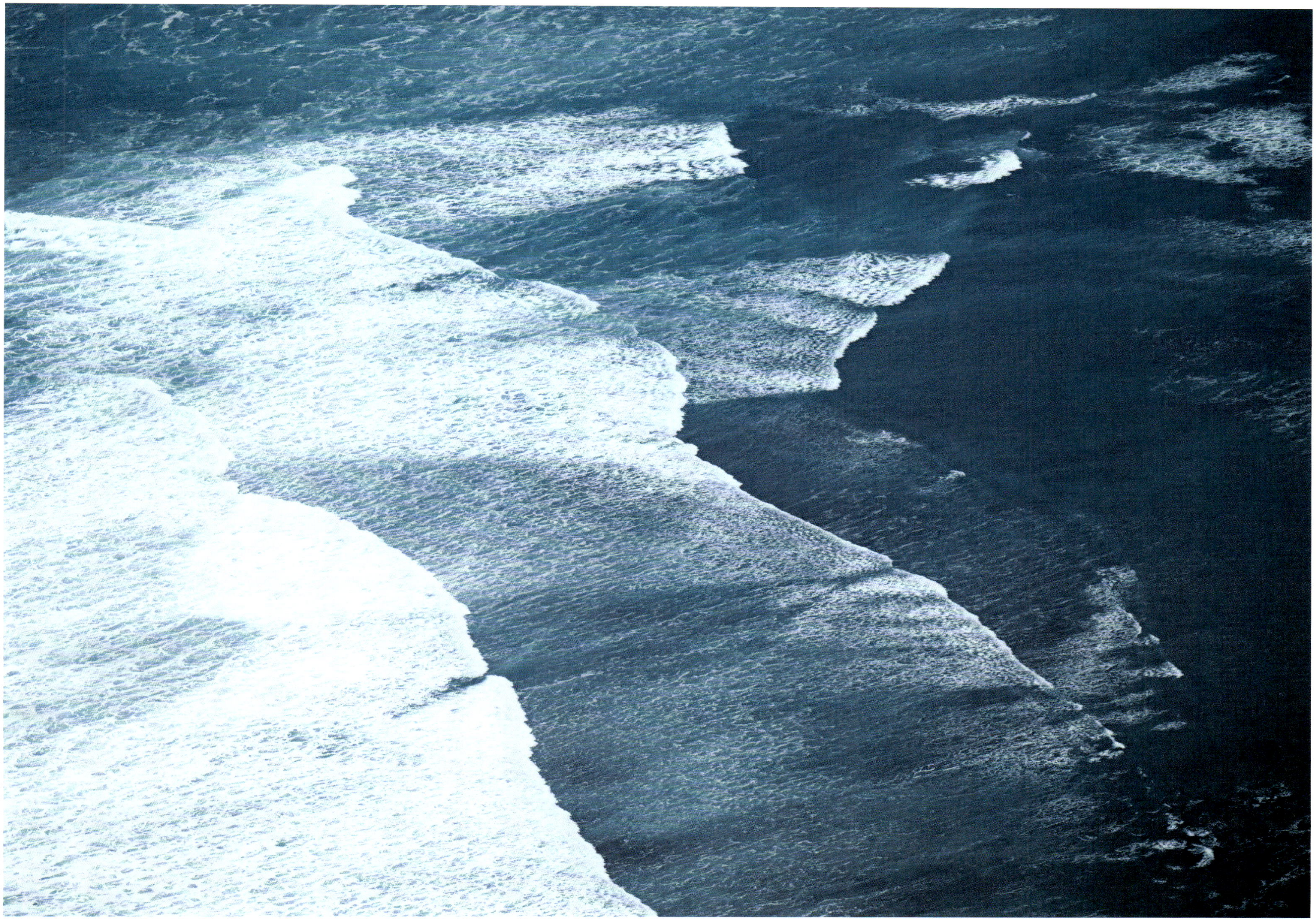

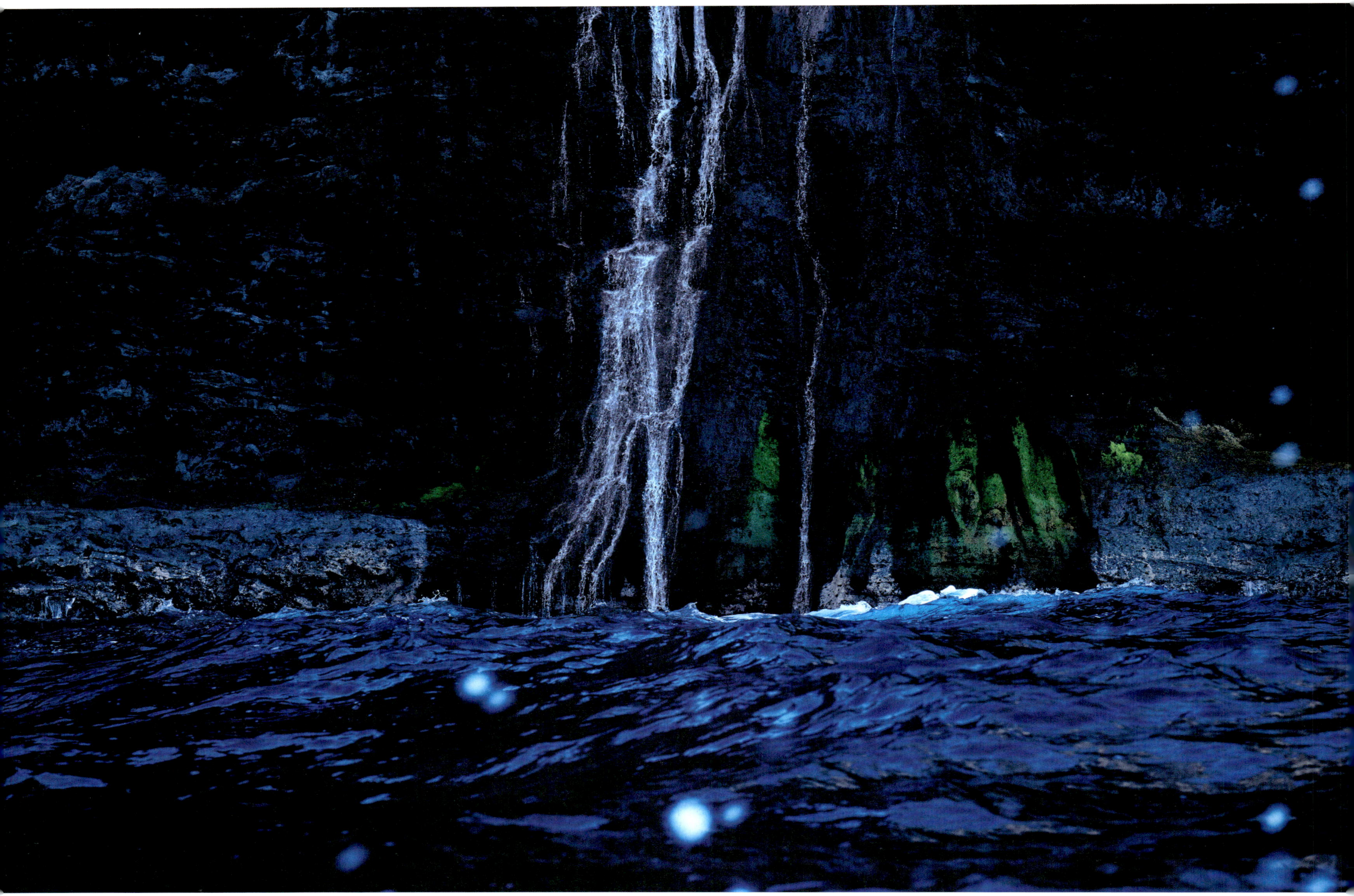

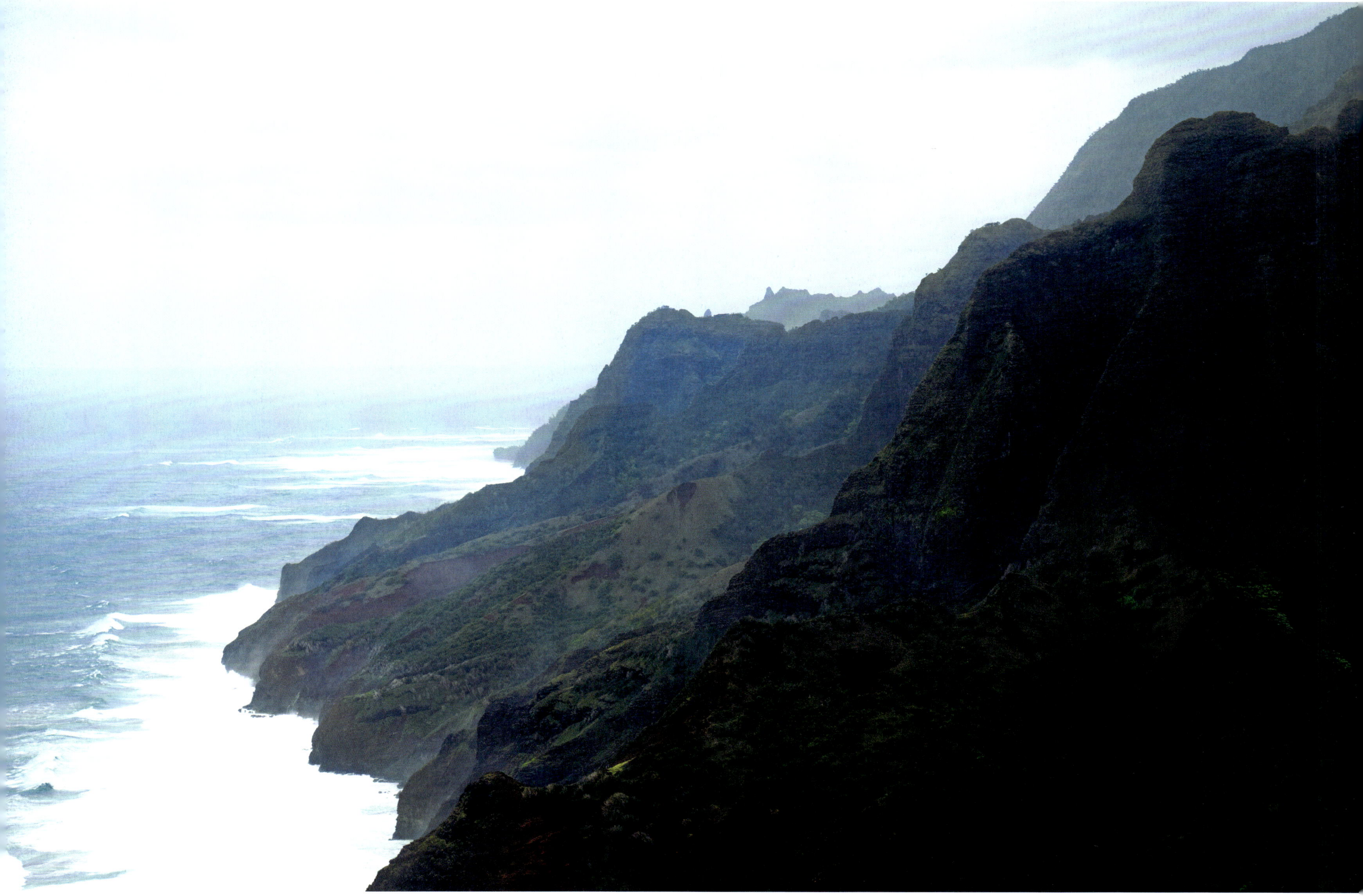

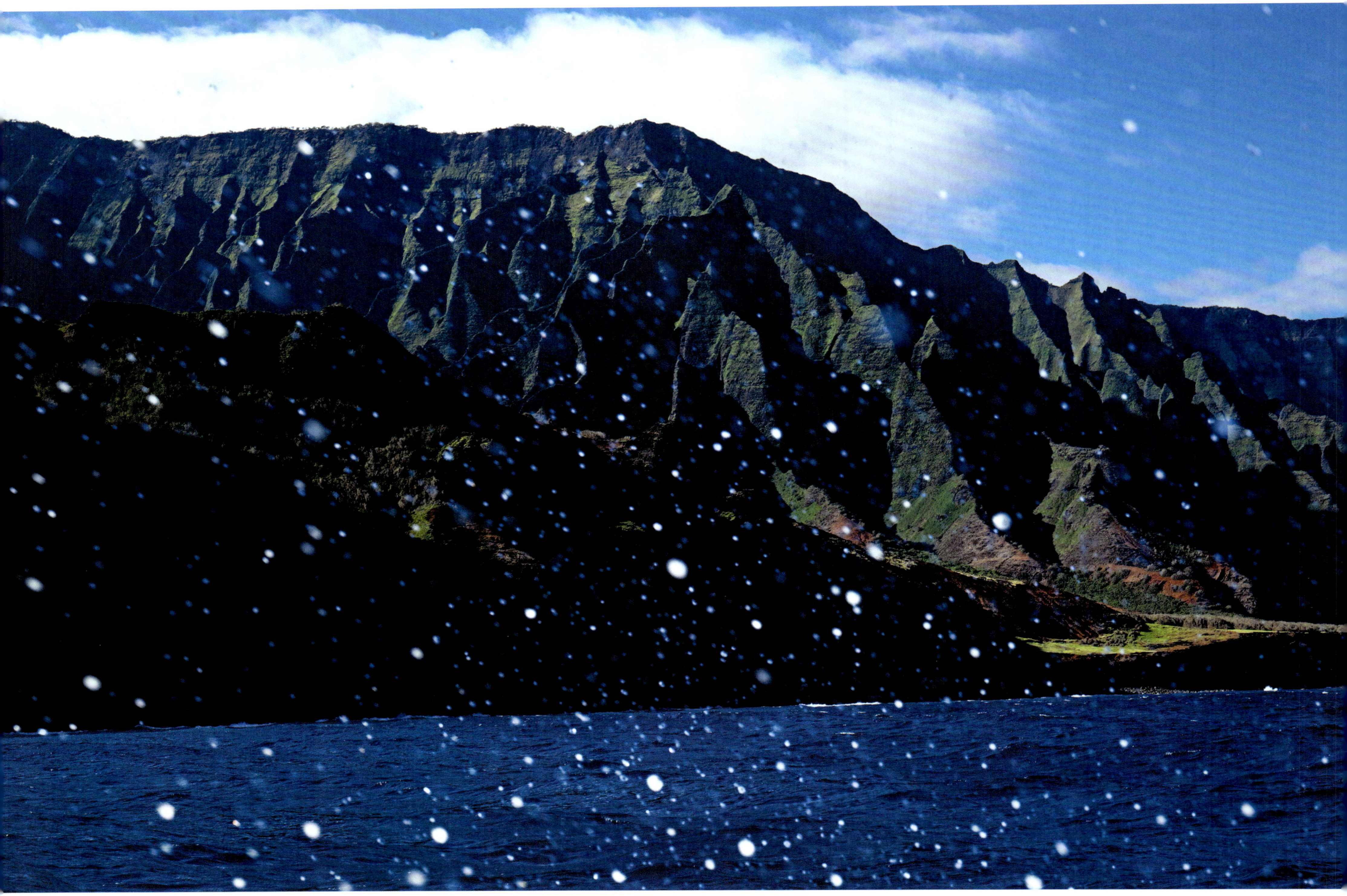

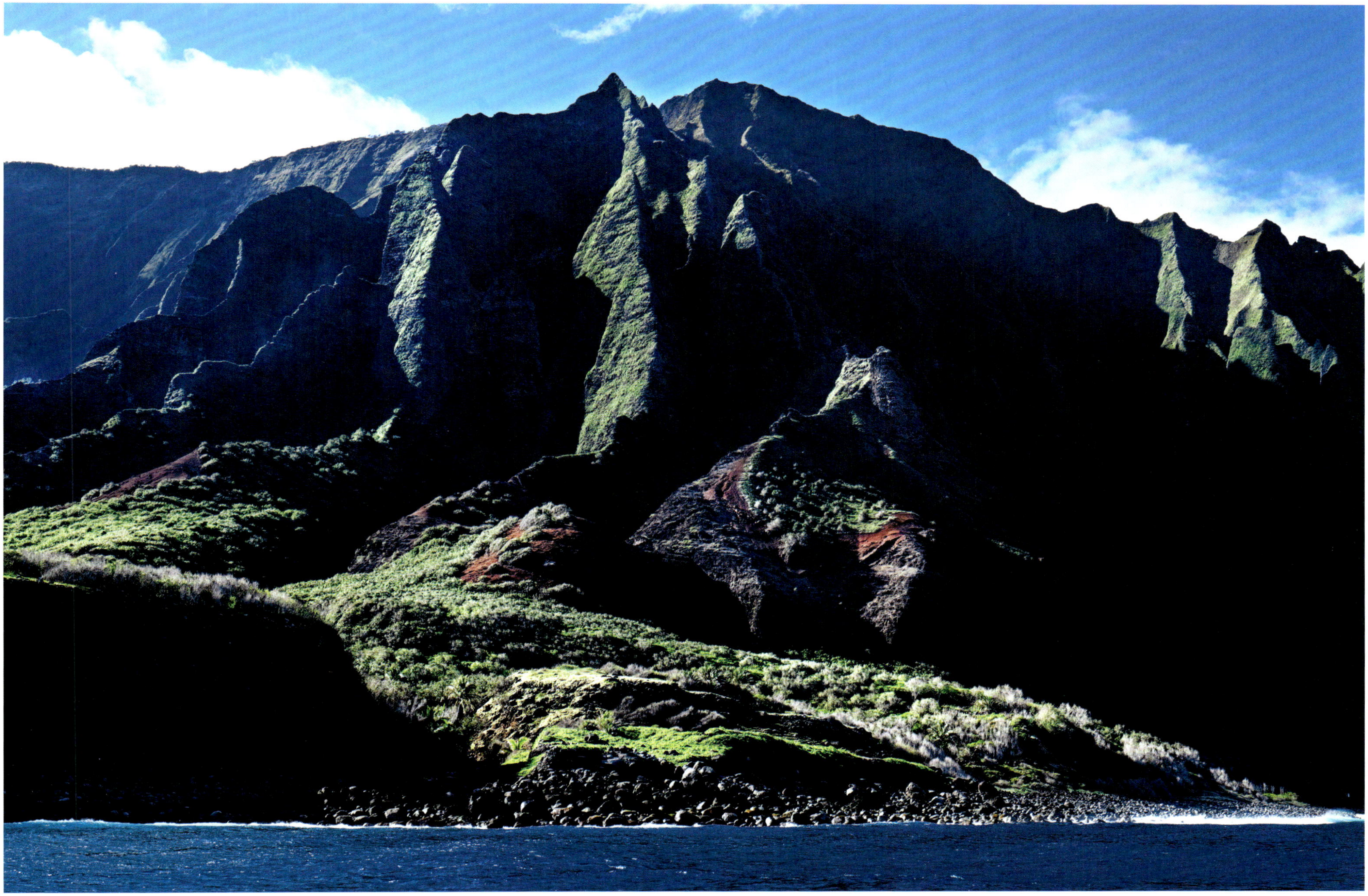

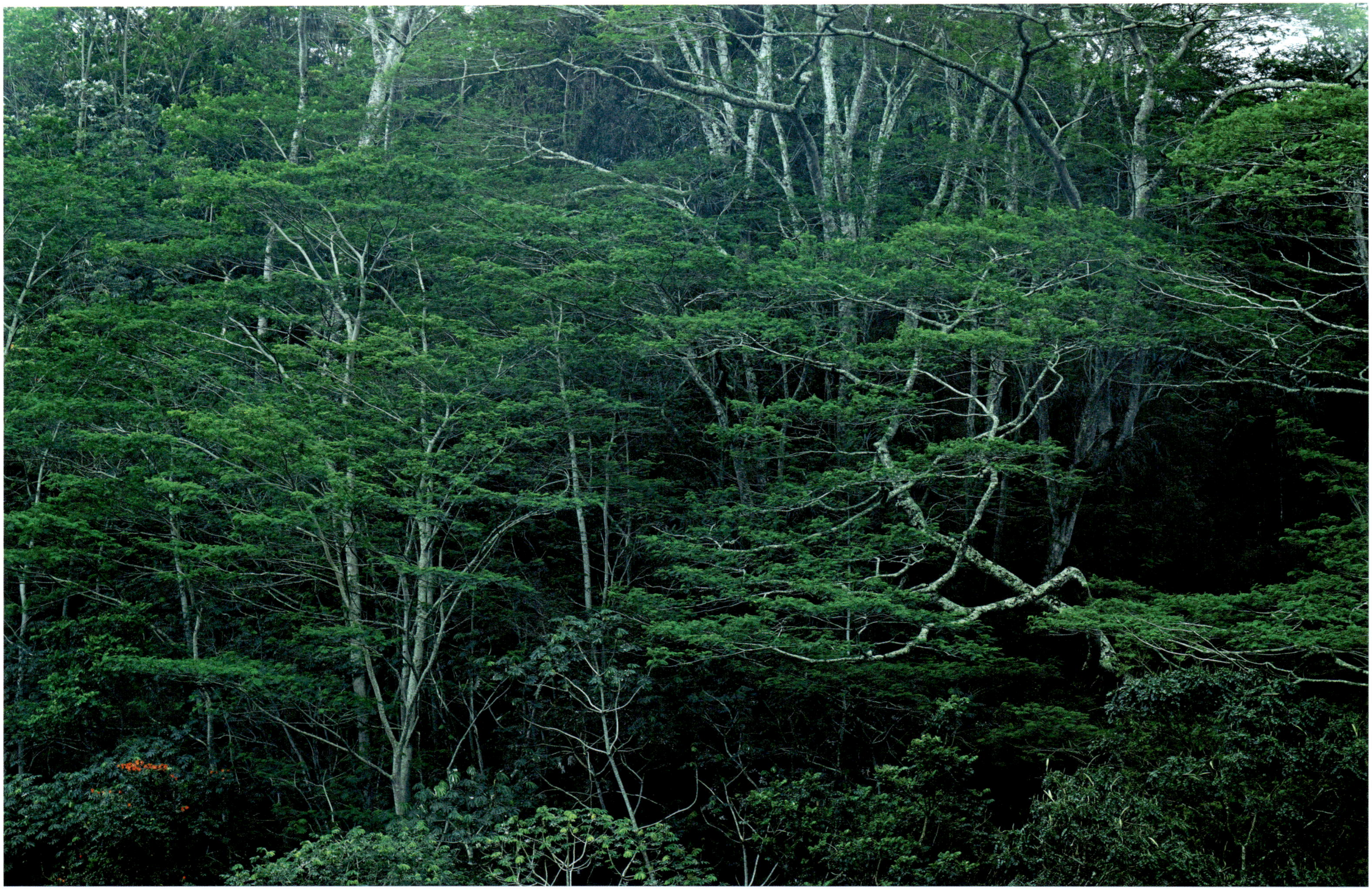

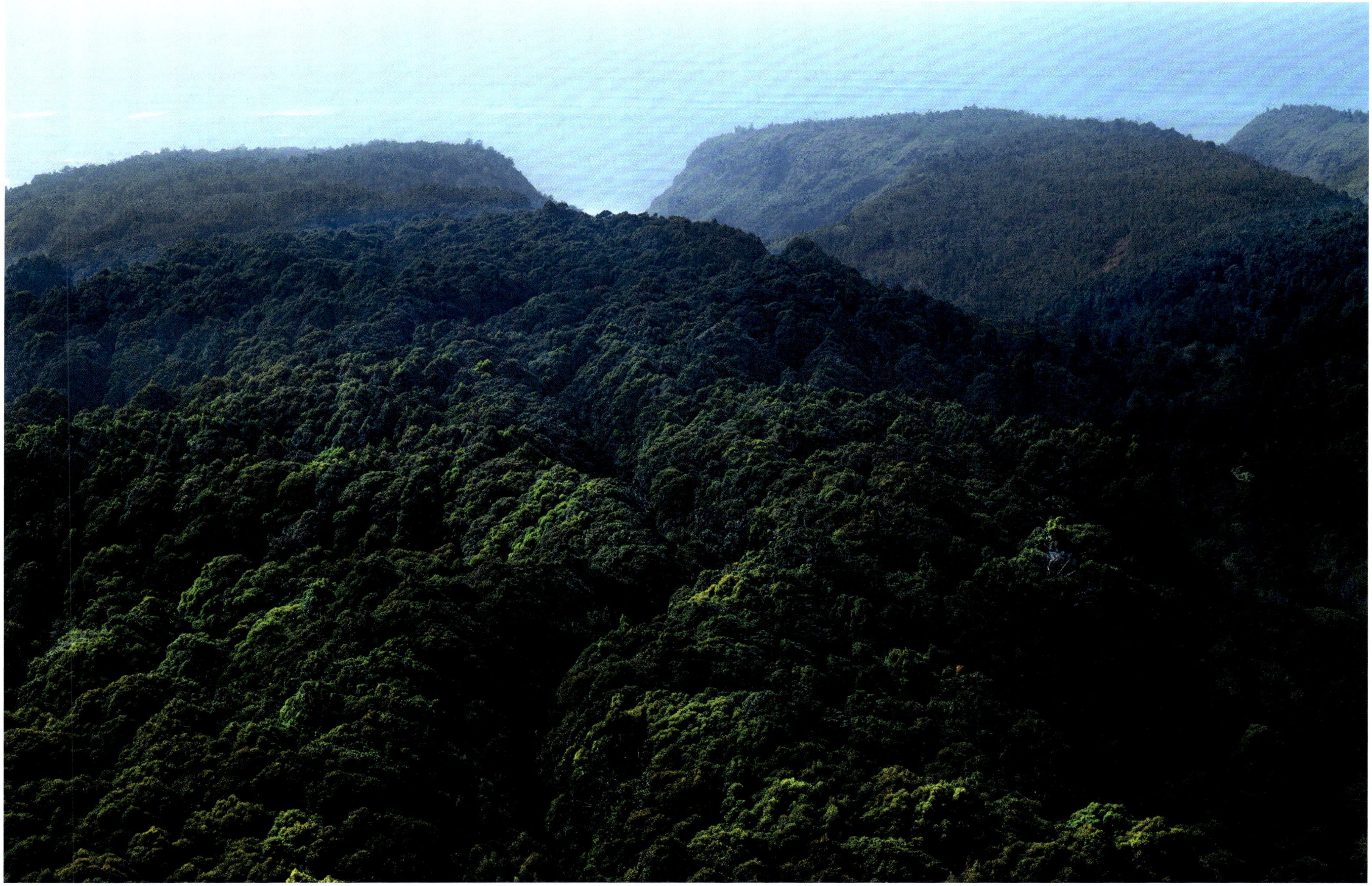

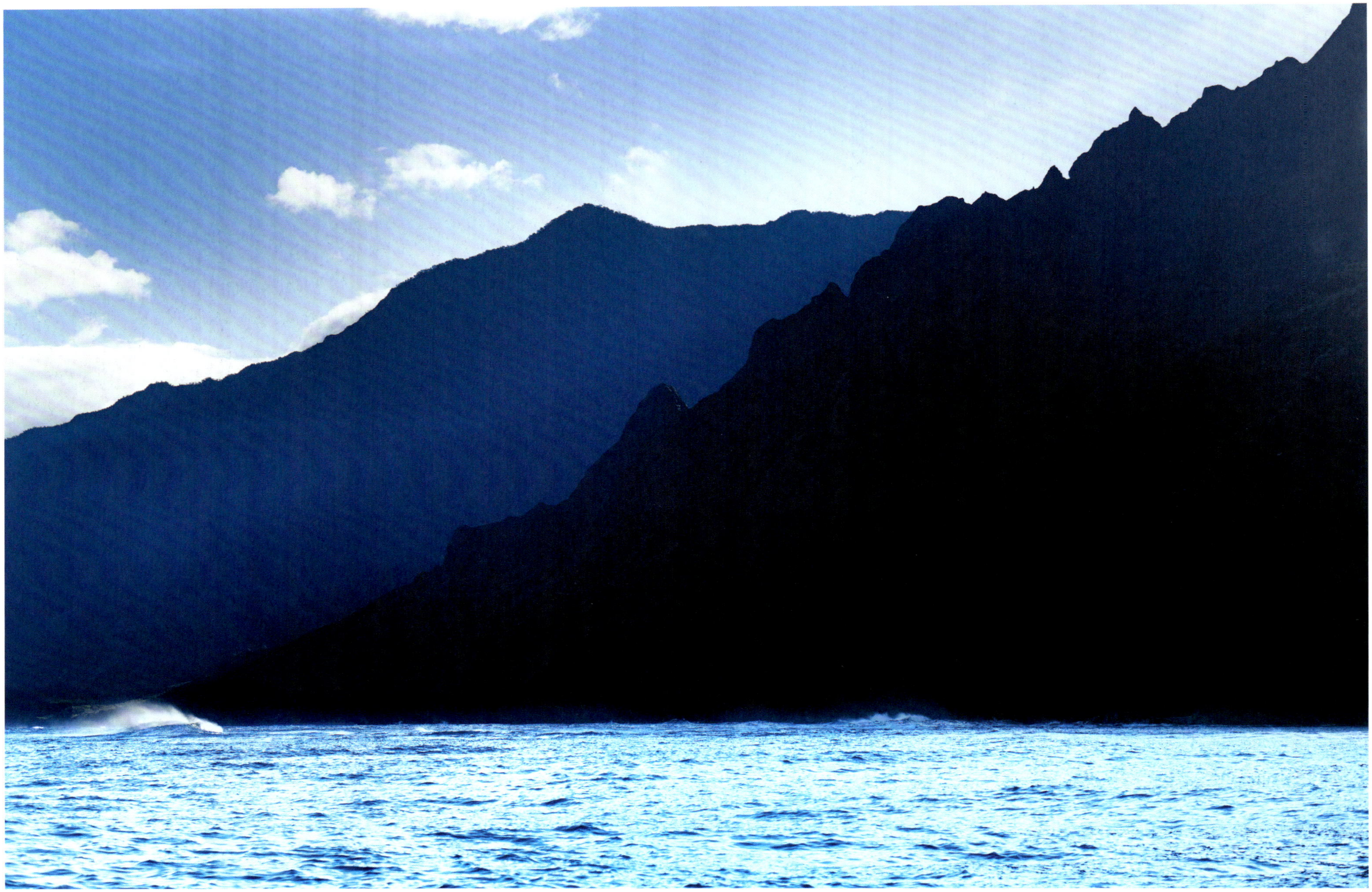

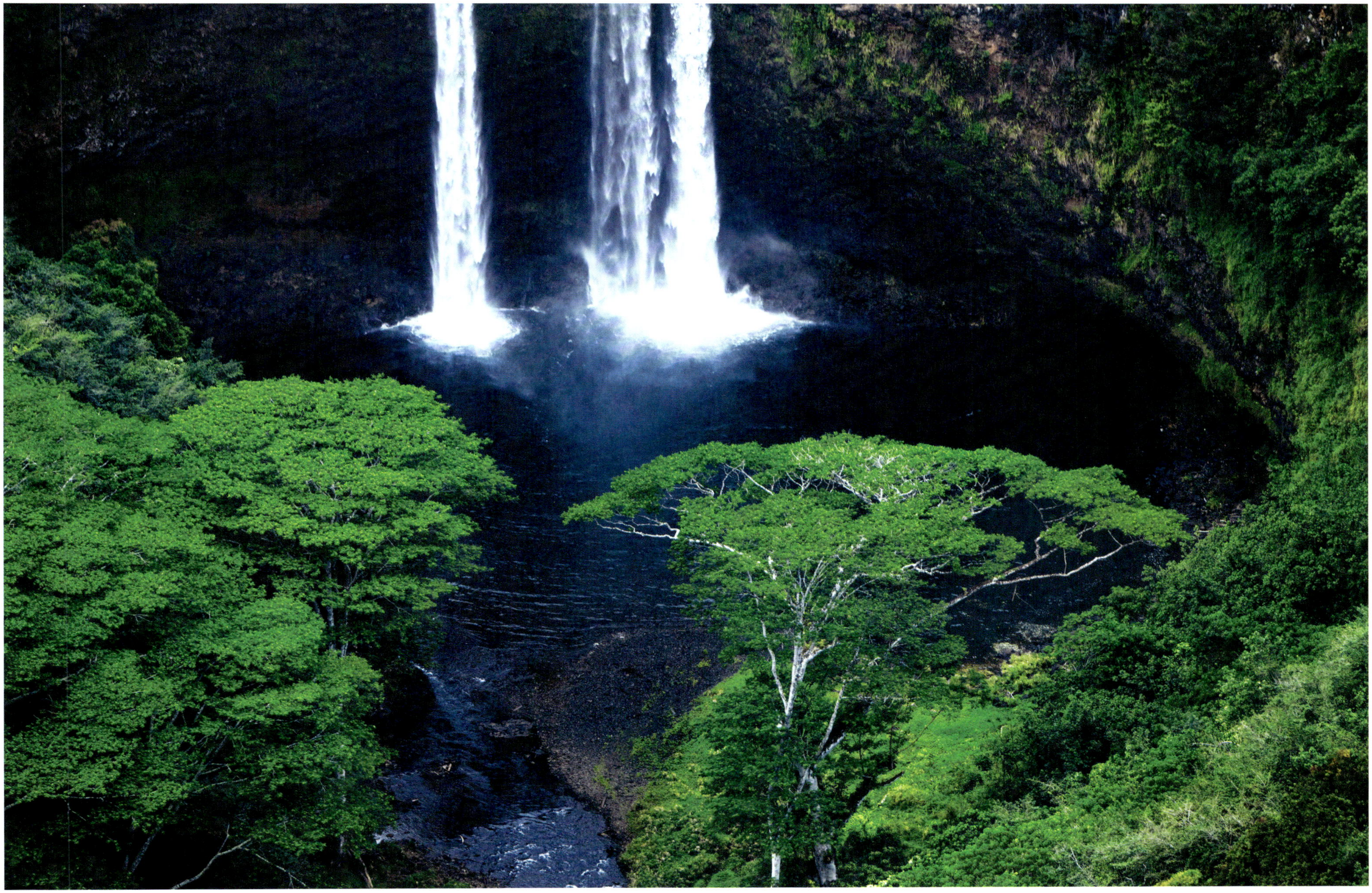

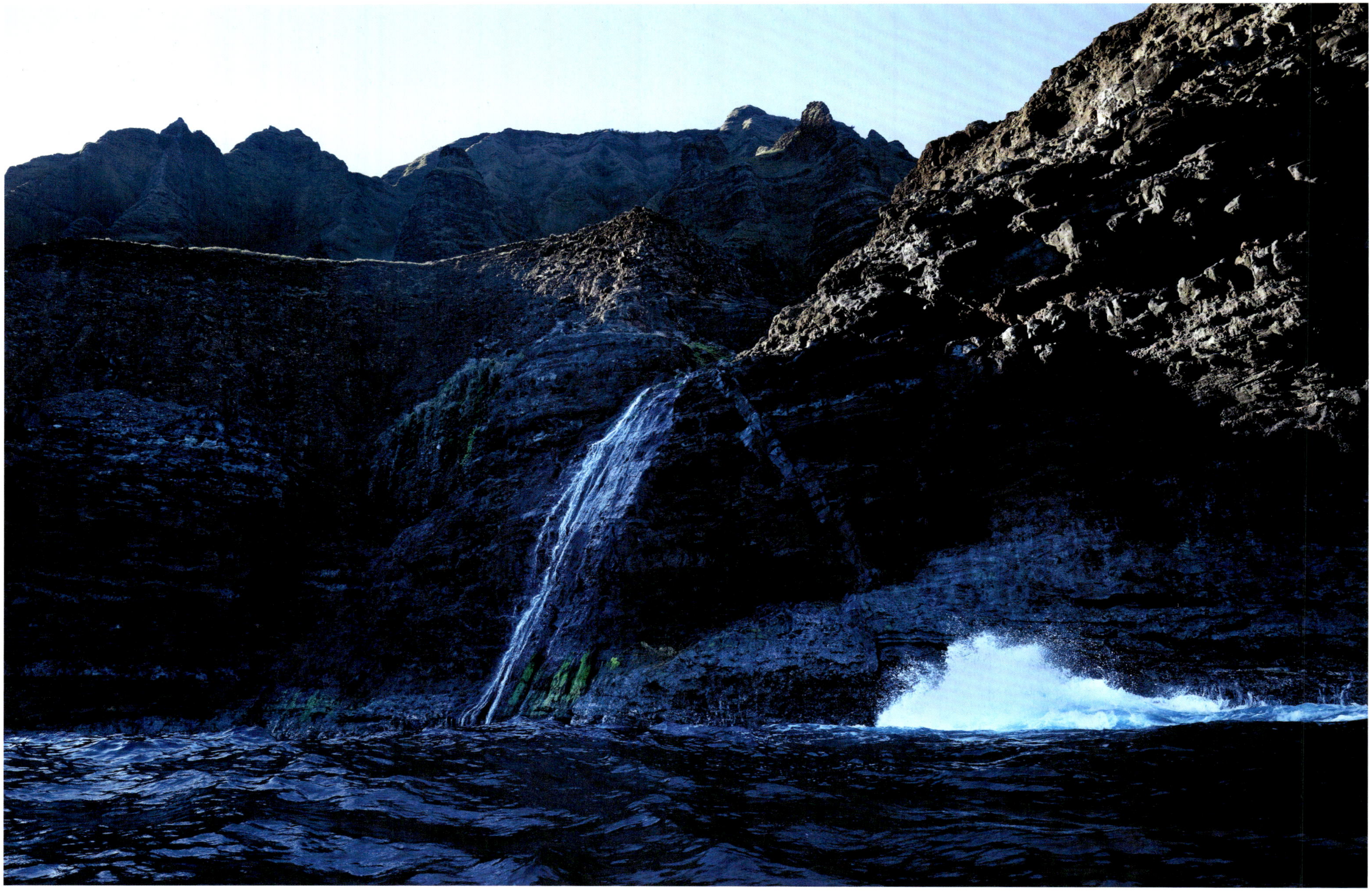

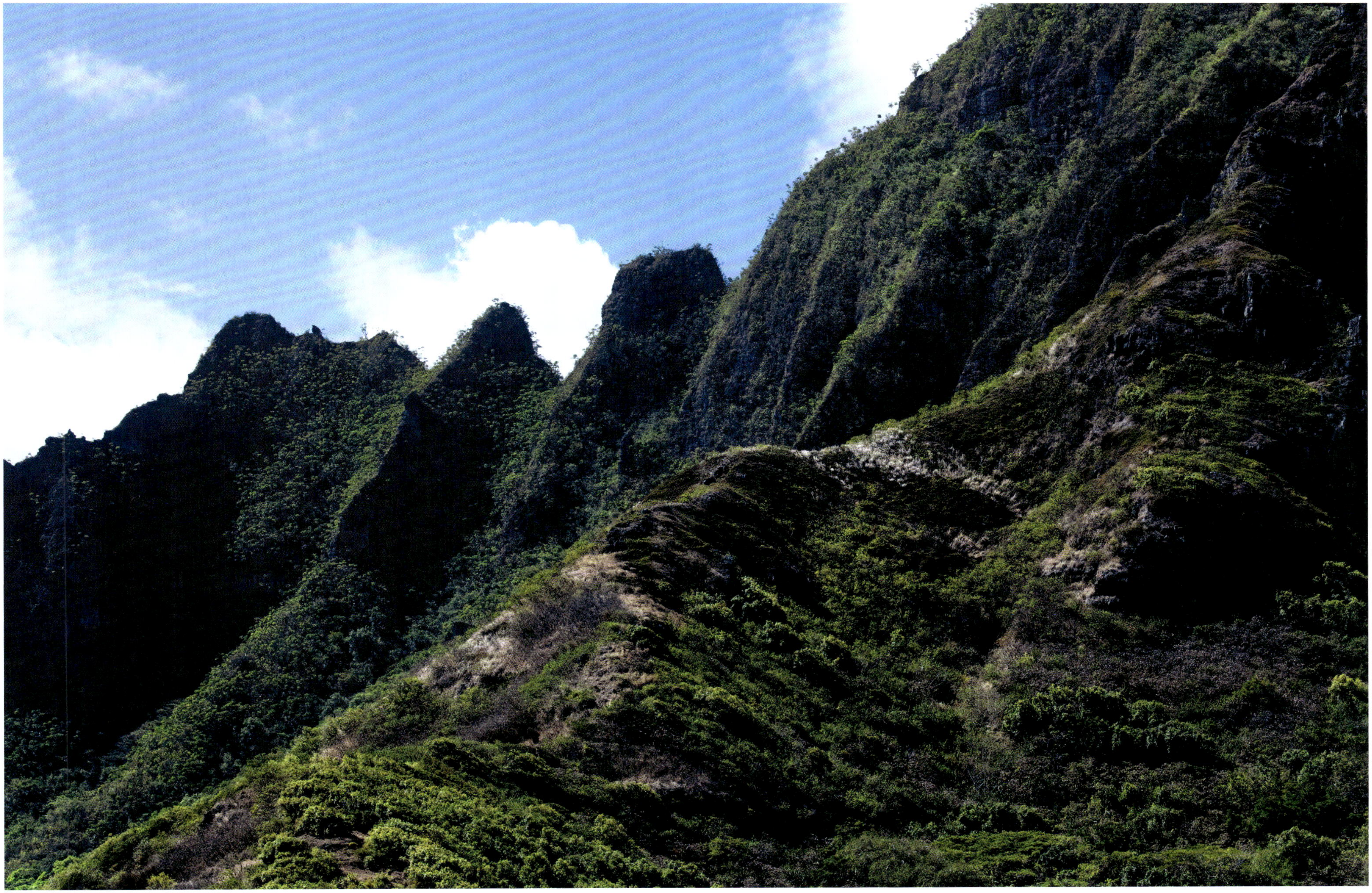

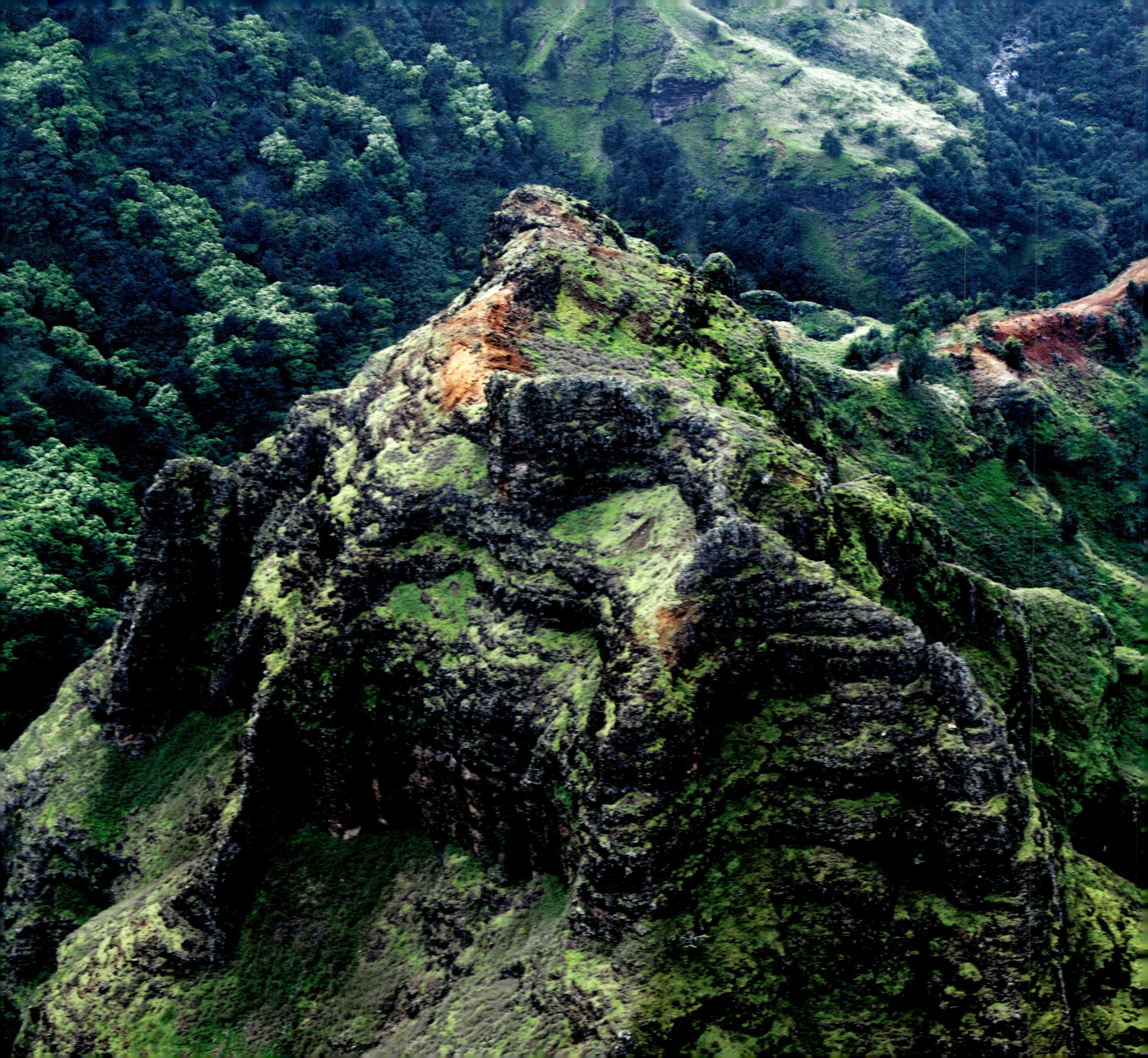

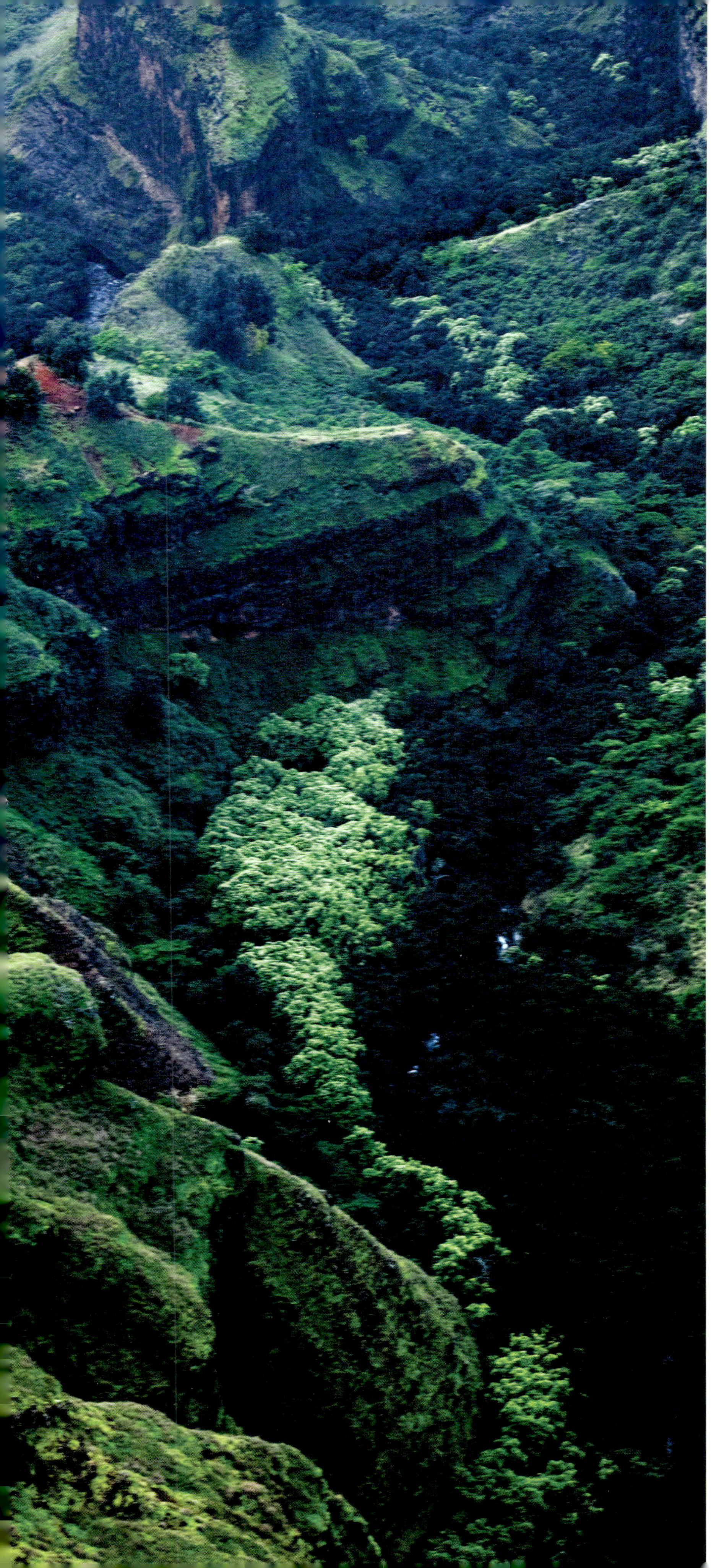

CLIMBING THE OCEAN

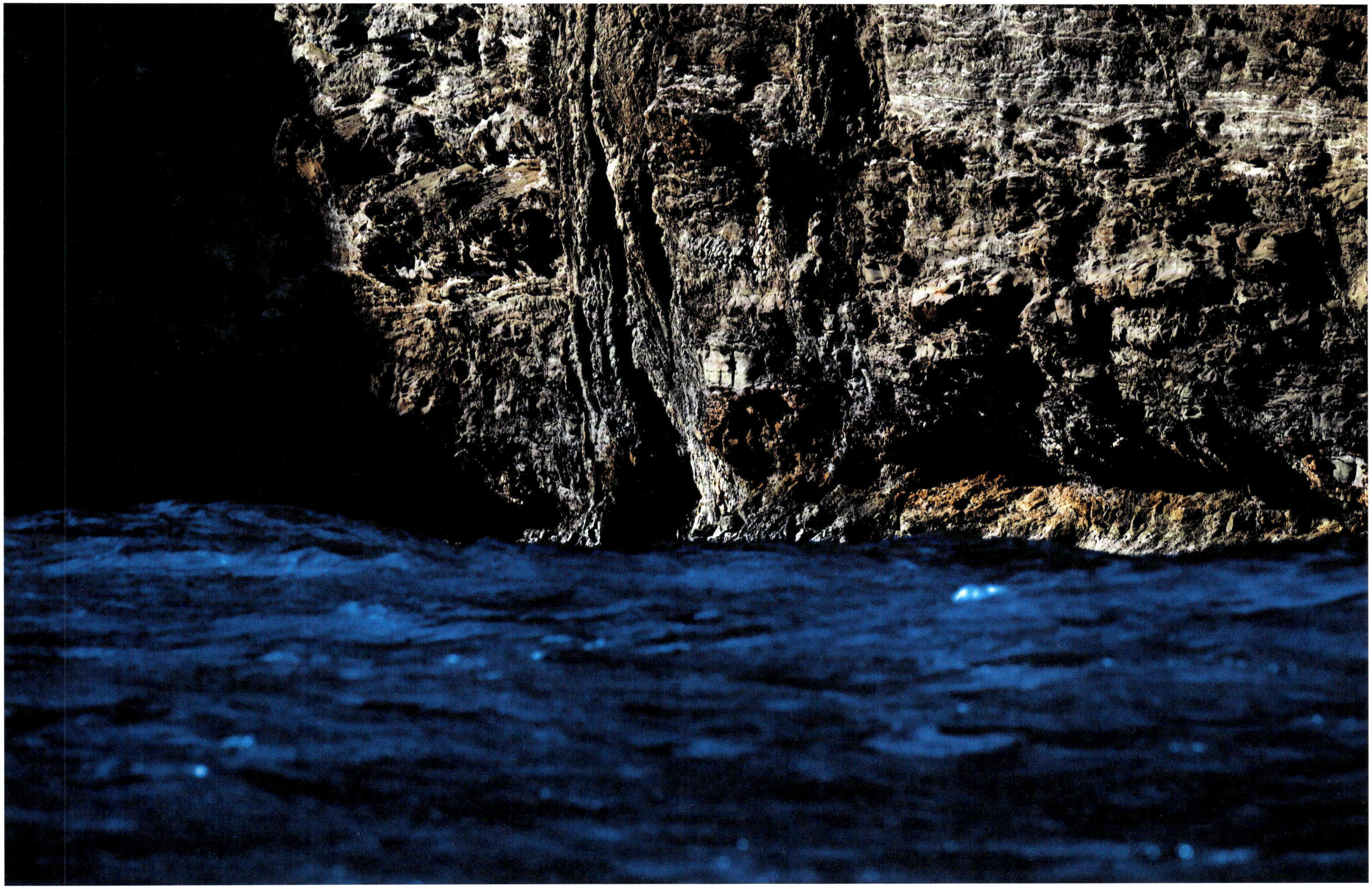

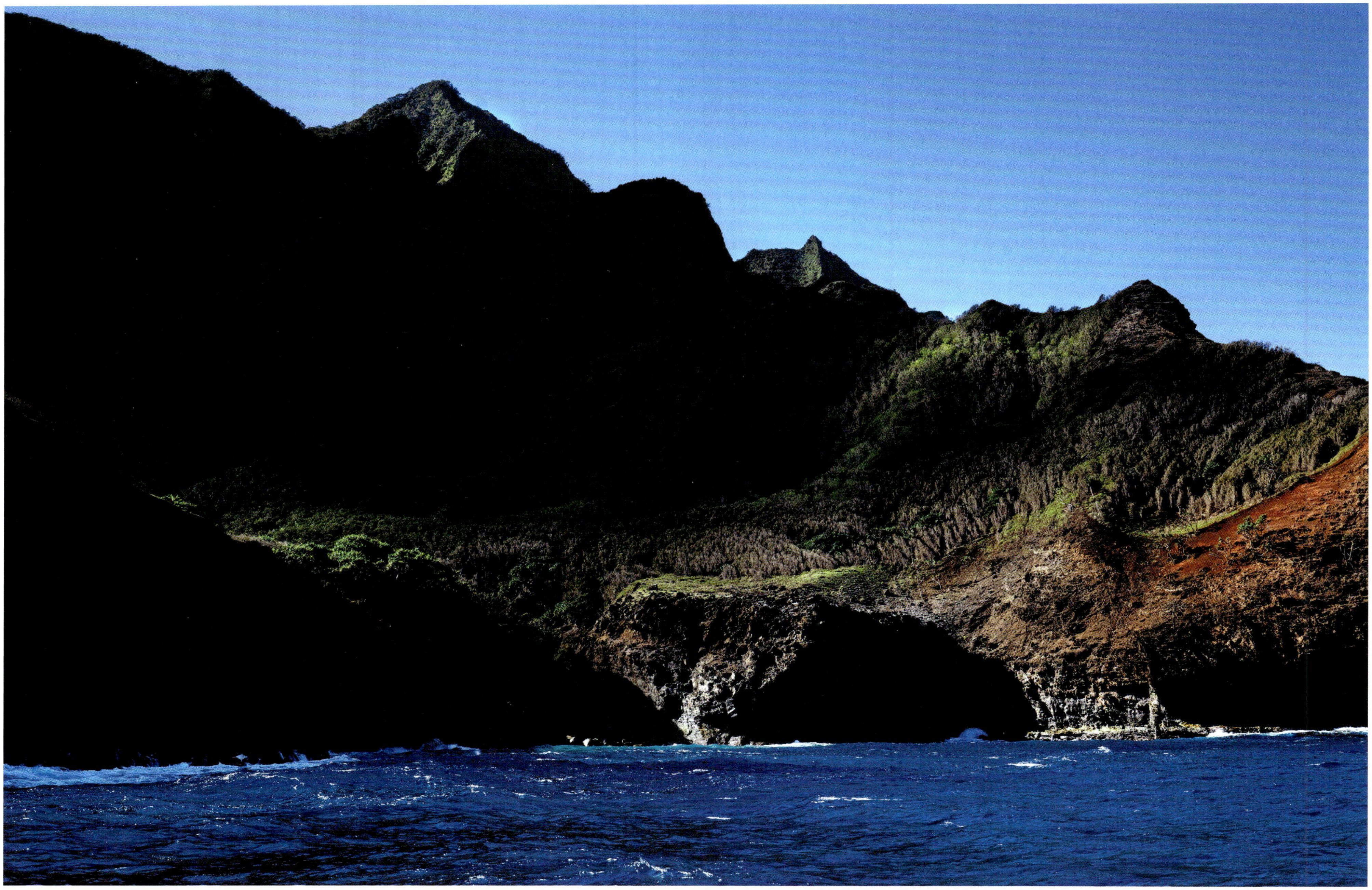

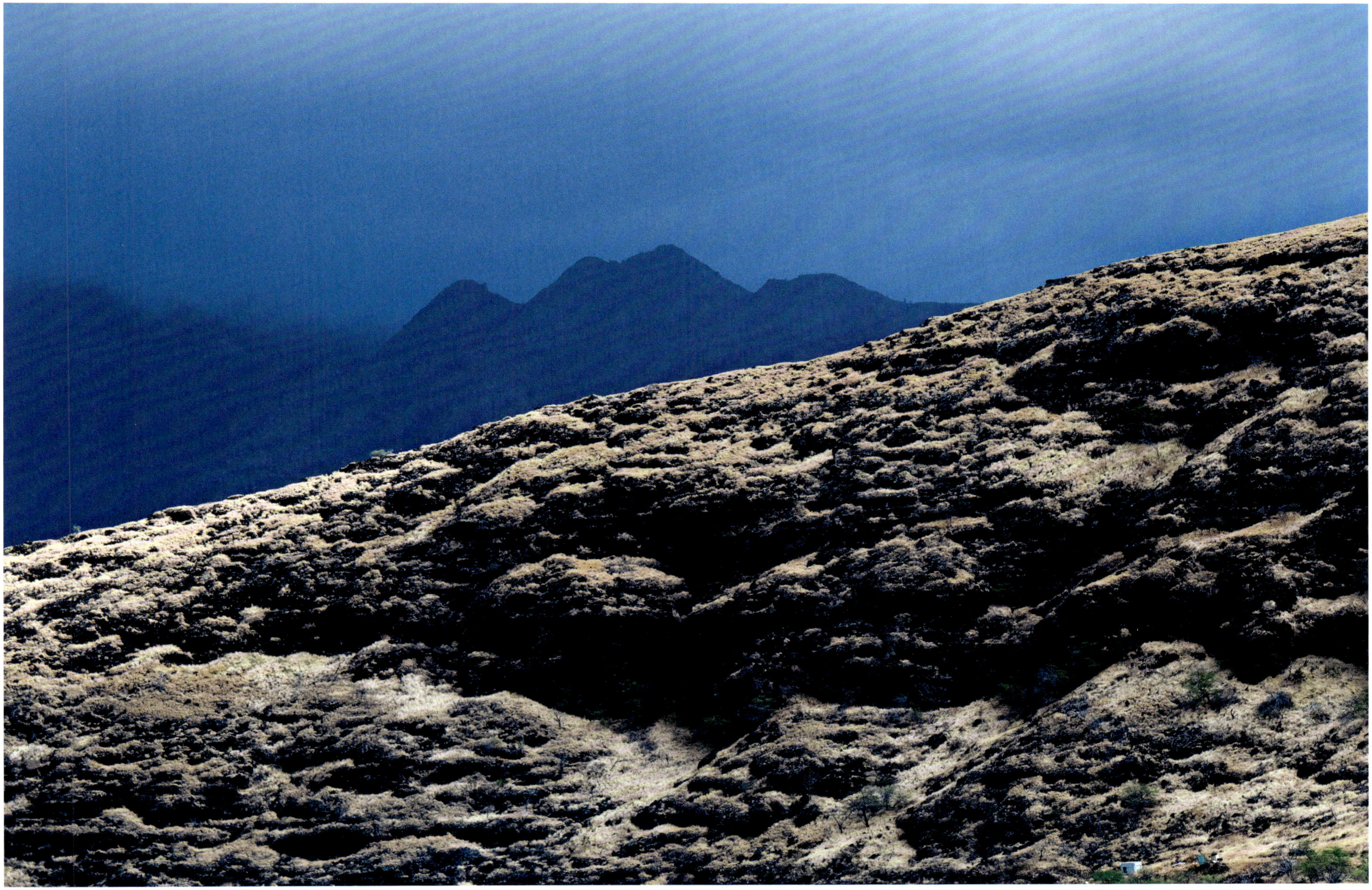

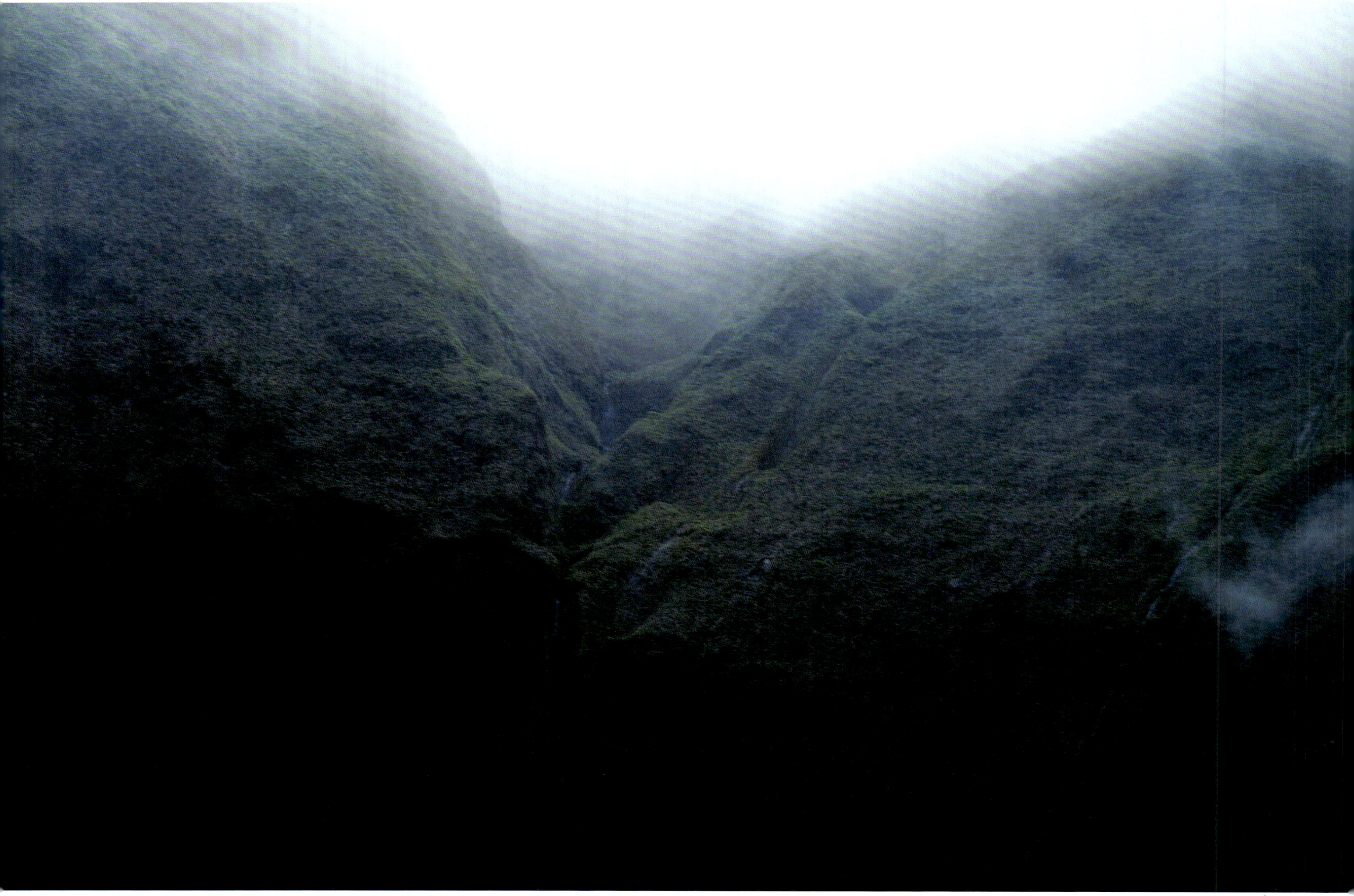

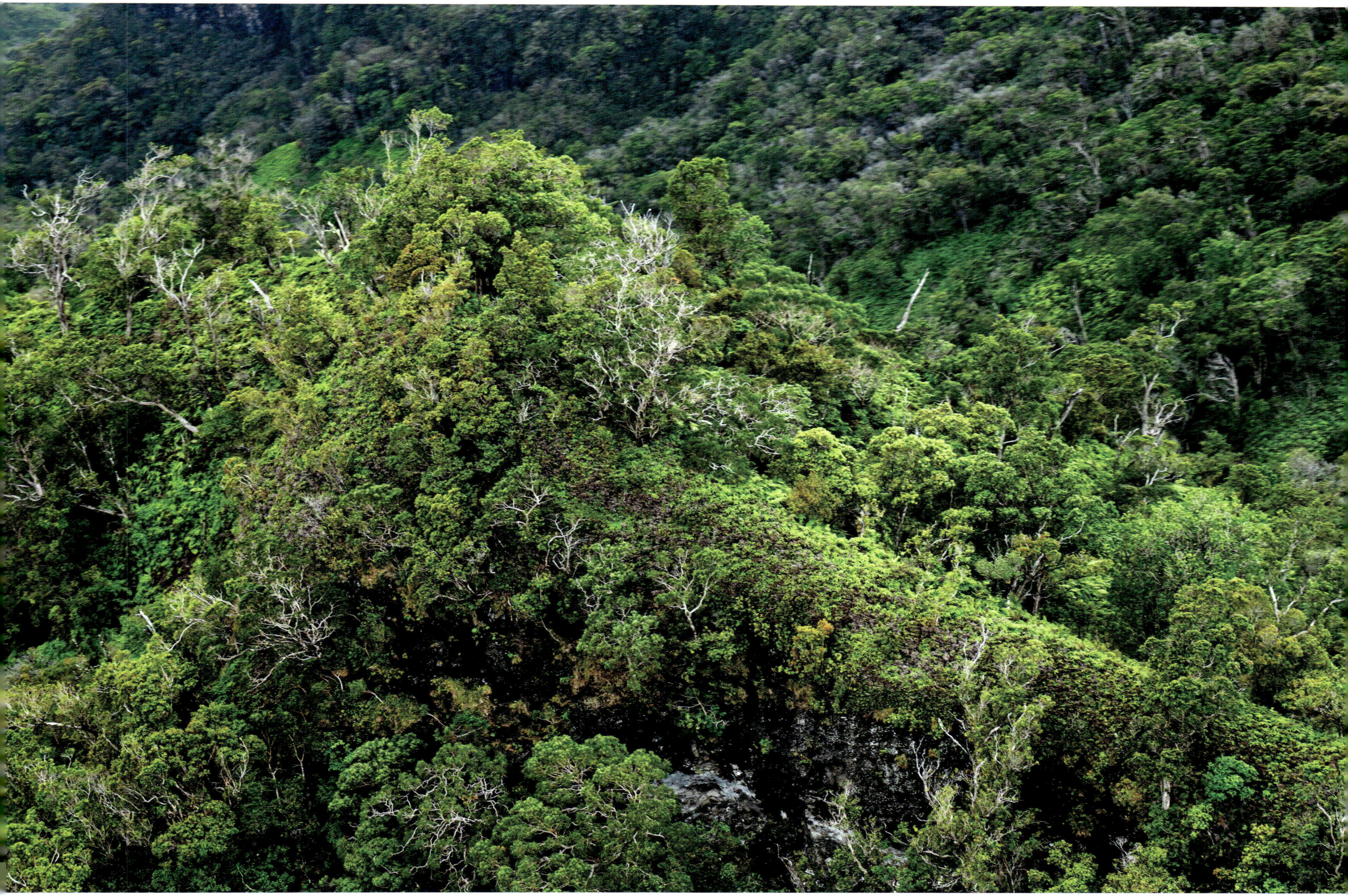

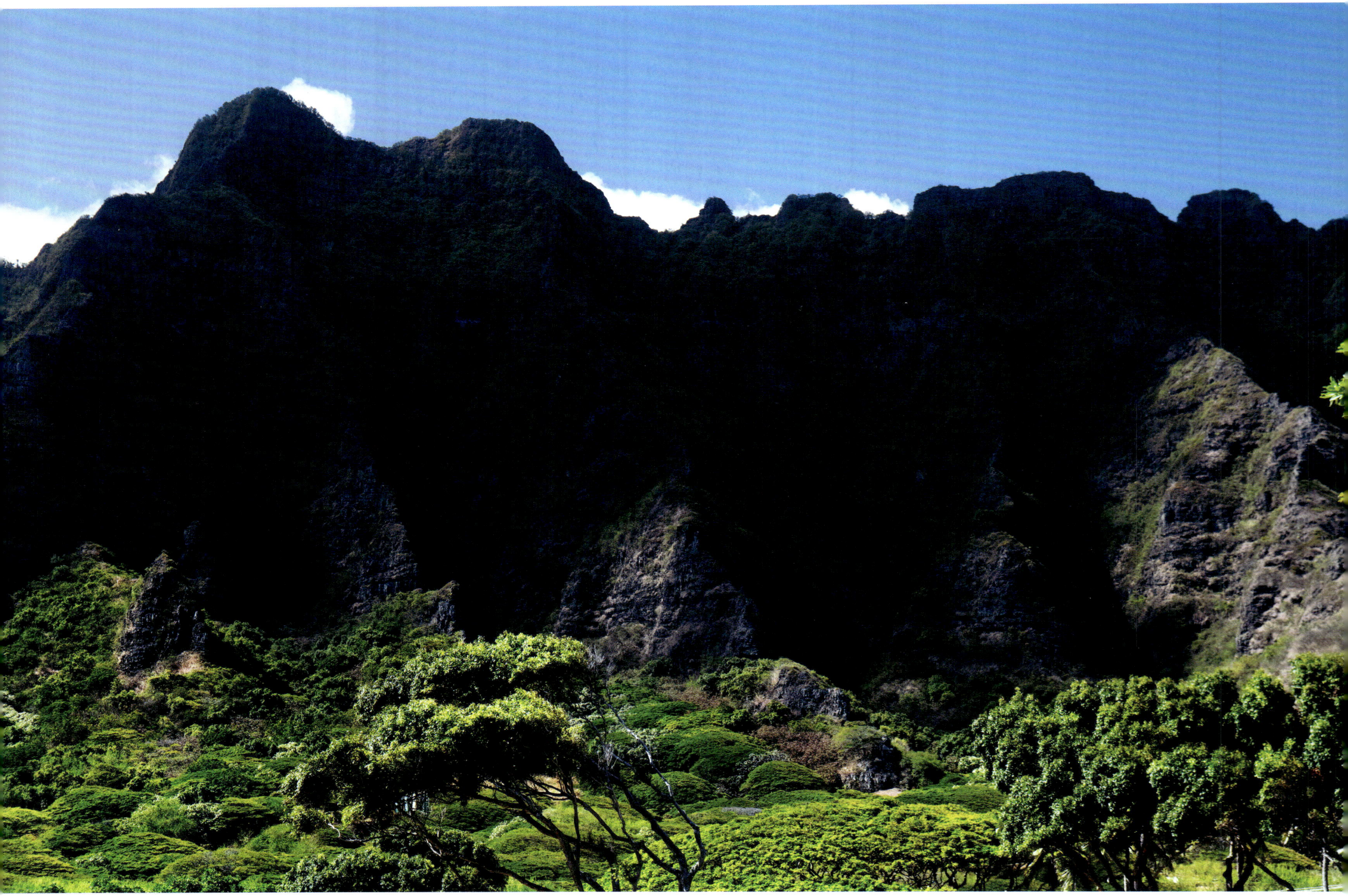

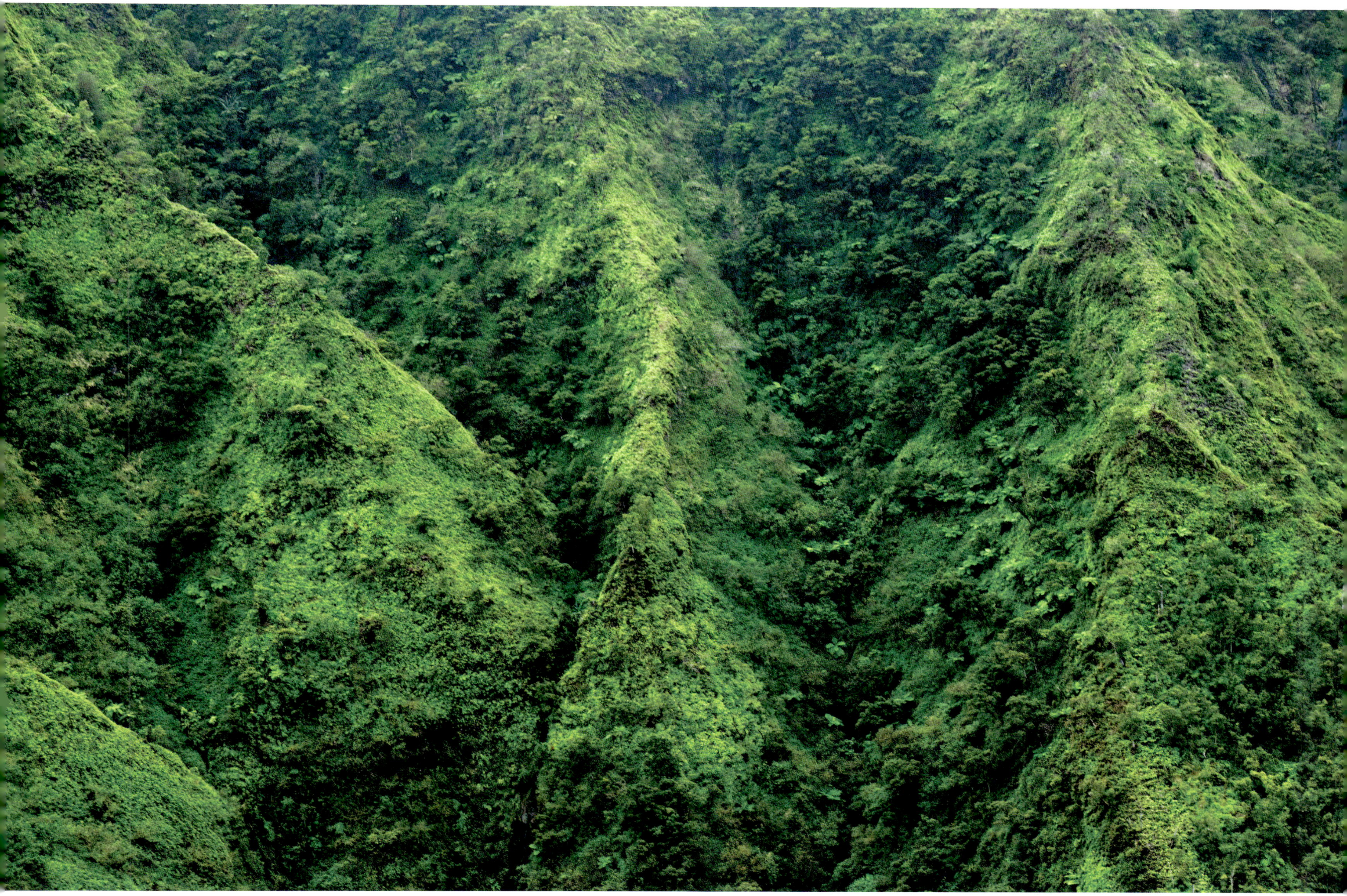

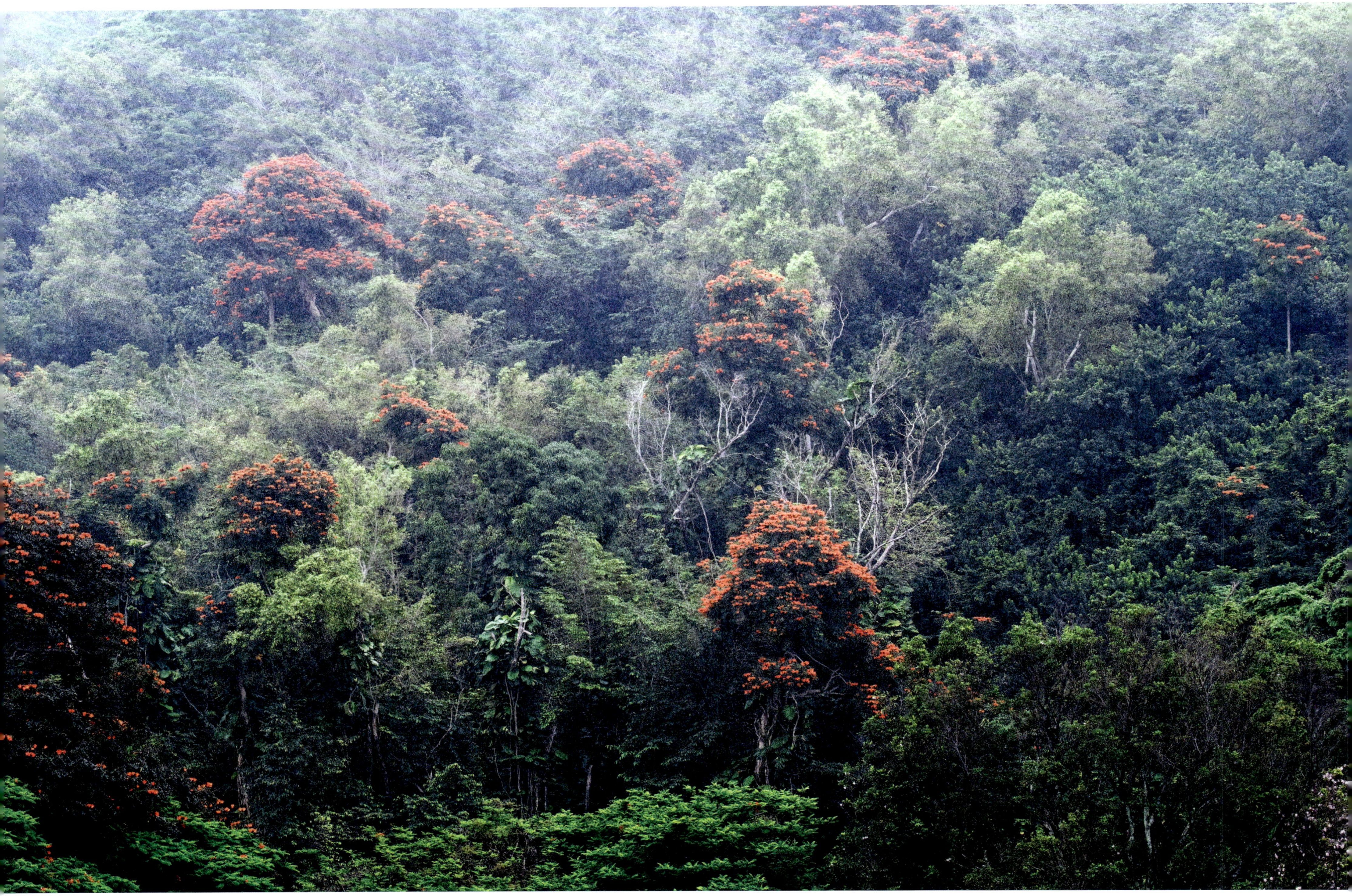

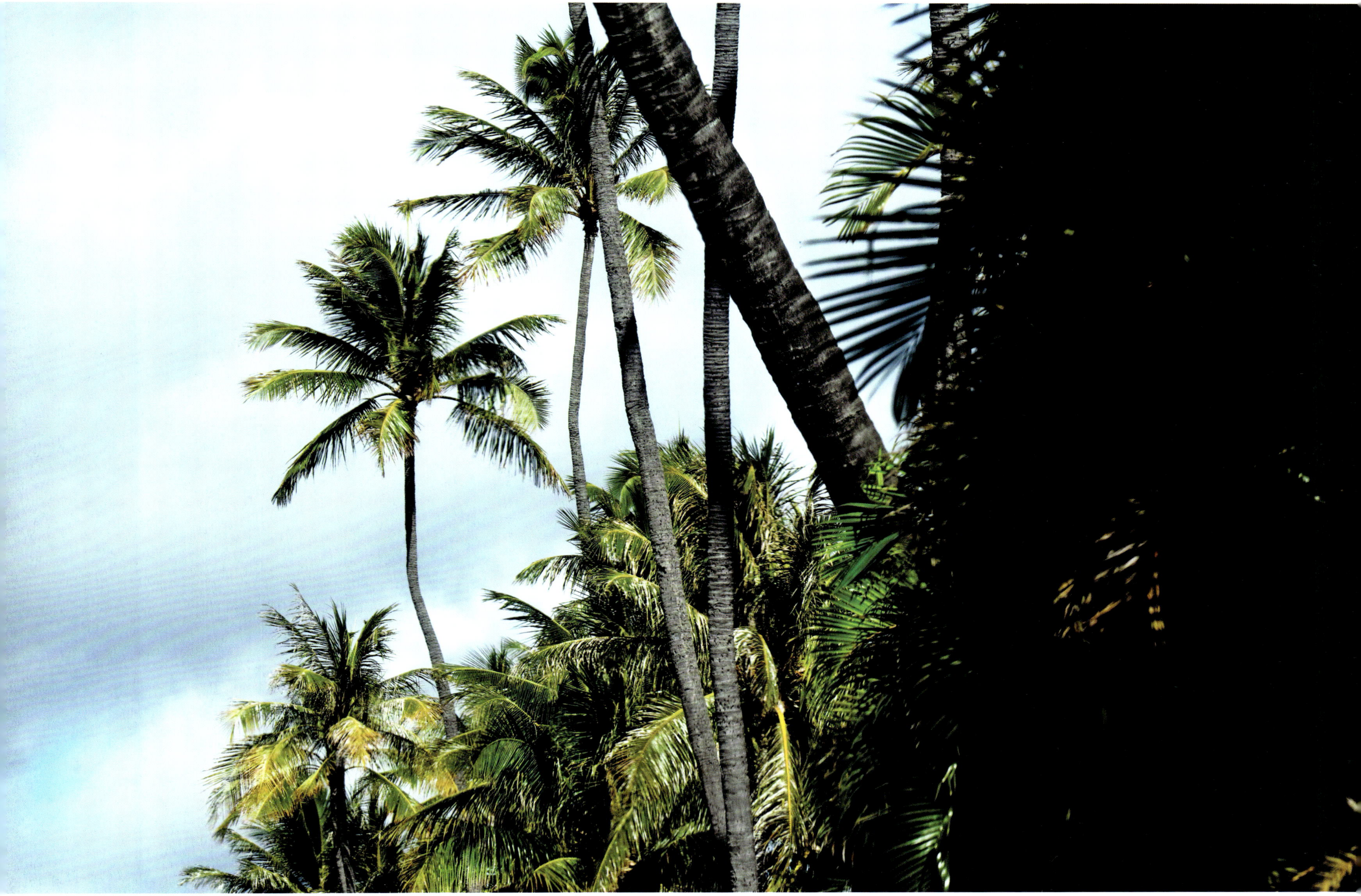

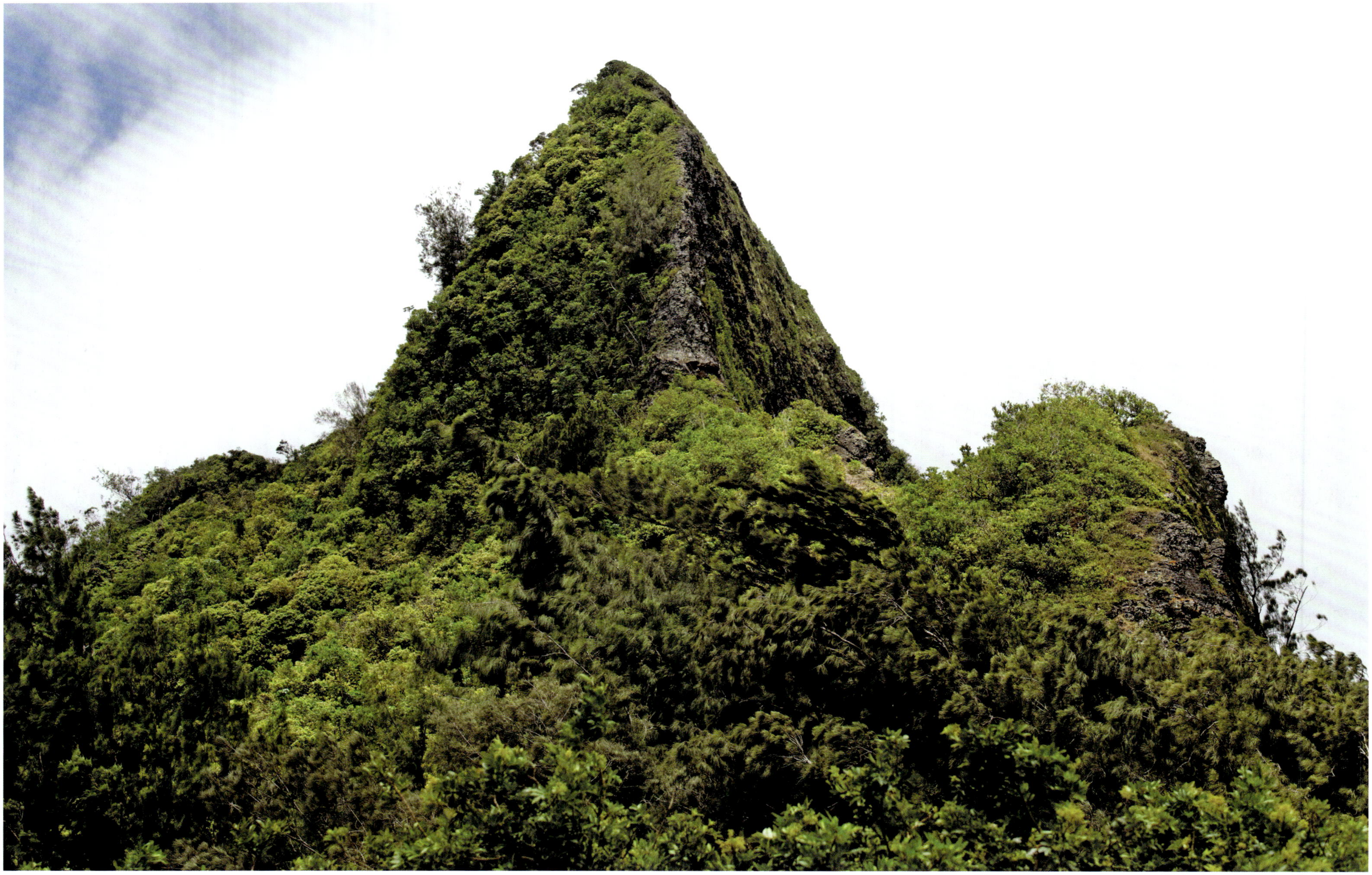

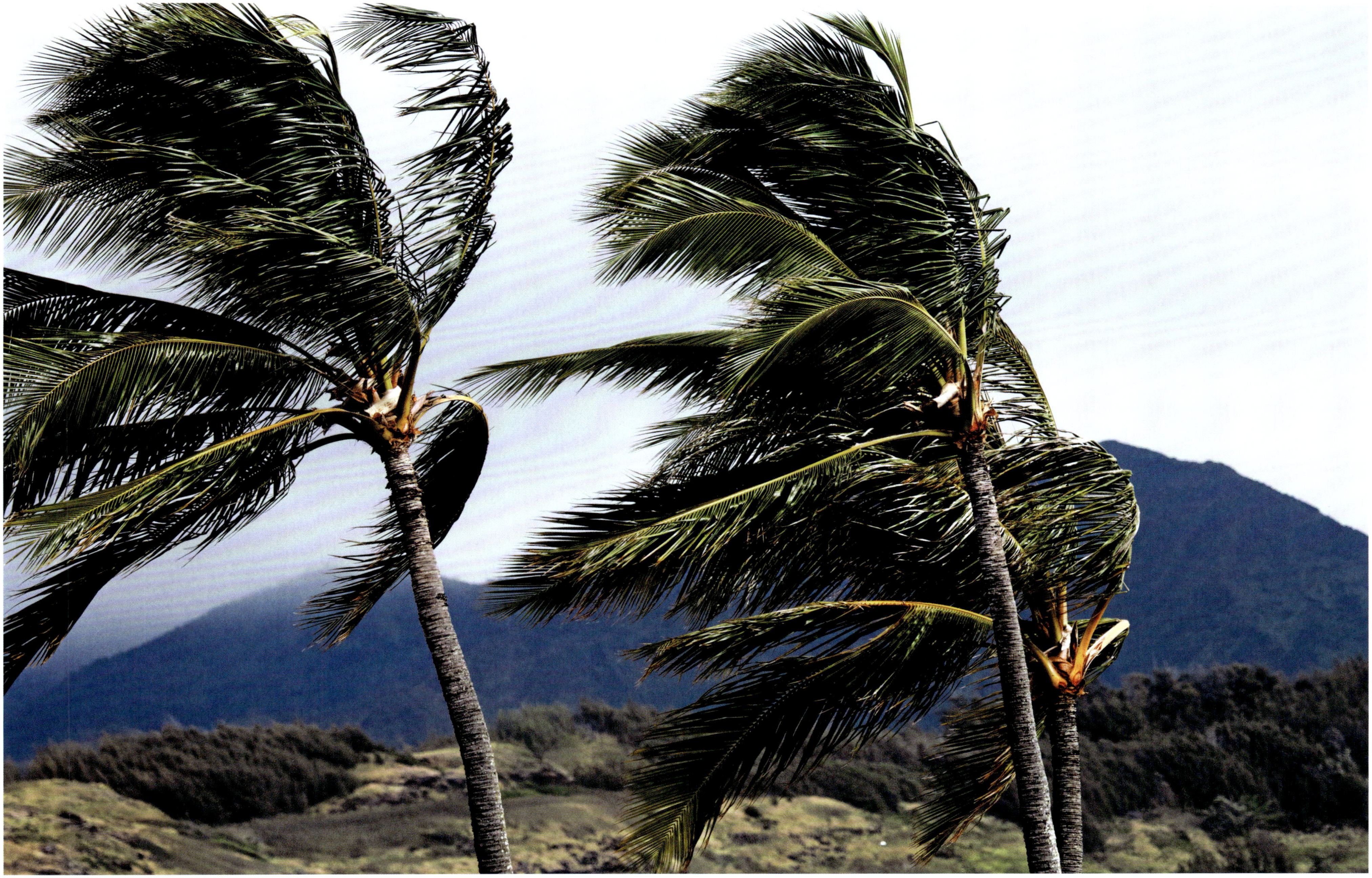

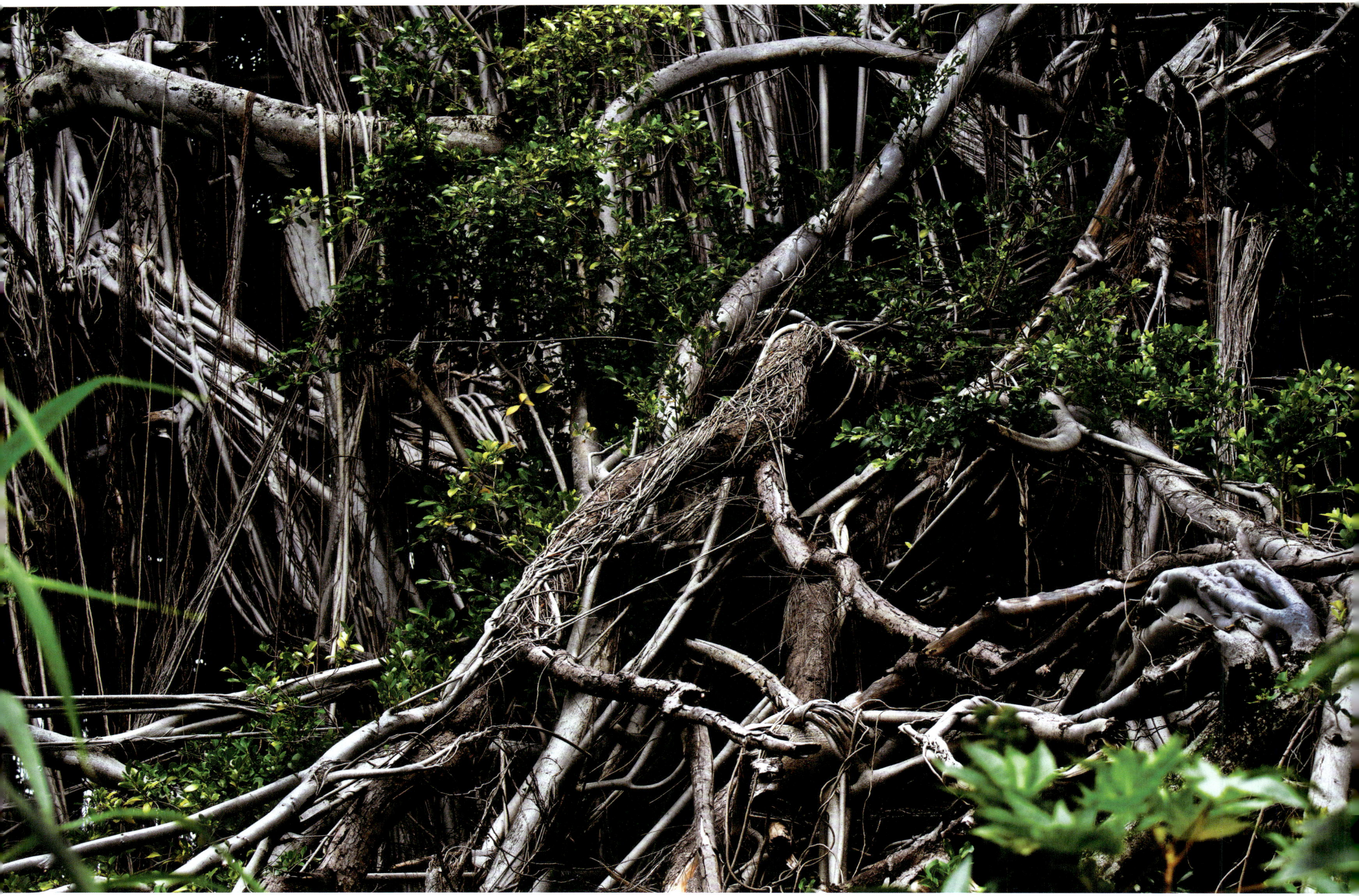

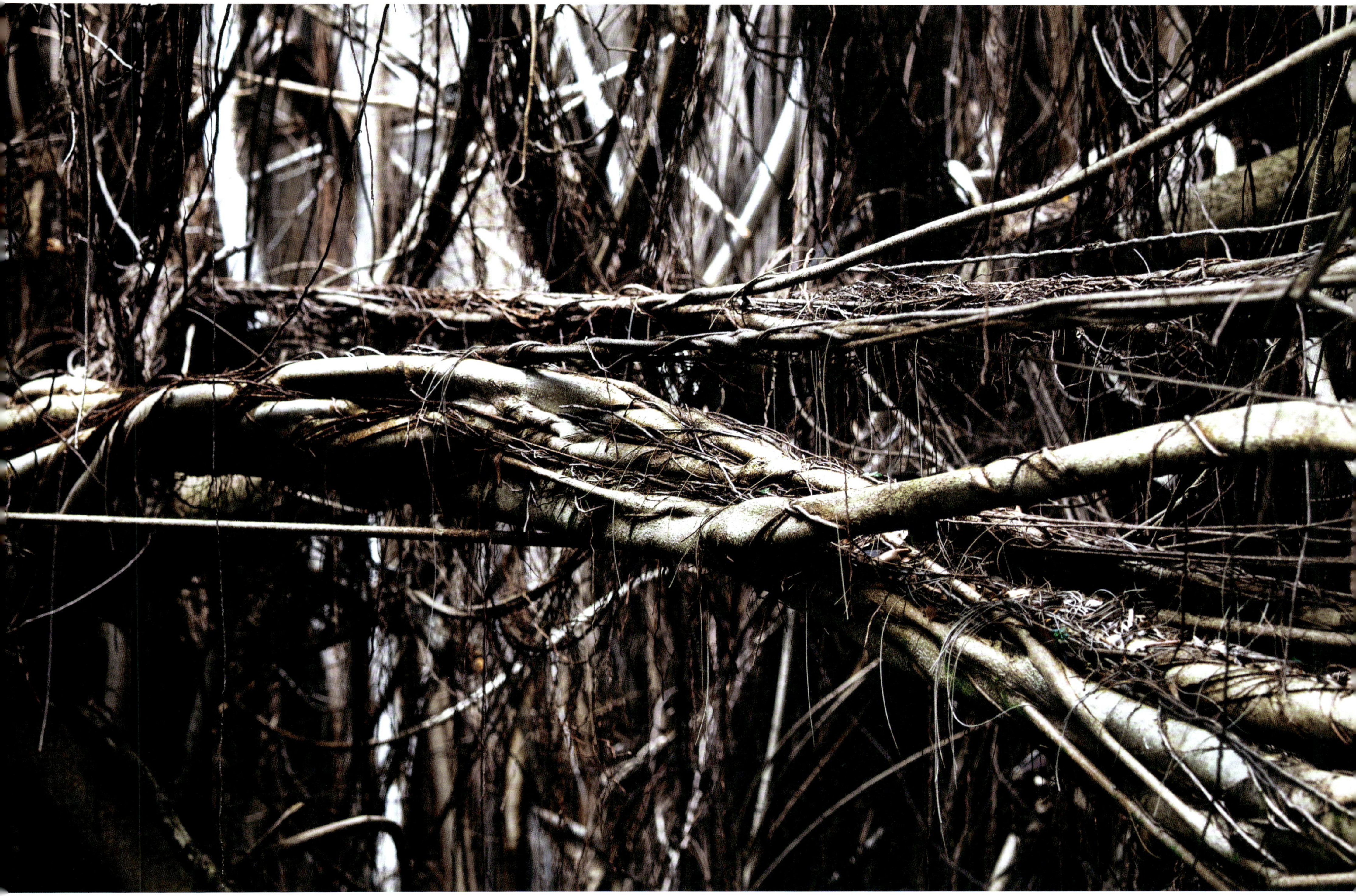

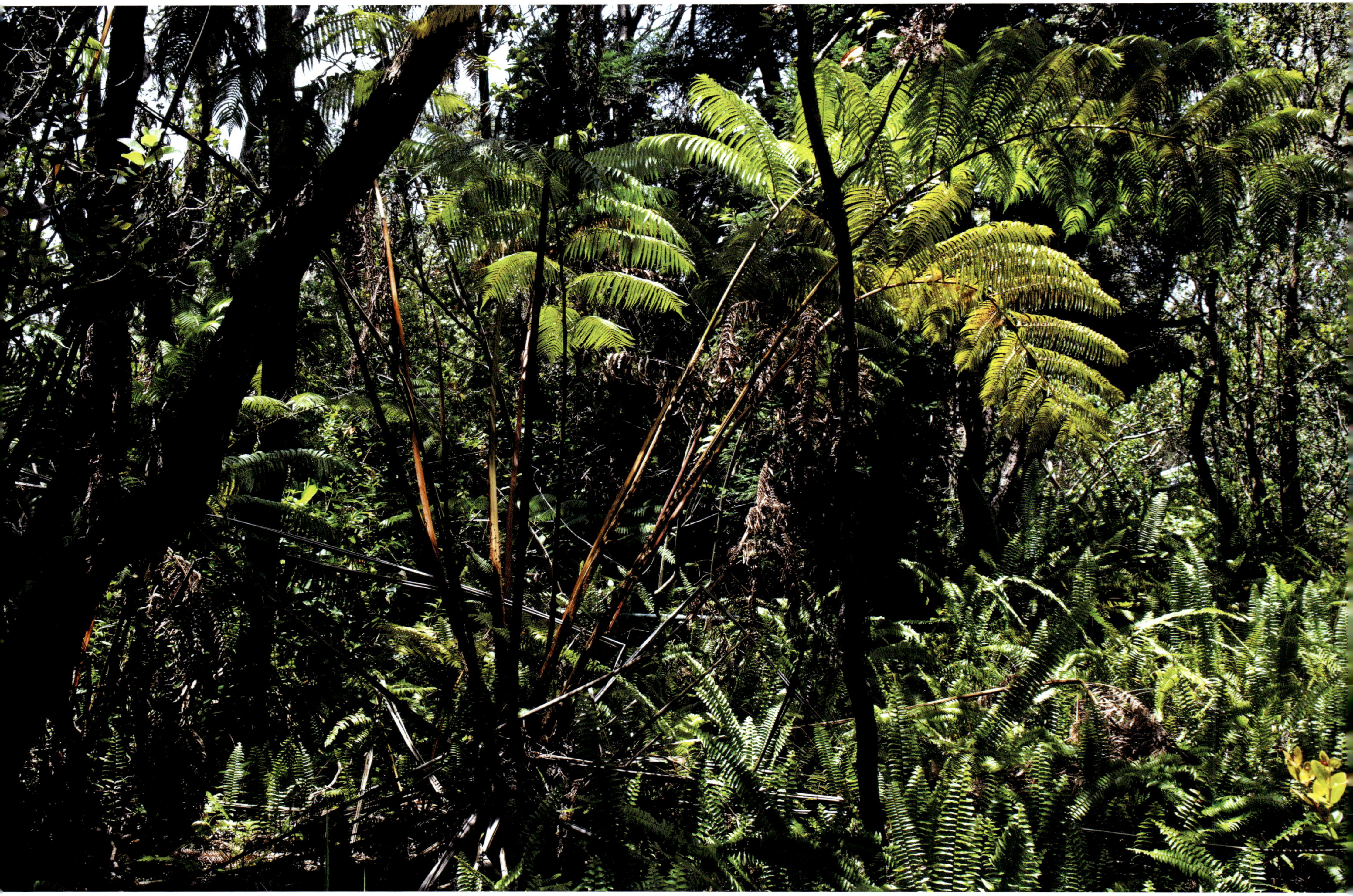

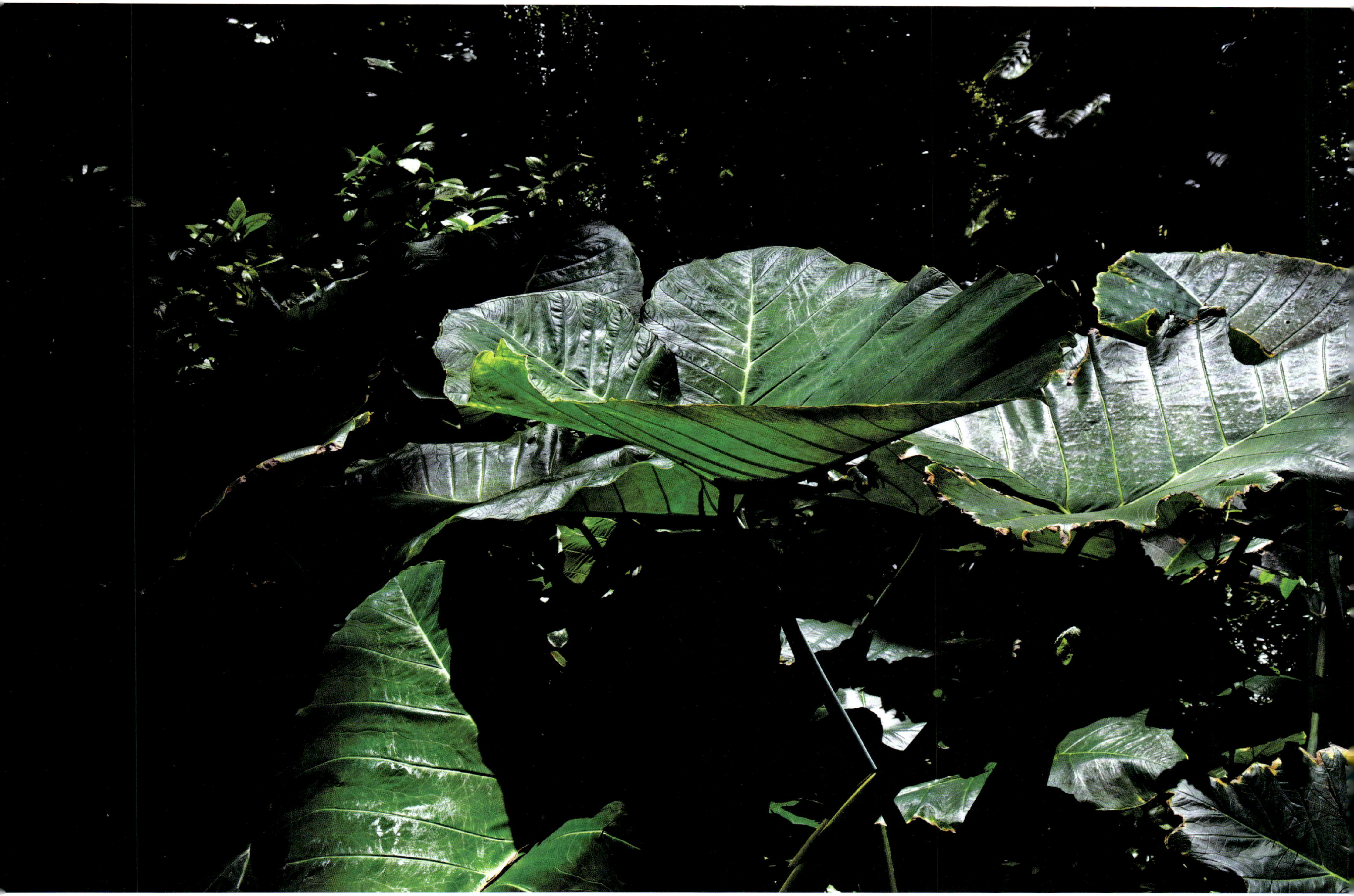

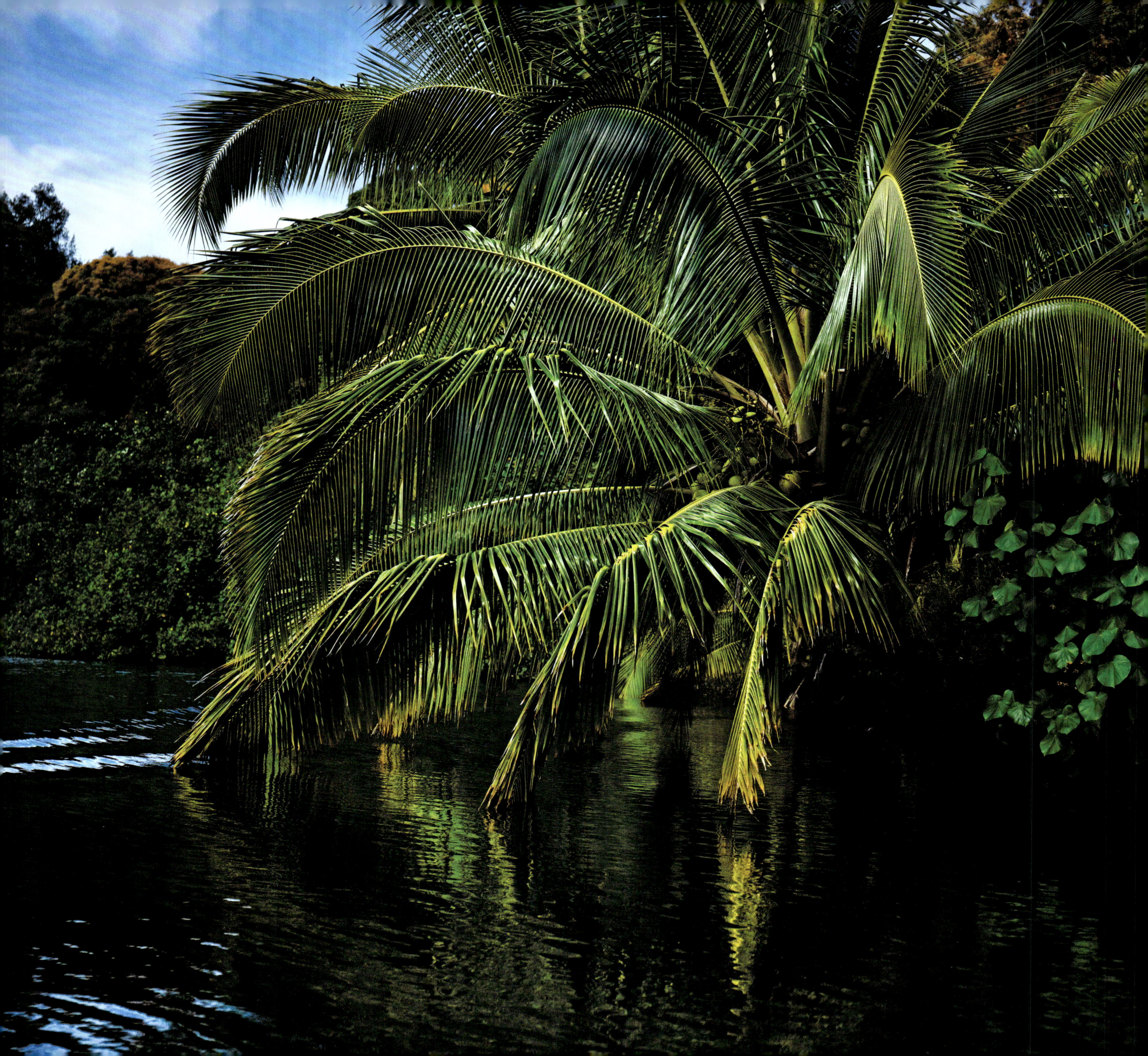

139

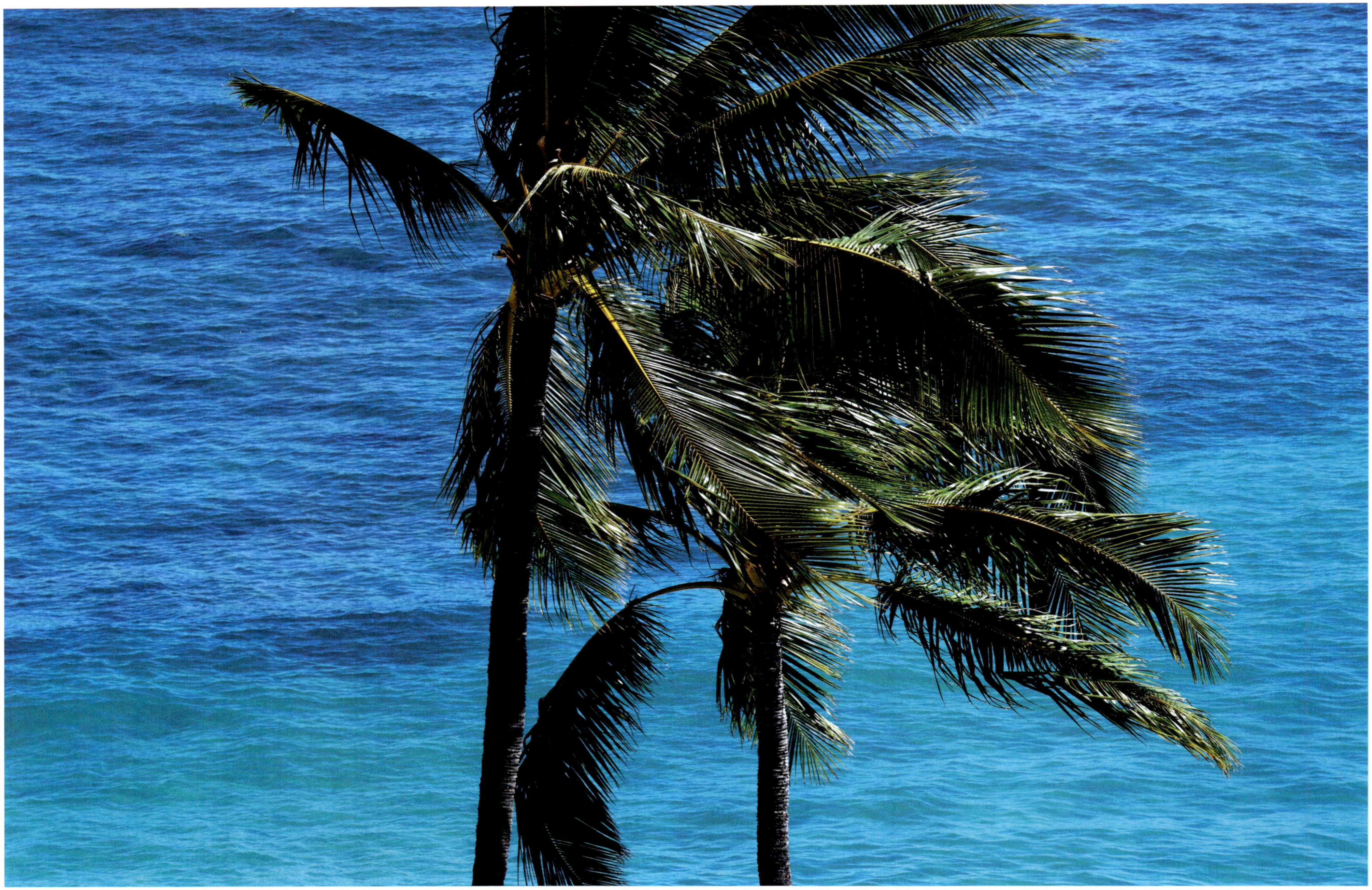

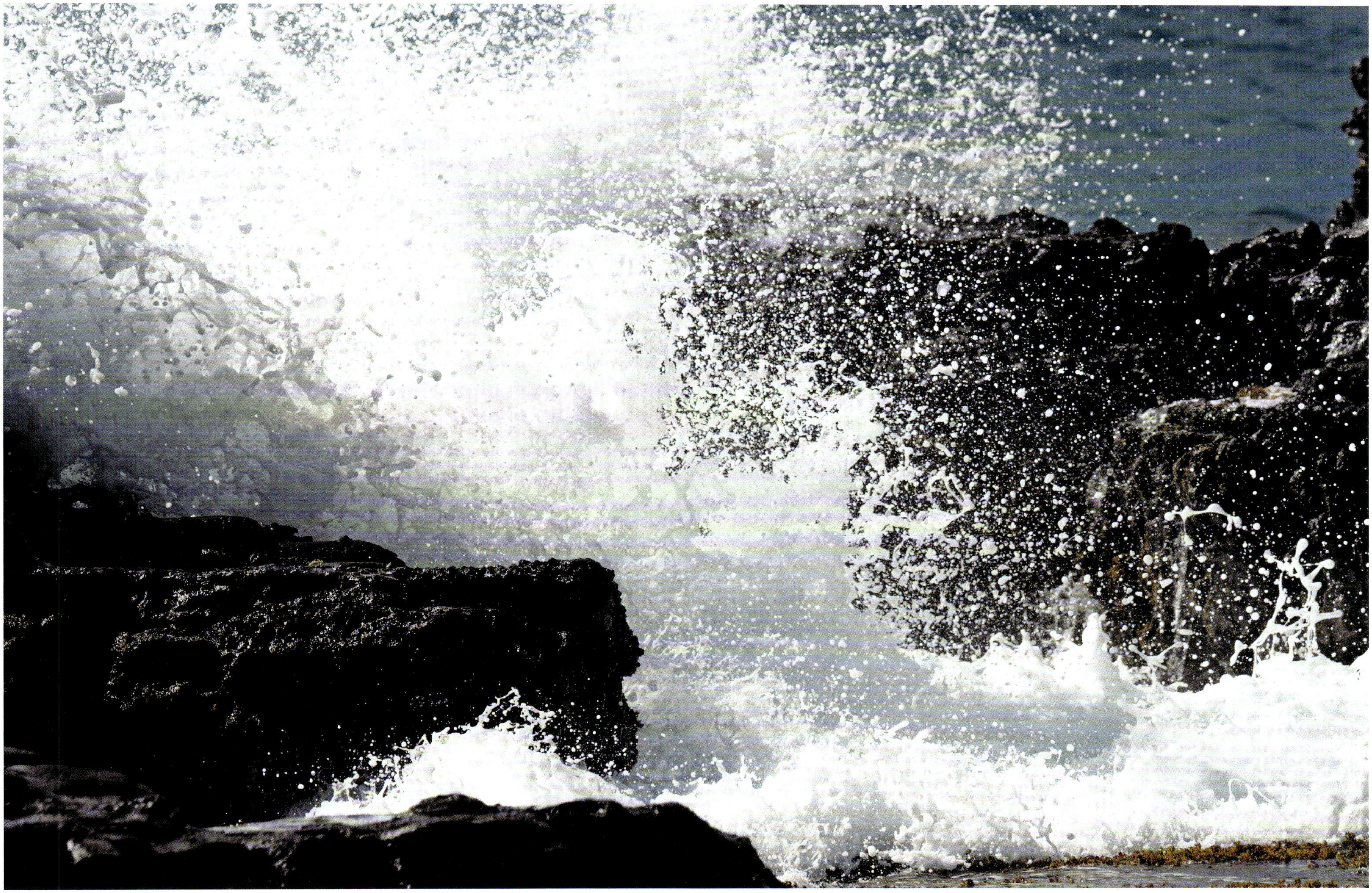

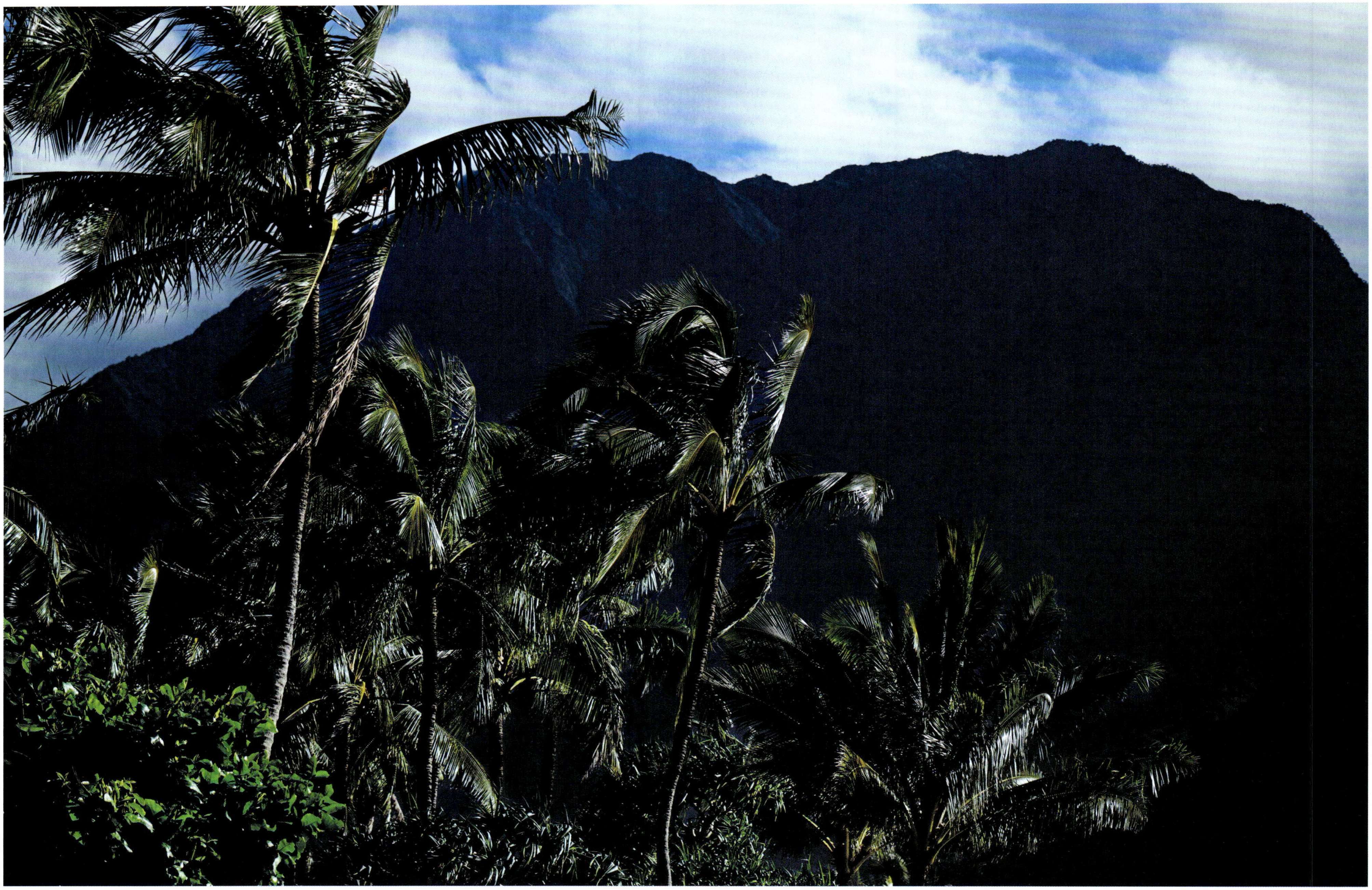

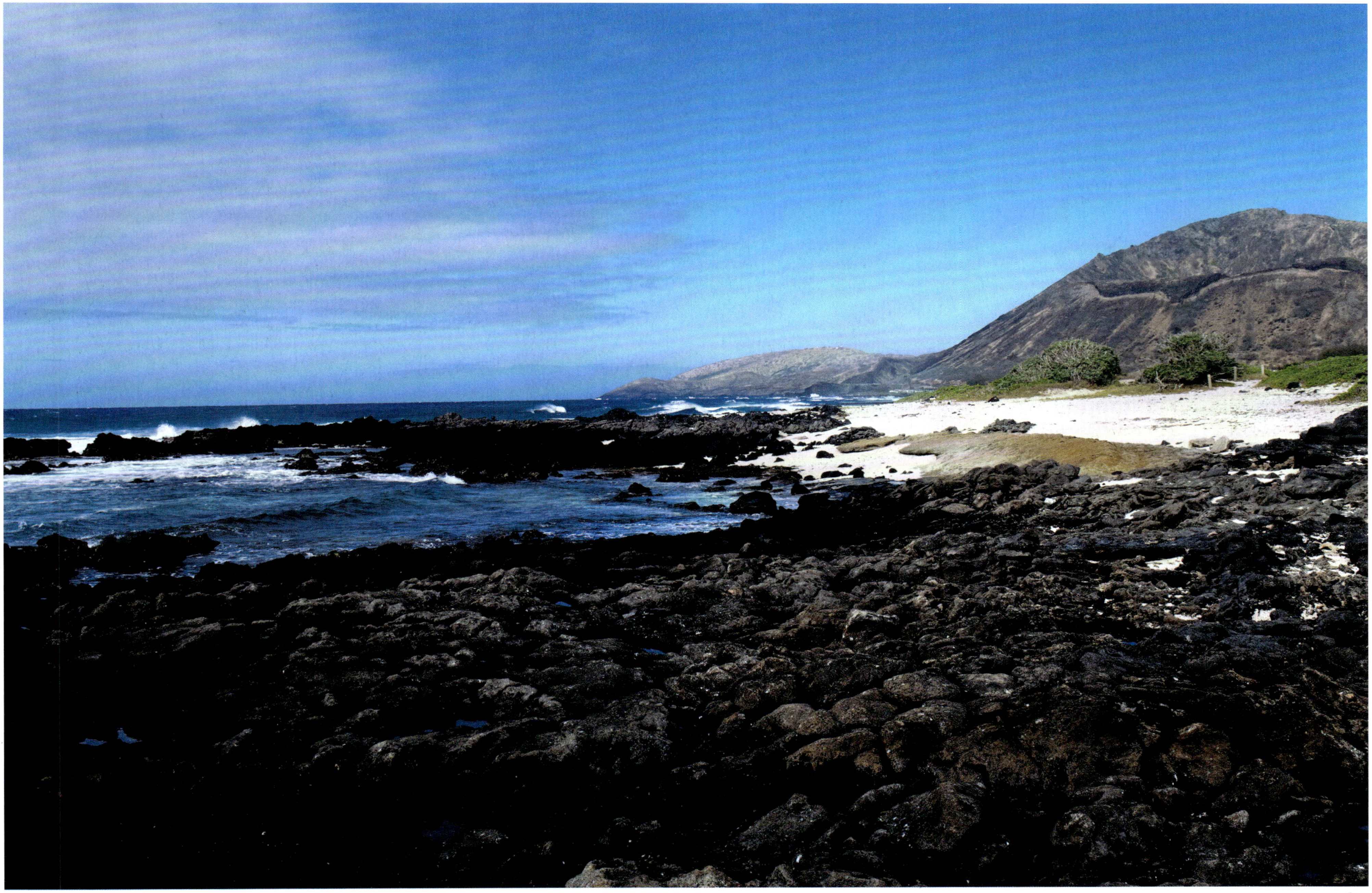

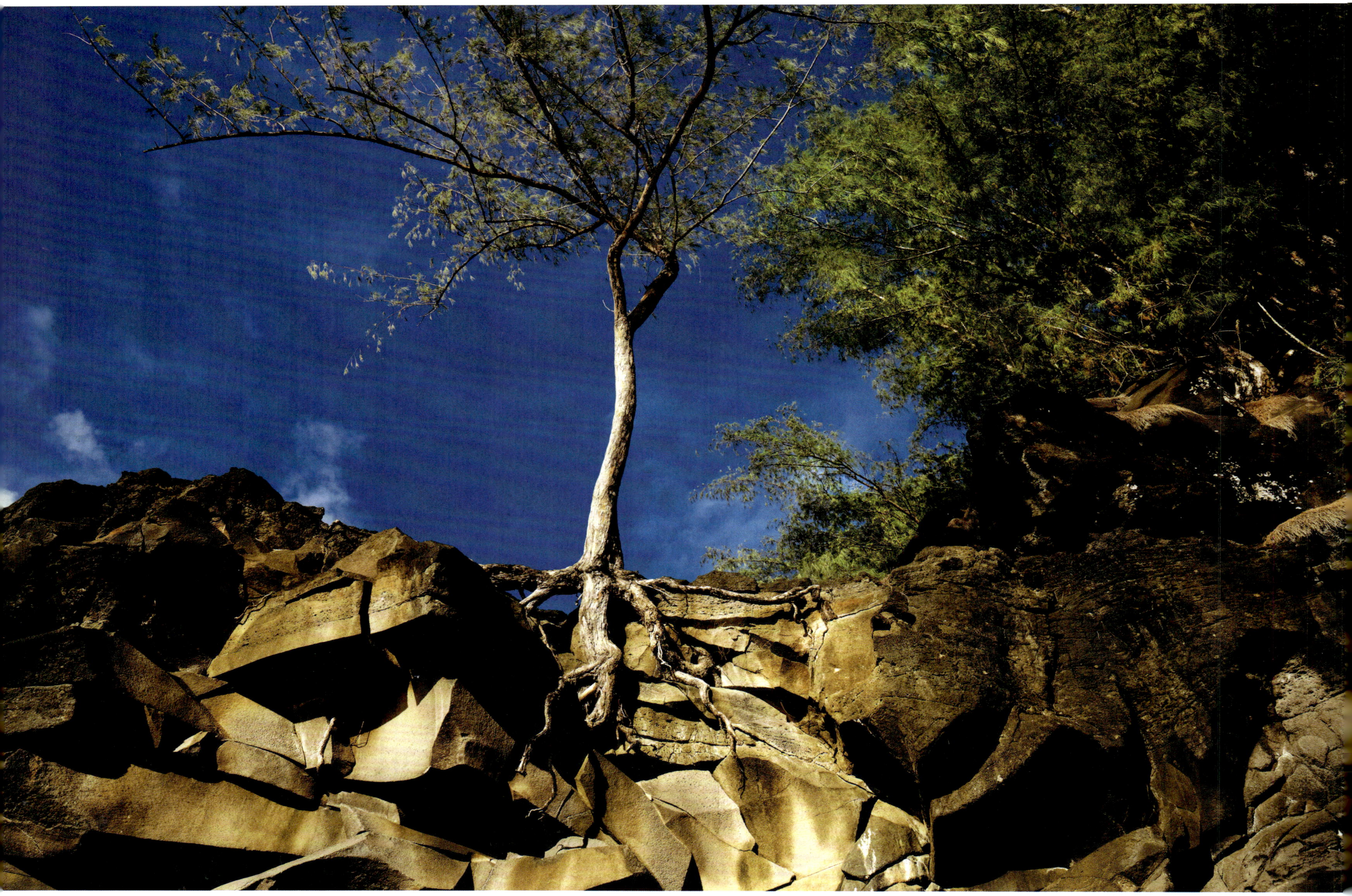

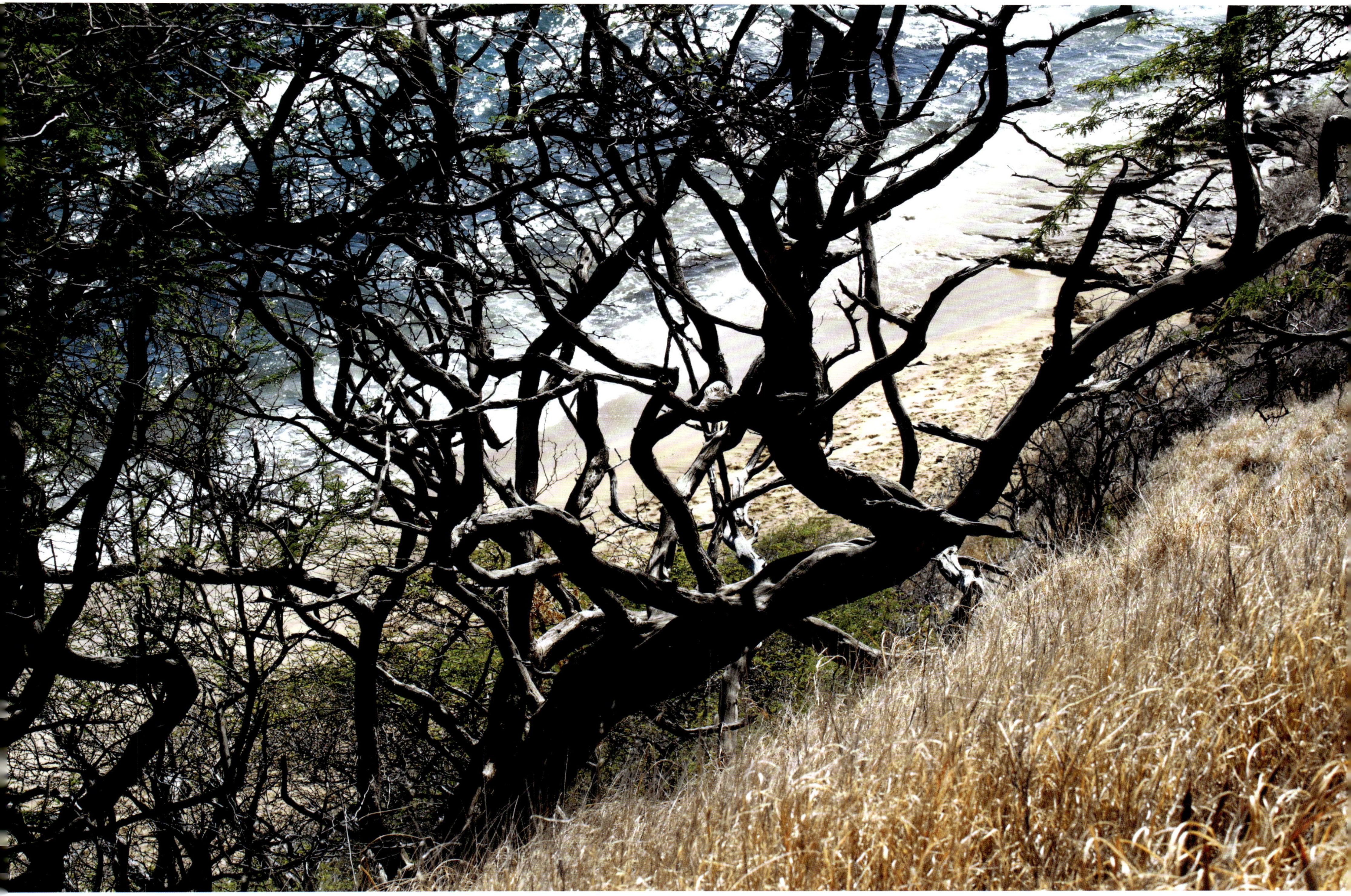

WE LISTEN WHEN THERE IS AN IMAGE

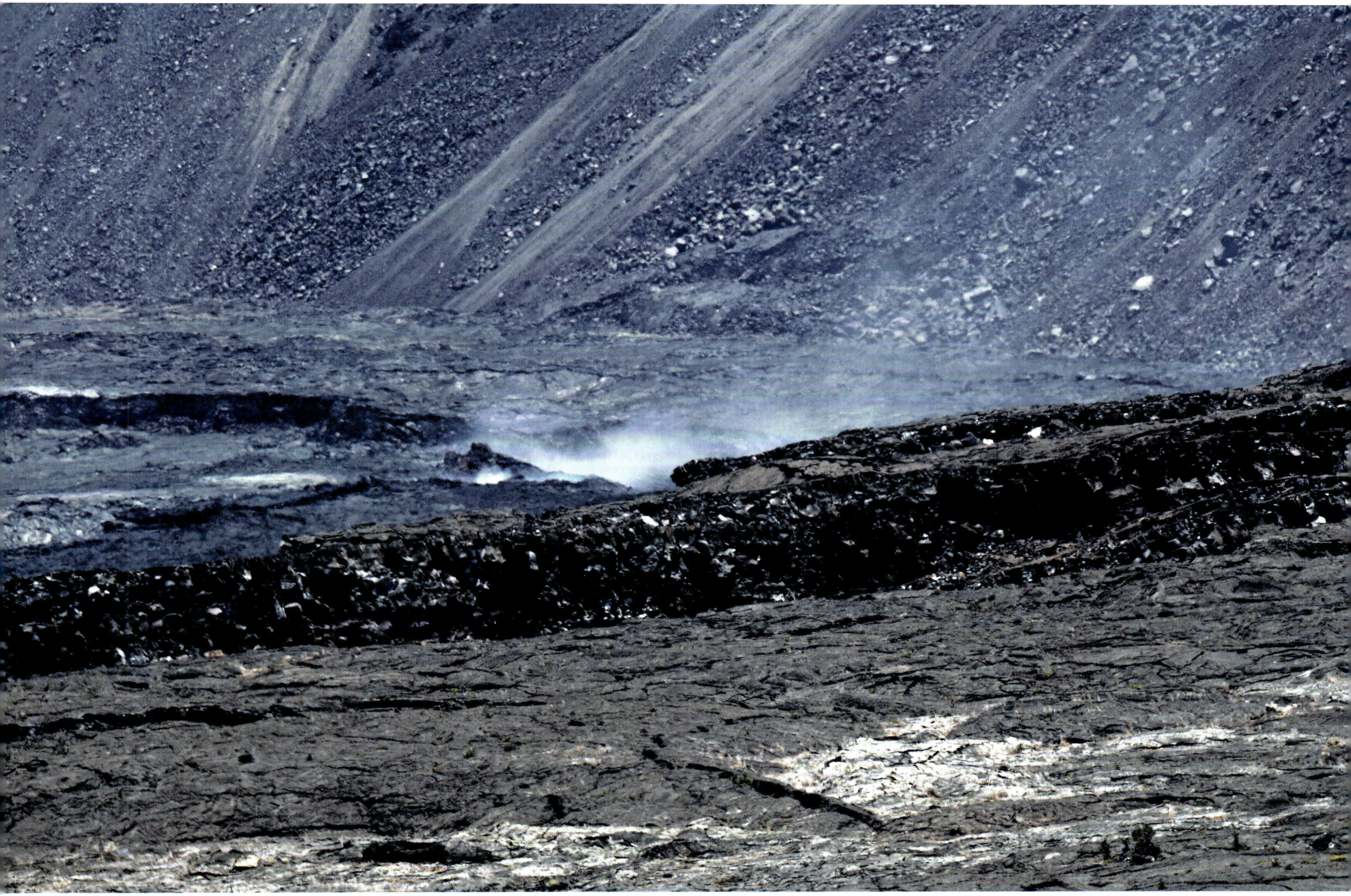

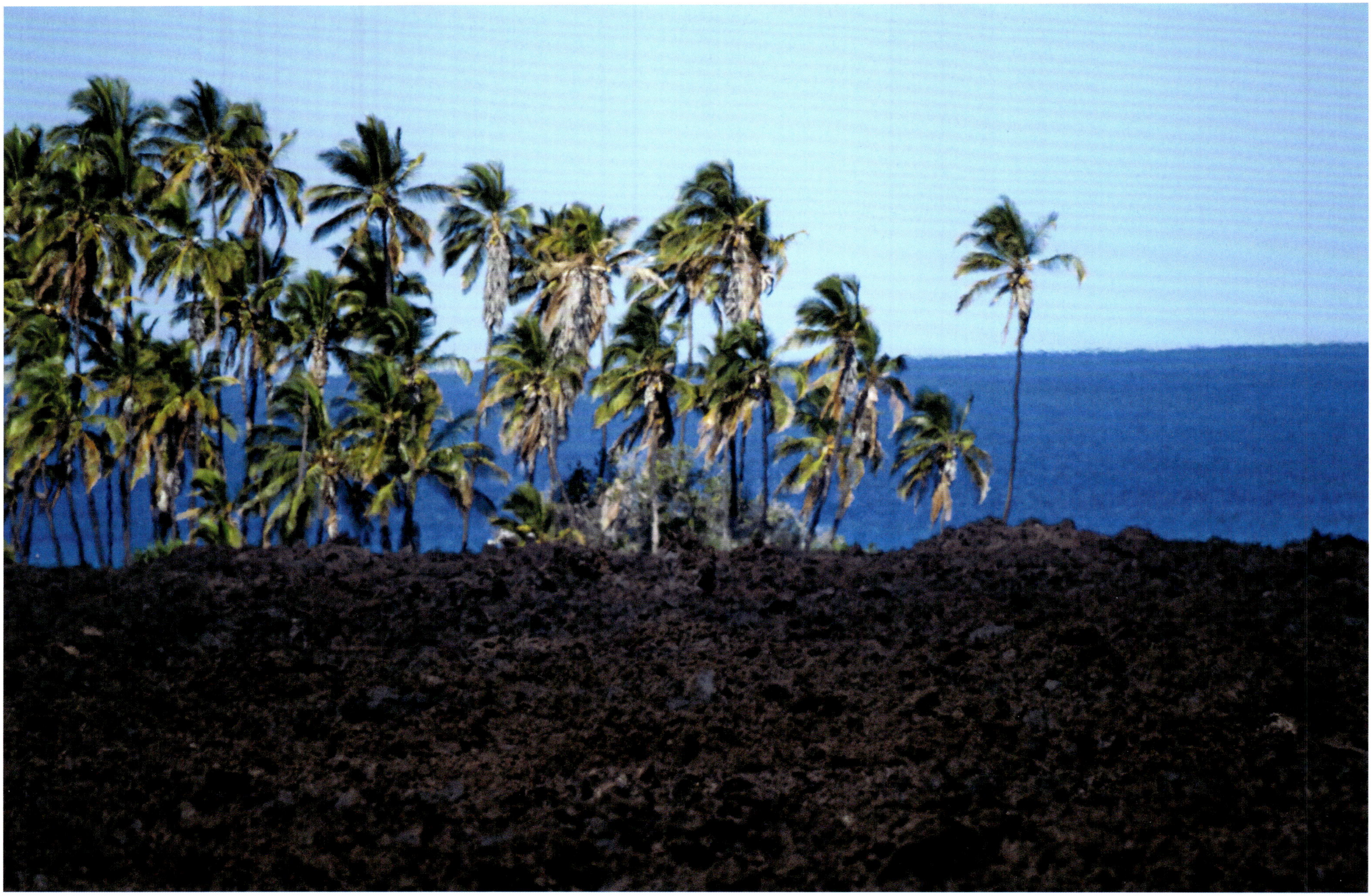

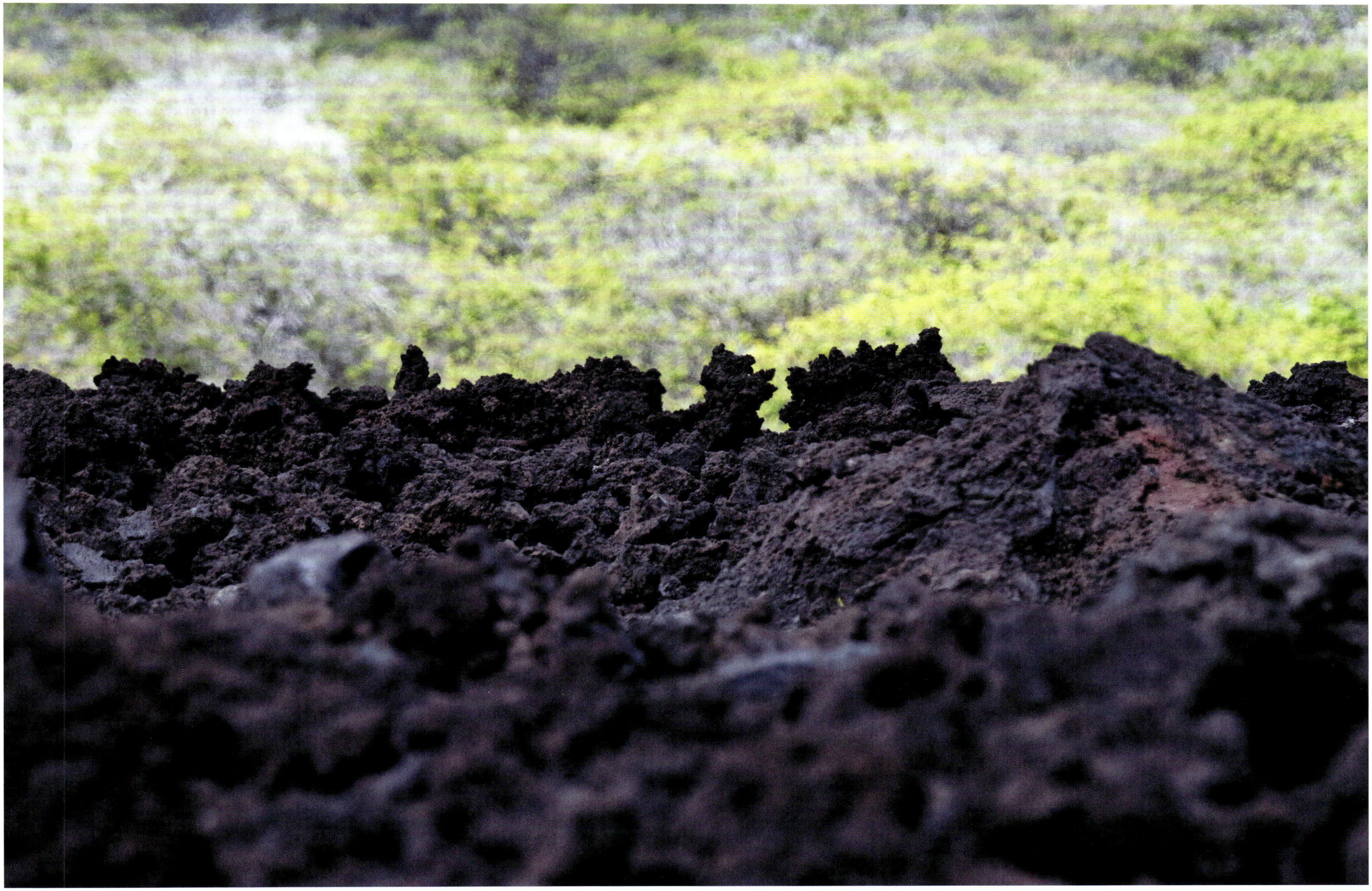

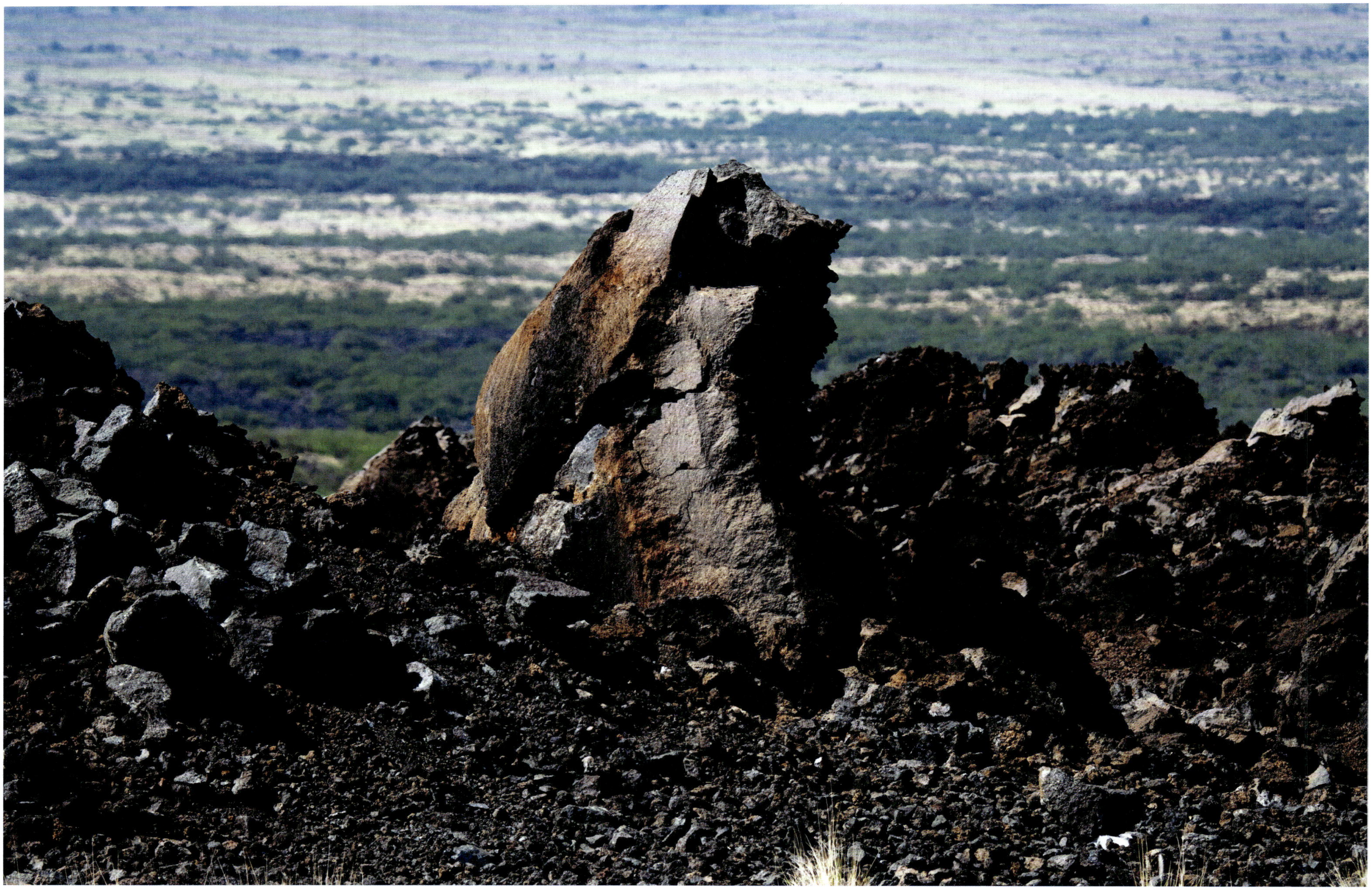

151

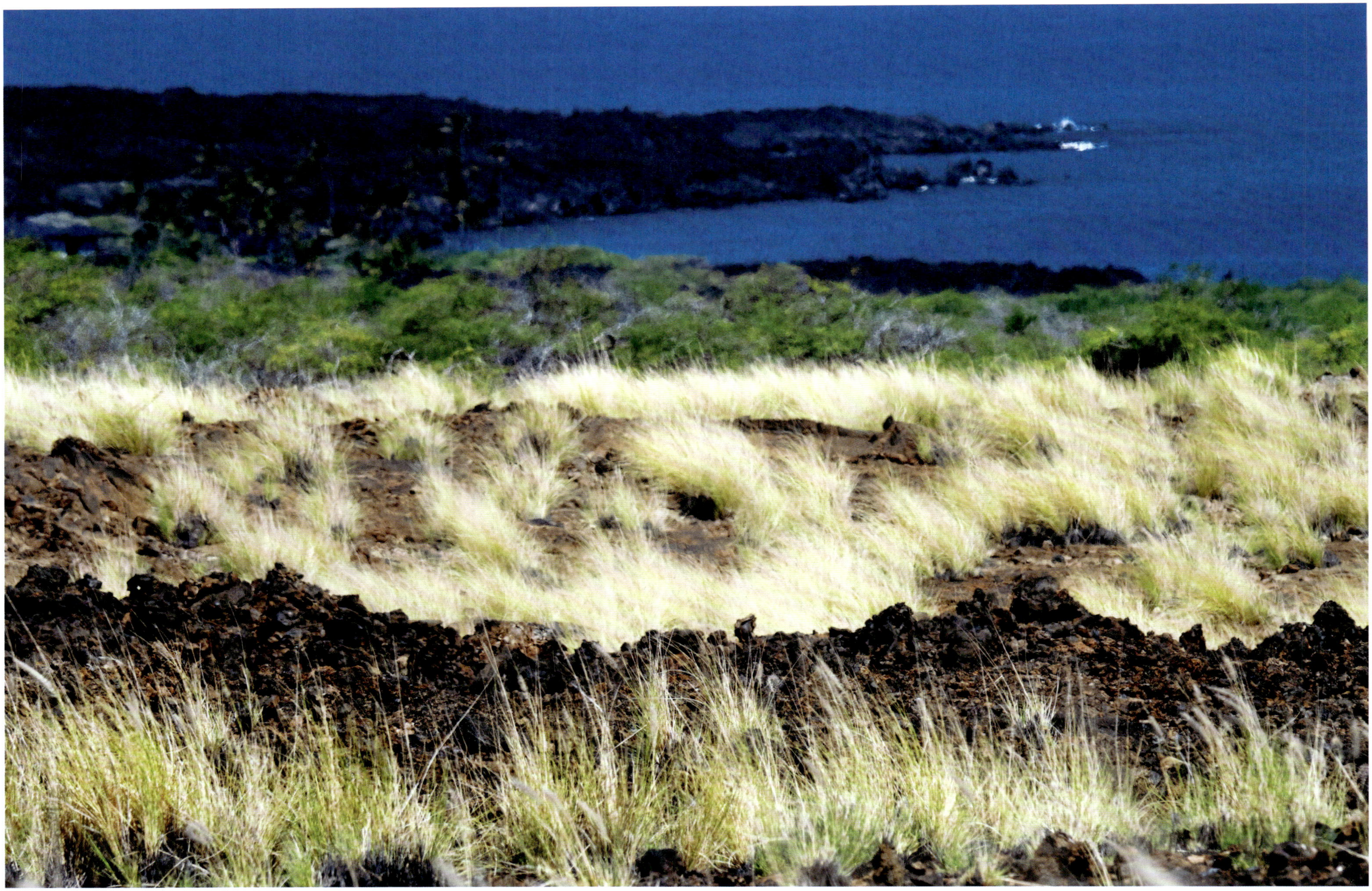

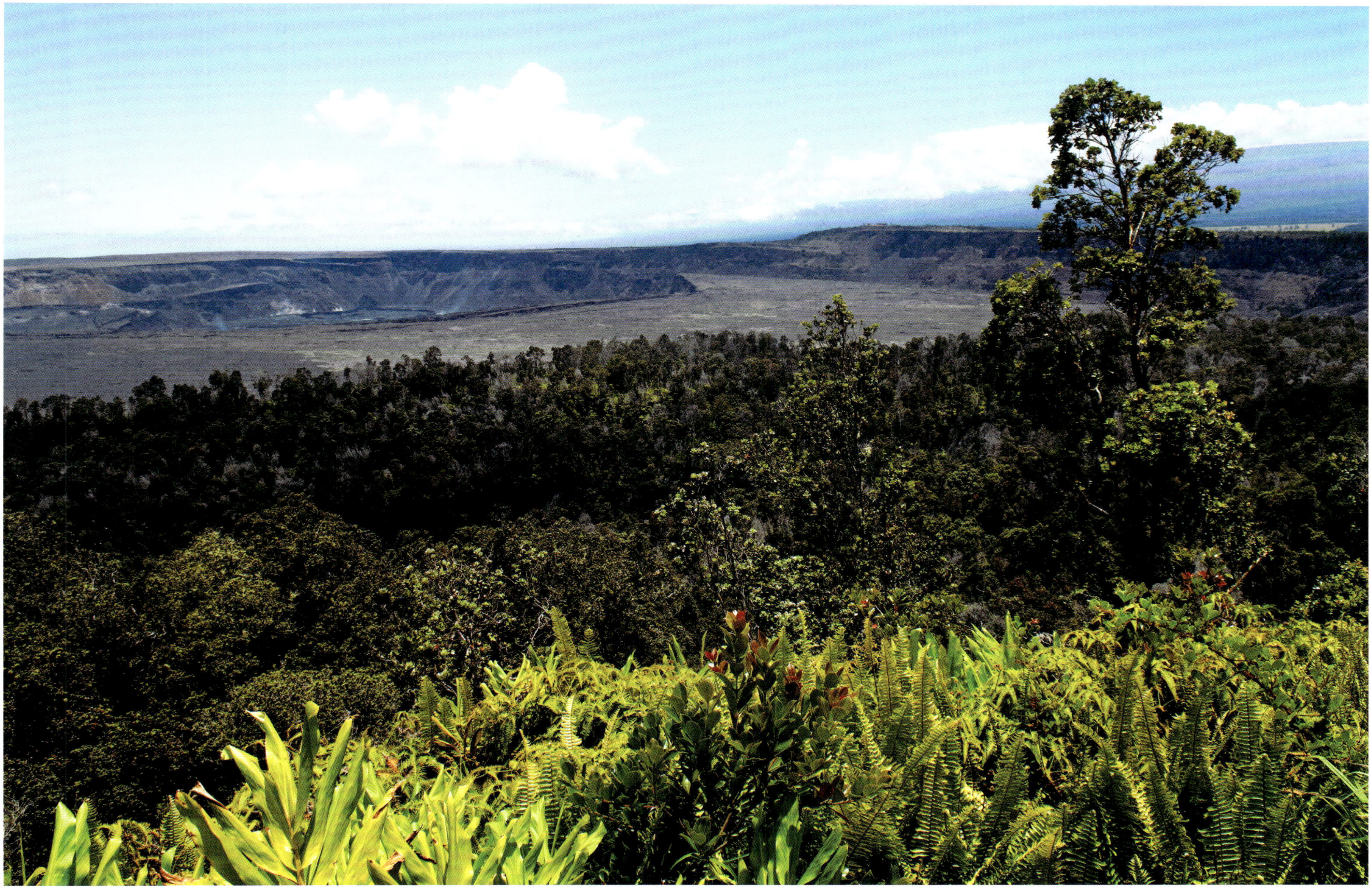

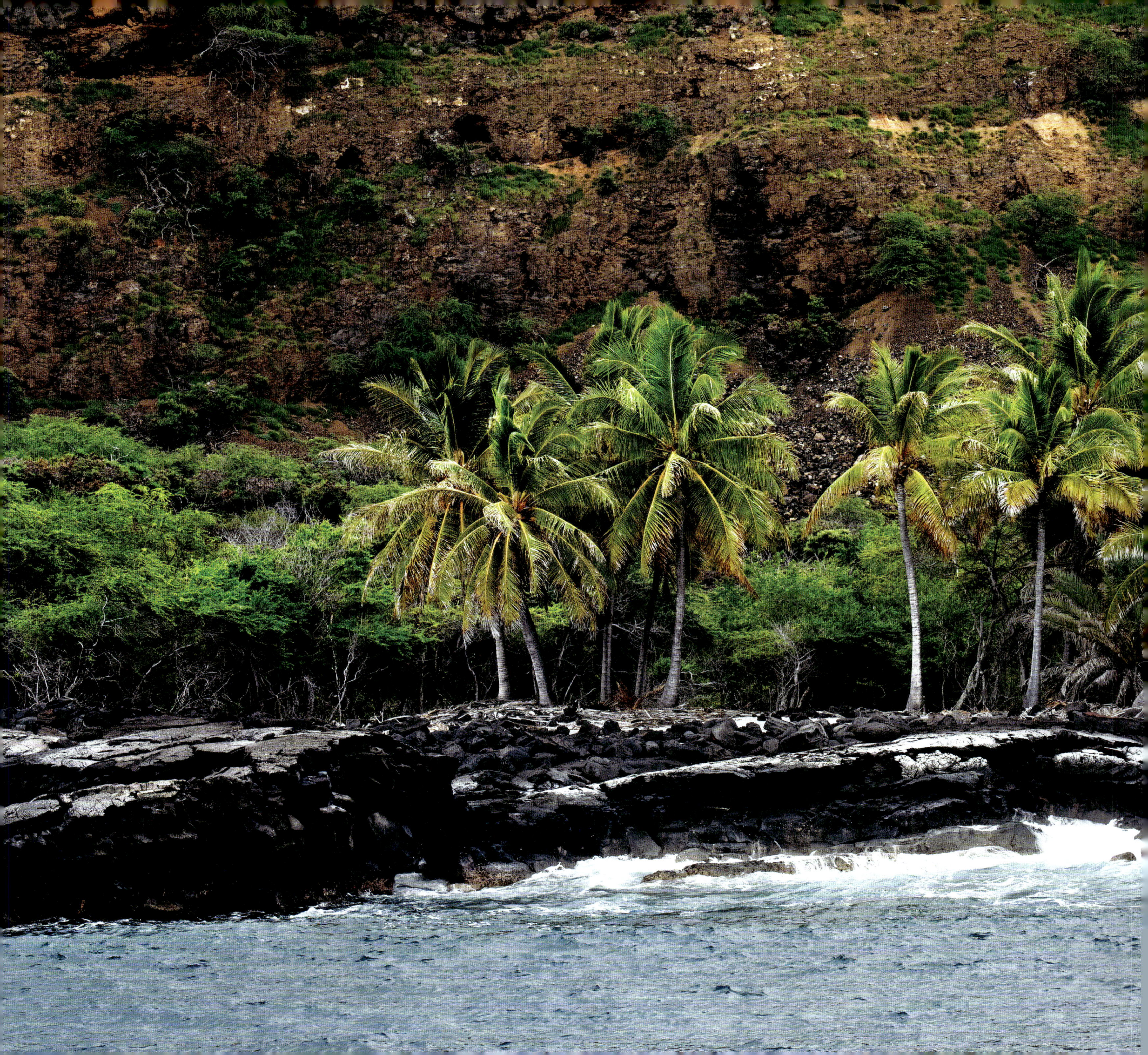

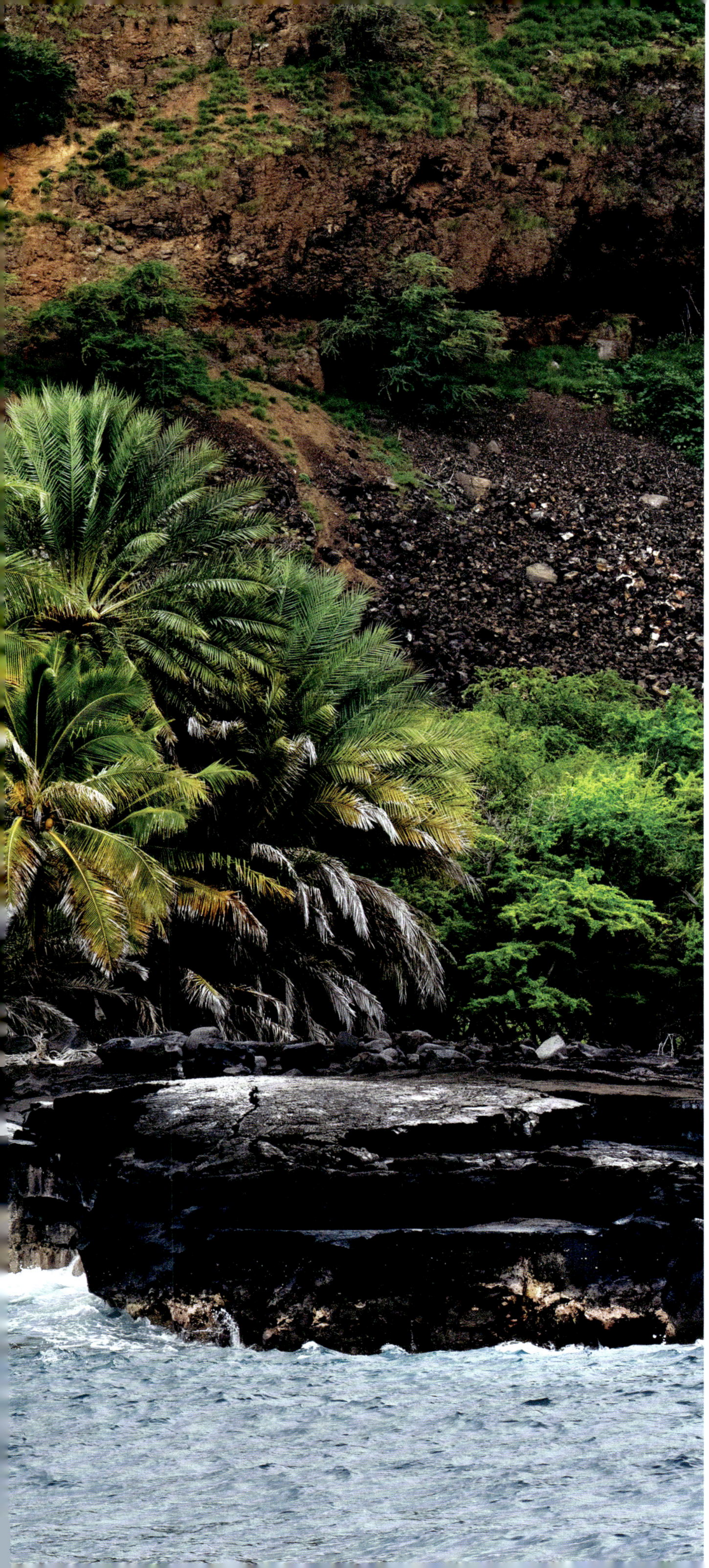

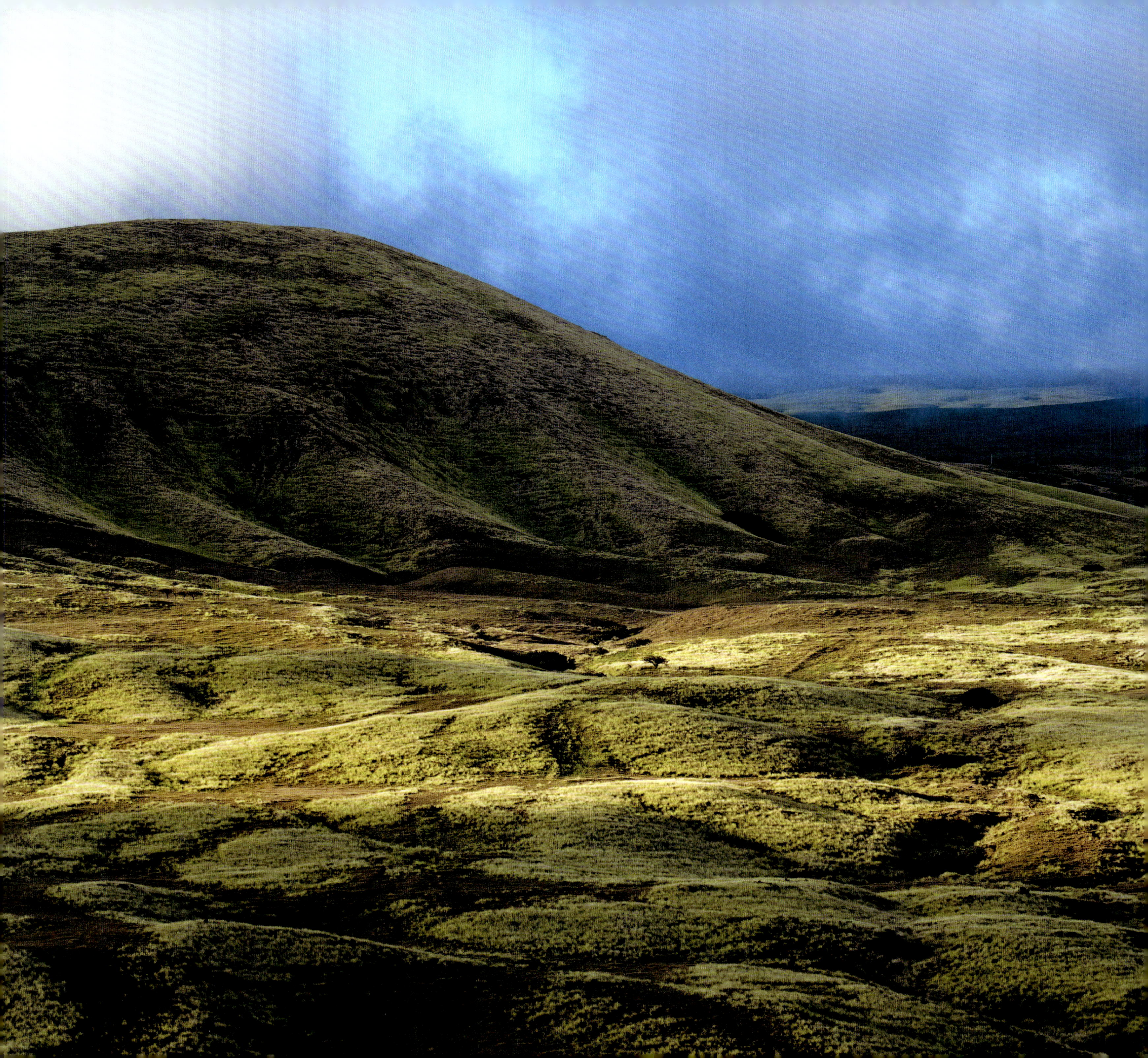

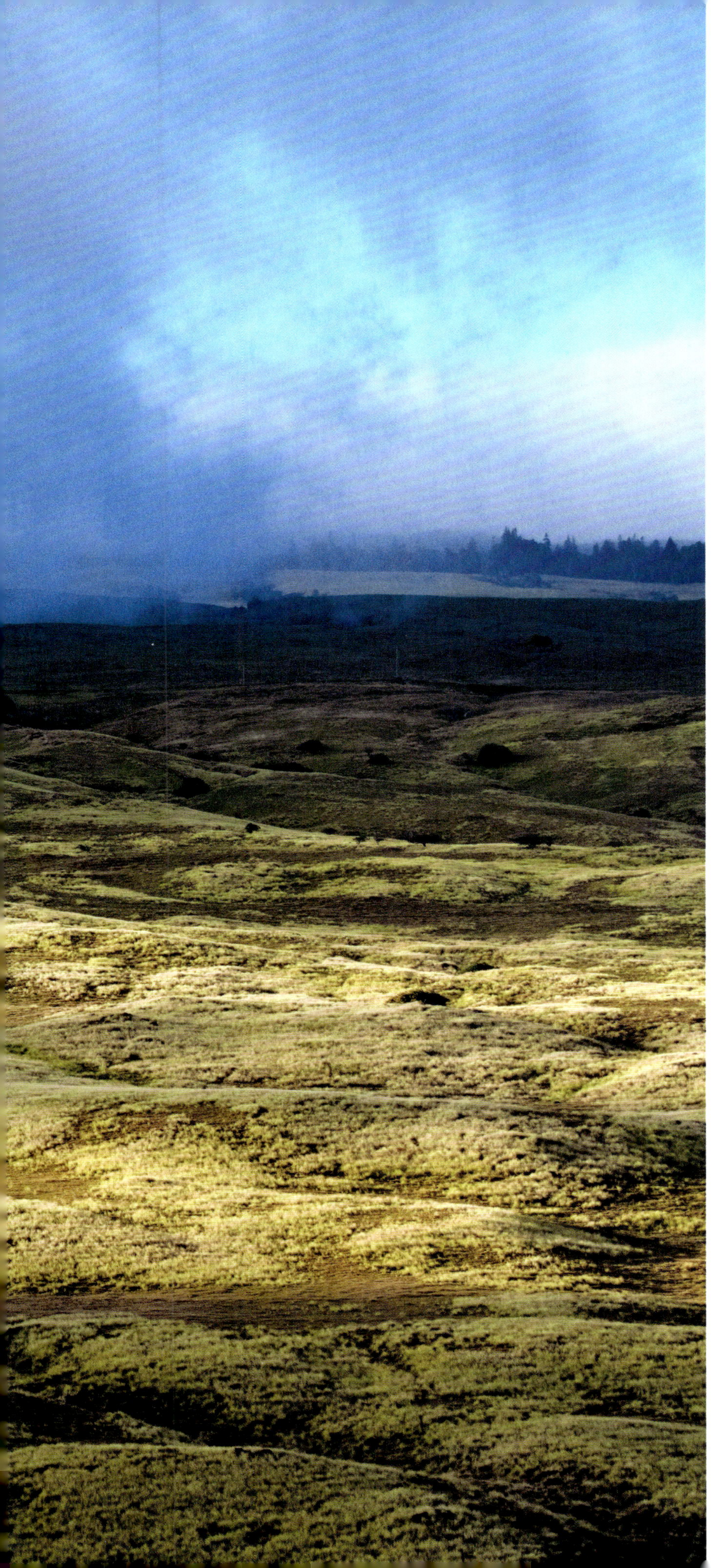

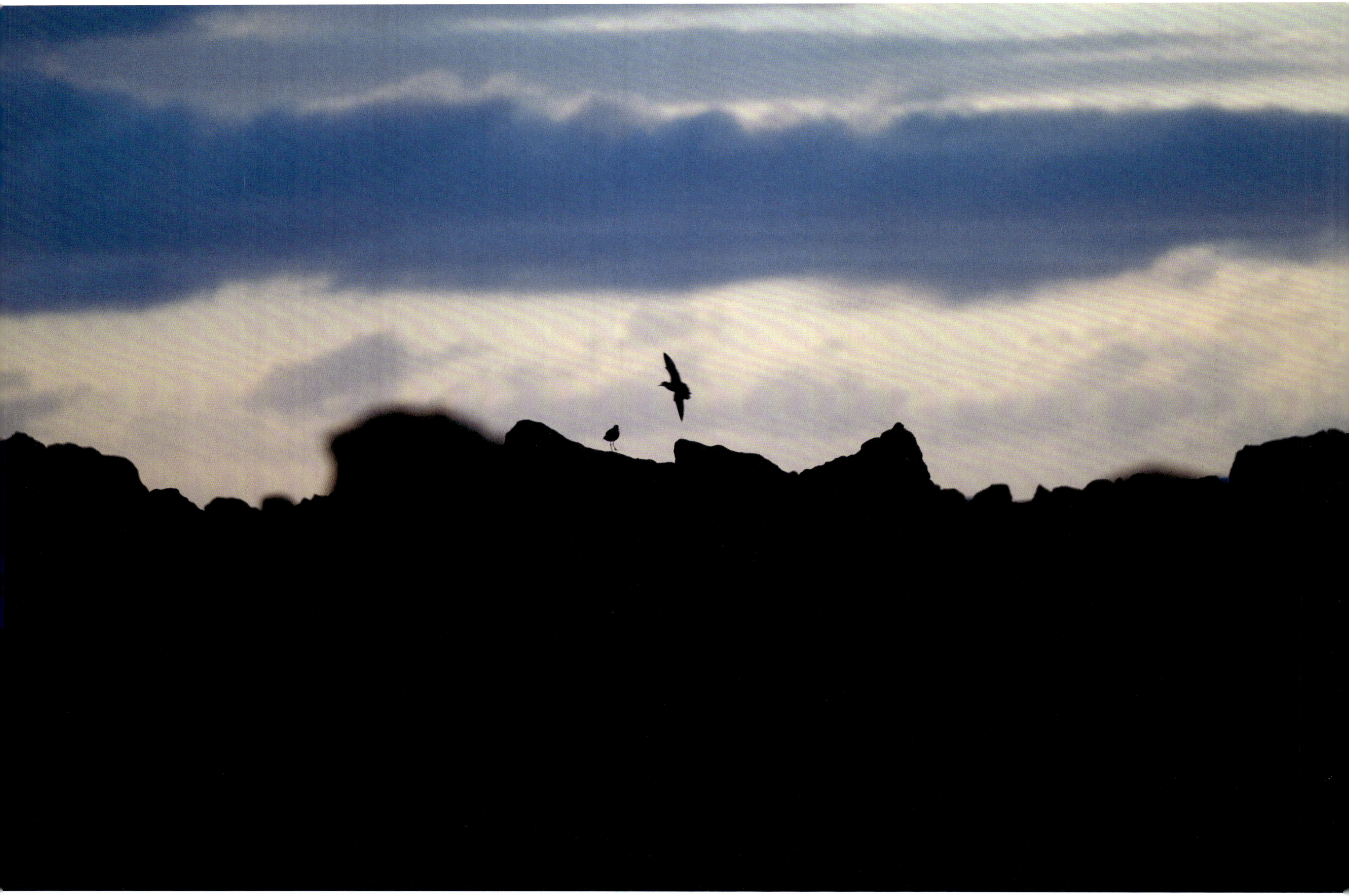

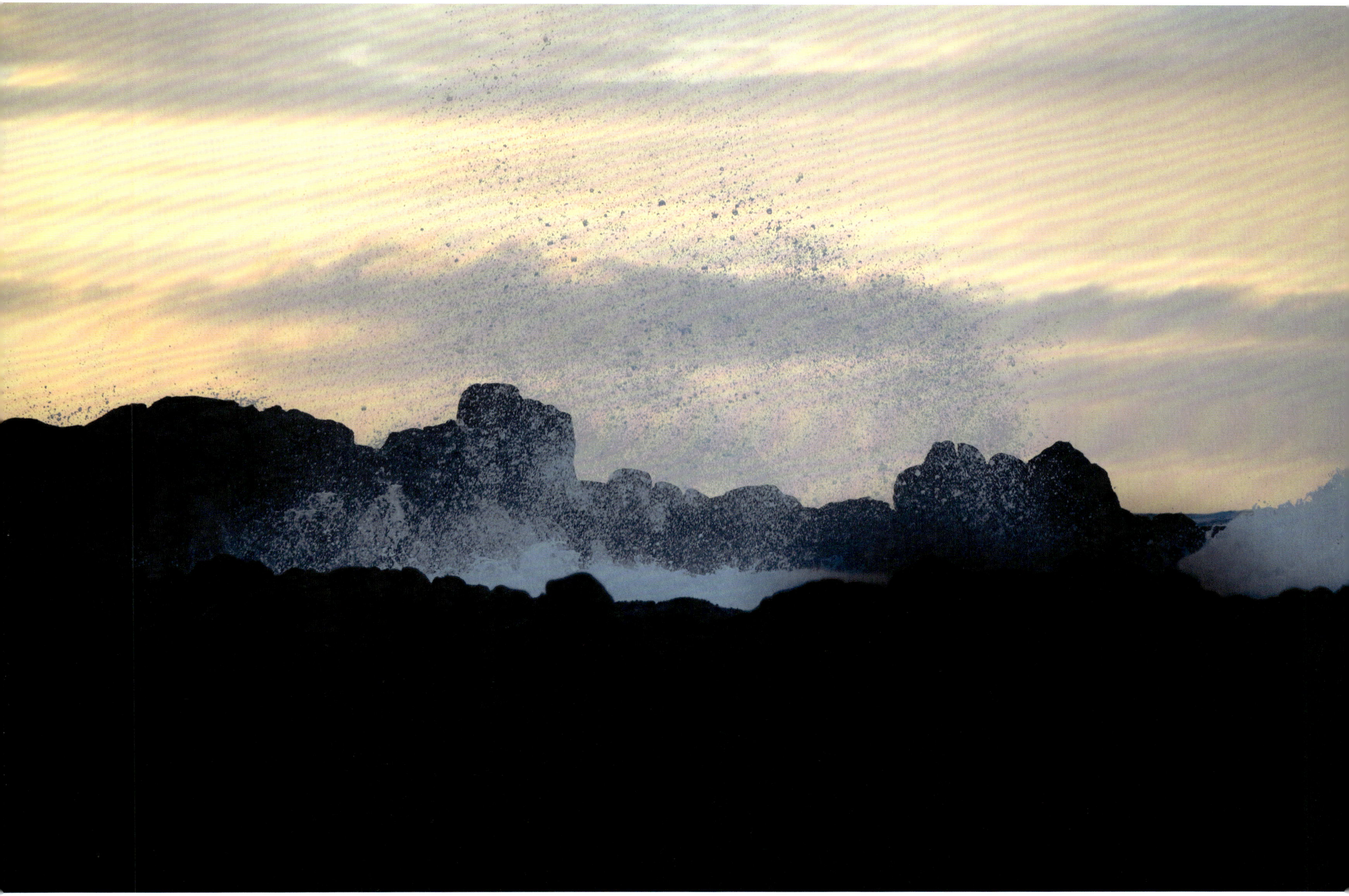

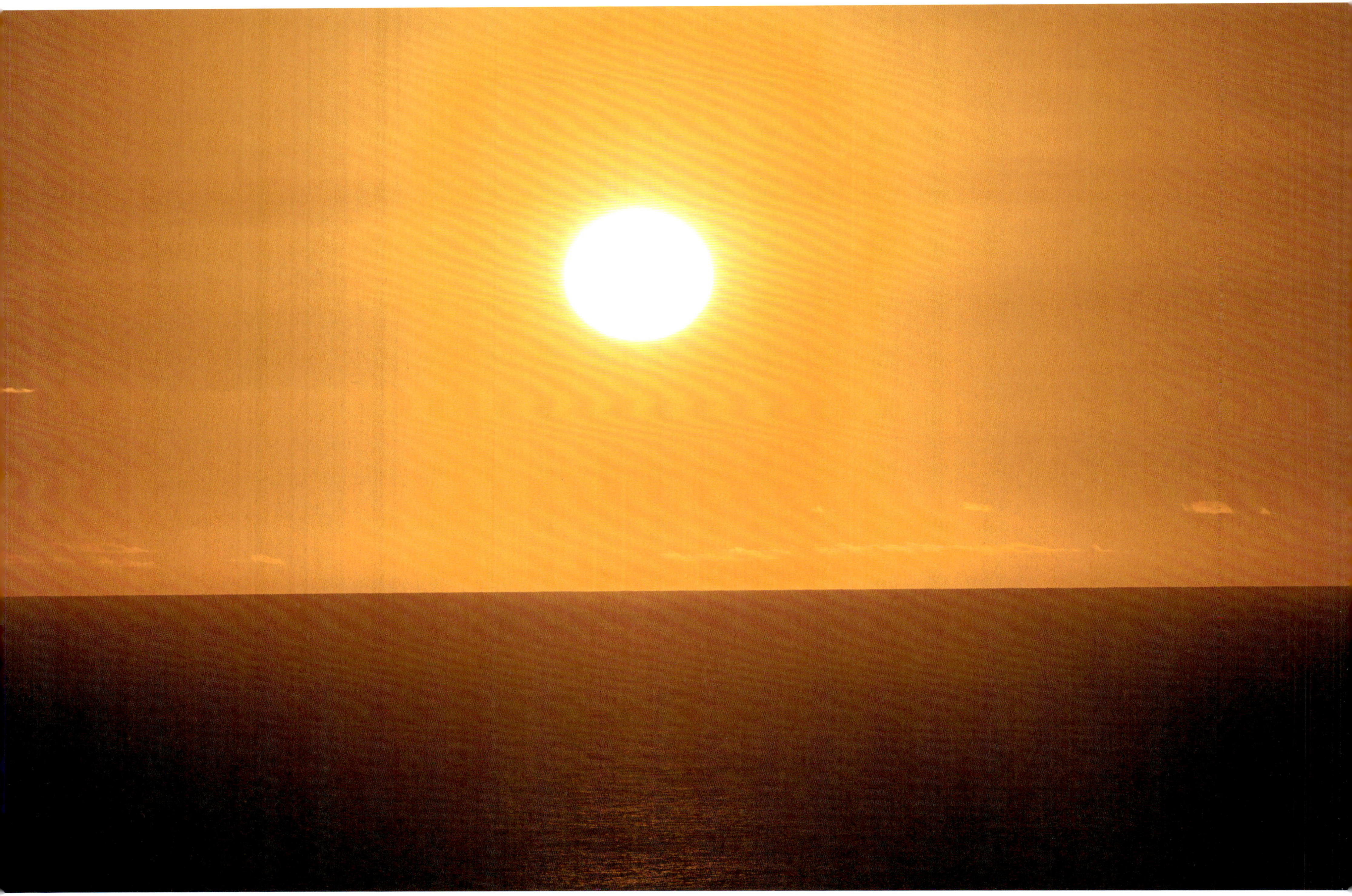

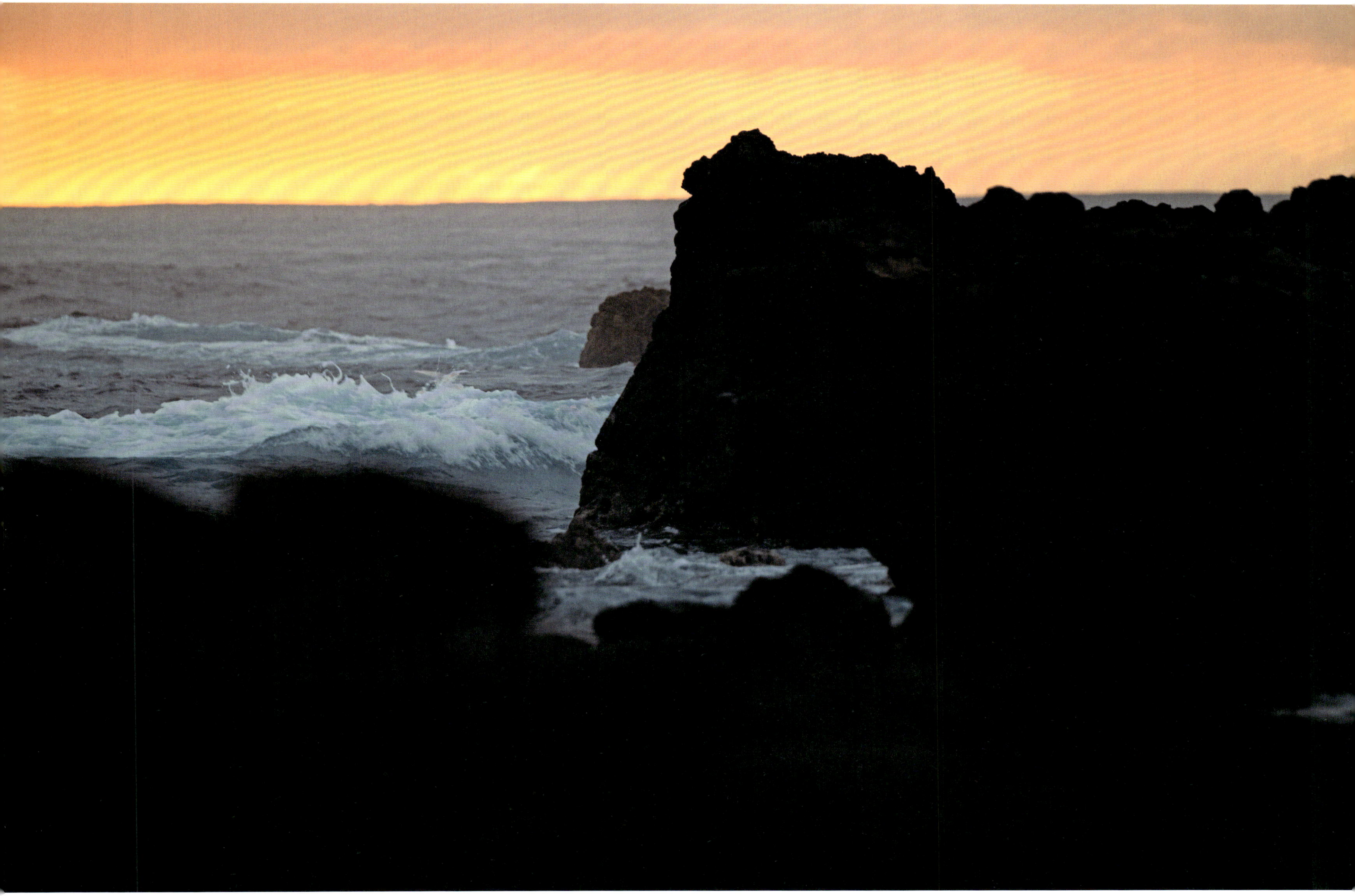

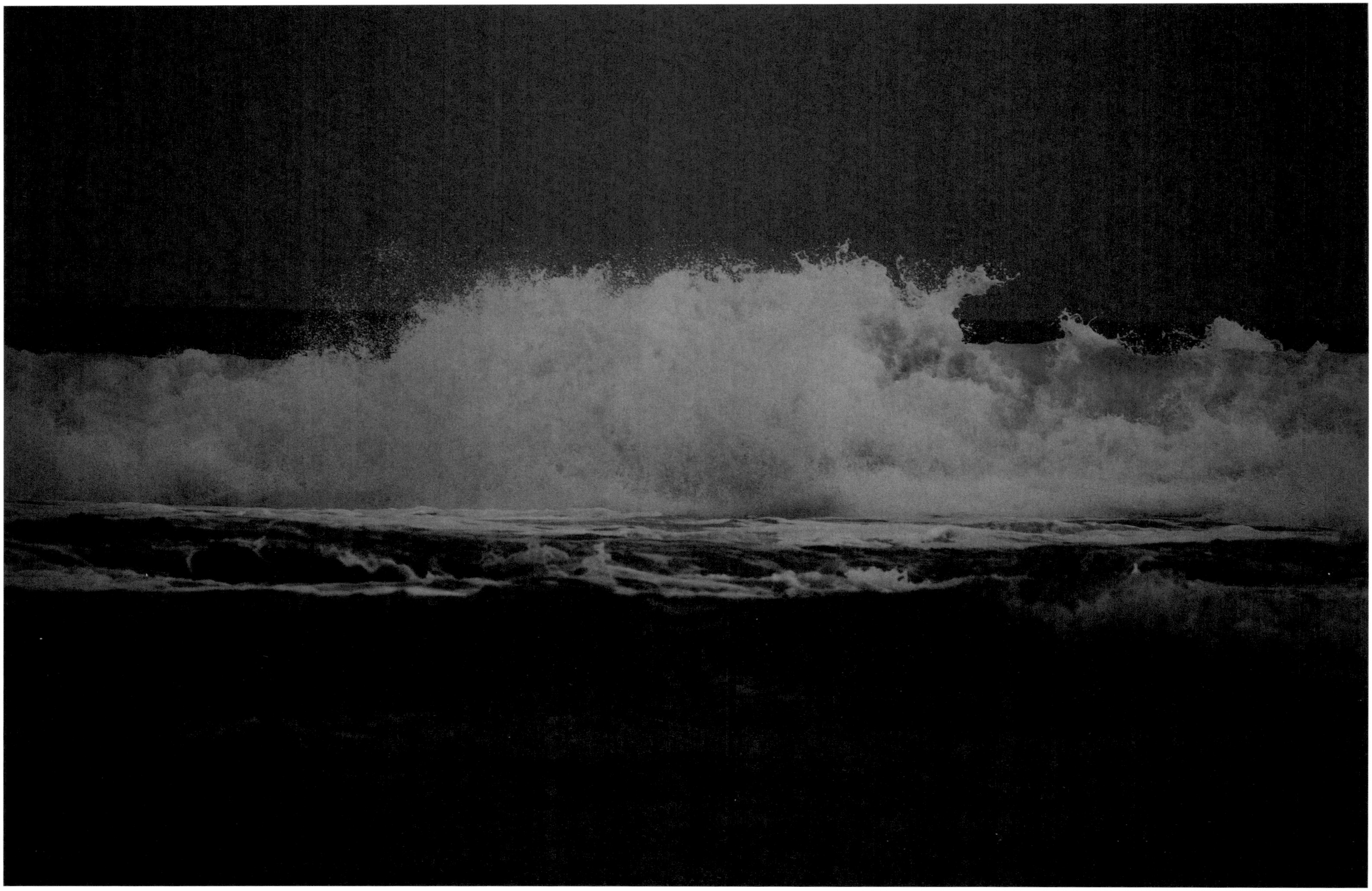

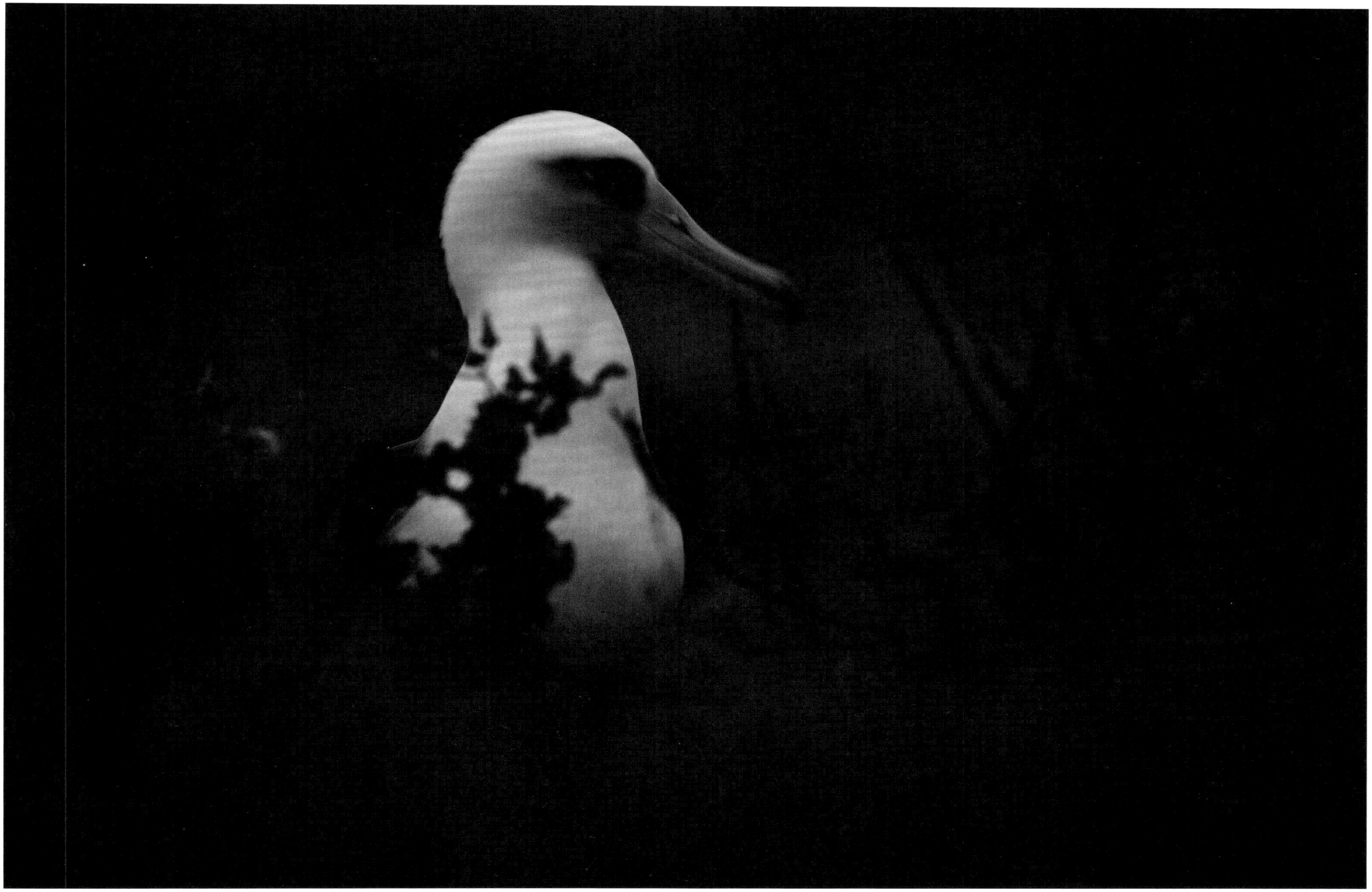

THE BLUE ON FIRE: HAWAI'I

Emmy-nominated photographer Enzo Barracco's latest artistic project to raise awareness of the world's extraordinary natural treasures takes us to Hawai'i. Through an absorbing series of remarkable images, The Blue on Fire: Hawai'i invites us to connect with the islands of this unique archipelago and the ocean that surrounds them; to immerse ourselves in extraordinary landscapes and to meet and hear the voices of those who live there.

Located in the middle of the vast Pacific Ocean, Hawai'i is a perfect location to explore how a land between fire and water, a land with a strong identity, can provoke a dialogue that inspires us to value and protect the natural world. Its overriding theme is the critical importance of maintaining the equilibrium and health of the ocean for the well-being of our planet. Through words and images, the book weaves stories, encouraging us to reflect and re-focus our lives and values to create the social change we need to safeguard our planet.

Enzo Barracco
Enzo is an Emmy-nominated photographer, and Author, as well as a "SEA BEYONDer", an ambassador of SEA BEYOND, the Prada Group's educational program conducted since 2019 in partnership with UNESCO's Intergovernmental Oceanographic Commission (IOC) to raise awareness of sustainability and ocean preservation. He lives and works in New York and London. After a career in the fashion and luxury industries, his focus and inspiration have shifted toward sustainability. His aim is to use his art to raise collective awareness. In recent years he has built a network of global excellence around his projects, involving key government organizations, cultural institutions, and philanthropic foundations from across the world. Enzo's mission is to create a body of work which documents and visualizes climate change and the transformation our planet is facing right now. A transformation in which we are deeply involved and by which we are deeply affected. Enzo's publications include The Skin of Rock: Galápagos (2023) and The Noise of Ice: Antarctica (2016). His work is in the permanent collection at LACMA Museum, Los Angeles and Mougins Museum, France, as well as many private collections. Enzo is also involved in corporate communication and has worked with leading companies including: PRADA, TIME Magazine, Shiseido, Vogue Italia, Vanity Fair, Lavazza, Phaidon Press, Boston Consulting Group, Barclays Bank, Estée Lauder Group, La Prairie Group, Park Hyatt Group, Dorchester Collection, Royal Marines UK, Royal Geographical Society, BIG Architects, The Royal Foundation, Yale University, European Union Delegation to The United Nations, New York, UNESCO, The European Commission Representation in Italy, EU and many other large institutions.

ACKNOWLEDGEMENTS

I would like to thank some very special friends who supported me in this project and book but first, a particularly special thanks to my beautiful daughter Rosa, Amore mio, who has inspired me in my life and my work every day, from the moment she arrived on this blue planet and even before.

A very special thanks to PRADA Group: Lorenzo Bertelli, Marta Monaco, Valentina Isme Piccato, Rebecca Mentana, Francesca Pacciani, Kathleen Box, Jillian Cook, Nikolas Pankau-Sirixay and Joscelin Yau.

I would also like to personally thank Ottavio Serena di Lapigio; Shwop.io; Laird Hamilton, Big Wave Surfer; Shyla Raghav, Chief Climate Officer, TIME Magazine; Mark Blackburn; Michael Govan, Wallis Annenberg Director of the Los Angeles County Museum of Art (LACMA); Nancy Thomas, Senior Deputy Director for Art Administration and Collections LACMA Museum Los Angeles; Britt Salvesen, Curator and Department Head, Wallis Annenberg Photography Department and Prints and Drawings Department, LACMA Museum Los Angeles; Corinne Erni, The Lewis B. and Dorothy Cullman Chief Curator of Art and Education, Deputy Director of Curatorial Affairs, Parrish Art Museum, Water Mill, NY; Daniele Foti, Vice President of Marketing, Lavazza North America; Jonathan Lehr, Marketing Director, Lavazza Group; Ambra Malagola, Marketing Manager, Lavazza; Conor Darcy; Paul Gallagher; Edwina Ehrman; Emma Lyandres; Mark Lee; Claudio Angelini; Andrea Zannoni; Malia Chung Zannoni; Dario Colombo; Greig Scott; James Francis-King; Mark Hertz; Shanti Nishimori Holland, Yuriko Nishimura Iruka, Hawaii Dolphin.com; Giorgia De Parolis, First Councillor, Permanent Mission of Italy to the United Nations; Raffaella Valentini, Consul General of Italy in Los Angeles; Sergio Strozzi, Consul General of Italy in San Francisco; Vitalba Gammicchia, Vice Consul of Italy in San Francisco; Josh Green M.D., Governor of Hawai'i (Ke Kia'aina o Hawai'i); Michele Carbone, Honorary Consul of Italy for the State of Hawaii; Michael Bruno, Provost and Professor of Ocean Engineering, University of Hawai'i at Mānoa; Kevin Aoki, Owner Aoki Group; Jon Bryan, Outrigger Canoe Surfer; Terry Chung, Kaua'i Waterman; Henk Rogers, Founder Blue Planet Companies; Bill Pratt; Elizabeth Cronin; Manua Kea Beach Hotel; The Explorers Club of New York; Tim Lana; Andy McComb, Redline Rafting; Air Kaua'i Helicopters; Victor Lee; David Erst; Skip Hill; Rick Lilley; David Barnes and Bonnie Bise, Halekulani Hotel Honolulu; Koa Fuller; Gianluigi Esposito; Giuseppe Stigliano; Paolo Taticchi and my family Carlo, Rosa and Antonio.

Being involved in a project of this size and scope has put me in contact with many people and organizations and I'm sure to have forgotten someone in preparing this list. My apologies to anyone I have missed, I couldn't have done it without you.

First published 2024 © EB BOOKS LLC, 2024

Main text, words, photographs, art direction © Enzo Barracco

www.enzobarracco.com

ISBN: 979-8-218-50434-2

All rights are reserved. No part of this publication may be reproduced, stored in a retrieval system, or transmitted, in any form or by any means, electronic, mechanical, photocopying, recording or otherwise, without the prior written permission of the publisher.

Editor: Edwina Ehrman
Designer and Pre Press: James Francis-King, The Logical Choice
www.thelogicalchoice.com

A copy of this book is available at:

The New York Public Library

The Explorers Club New York

Printed and bound in Italy by Rotolito